Queer Lovers and Hateful Others

Decolonial Studies, Postcolonial Horizons

Series editors:
Ramón Grosfoguel (University of California at Berkeley)
Barnor Hesse (Northwestern University)
S. Sayyid (University of Leeds)

Since the end of the Cold War, unresolved conjunctures and crises of race, ethnicity, religion, diversity, diaspora, globalization, the West and the non-West, have radically projected the meaning of the political and the cultural beyond the traditional verities of Left and Right. Throughout this period, Western developments in 'international relations' have become increasingly defined as corollaries to national 'race-relations' across both the European Union and the United States, where the reformation of Western imperial discourses and practices have been given particular impetus by the 'war against terror'. At the same time hegemonic Western continuities of racial profiling and colonial innovations have attested to the incomplete and interrupted institutions of the postcolonial era. Today we are witnessing renewed critiques of these postcolonial horizons at the threshold of attempts to inaugurate the political and cultural forms that decolonization now needs to take within and between the West and the 'non-West'. This series explores and discusses radical ideas that open up and advance understandings of these politically multicultural issues and theoretically interdisciplinary questions.

Also available

Religion without Redemption:
Social Contradictions and Awakened Dreams in Latin America
Luis Martínez Andrade

Rewriting Exodus
American Futures from Du Bois to Obama
Anna Hartnell

The Dutch Atlantic
Slavery, Abolition and Emancipation
Kwame Nimako and Glenn Willemsen

Islam and the Political
Theory, Governance and International Relations
Amr G.E. Sabet

The Politics of Islamophobia
Race, Power and Fantasy
David Tyrer

Queer Lovers and Hateful Others

Regenerating Violent Times and Places

Jin Haritaworn

www.plutobooks.com

First published 2015 by Pluto Press
345 Archway Road, London N6 5AA

www.plutobooks.com

British Library Cataloguing in Publication Data
A catalogue record for this book is available from the British Library

ISBN 978 0 7453 3062 4   Hardback
ISBN 978 0 7453 3061 7   Paperback
ISBN 978 1 7837 1269 4   PDF eBook
ISBN 978 1 7837 1271 7   Kindle eBook
ISBN 978 1 7837 1270 0   EPUB eBook

This book is printed on paper suitable for recycling and made from fully
managed and sustained forest sources. Logging, pulping and manufacturing
processes are expected to conform to the environmental standards of the
country of origin.

Typeset by Stanford DTP Services, Northampton, England
Text design by Melanie Patrick
Simultaneously printed by CPI Antony Rowe, Chippenham, UK
and Edwards Bros in the United States of America

CONTENTS

LIST OF FIGURES

ACKNOWLEDGEMENTS

What does it take to invent our bodies, desires and communities from the ashes of racism, colonialism and the gender violence that accompanies them, and beyond white moulds that are often premised on racialised death? *After the shower*, the image by Charlie Abdullah Haddad that is featured on the cover of this book, depicts the artist on their own. Hands wrapped around their naked torso, looking calmly at the camera, their stance conveys self-love and self-sufficiency. The work of surviving violence and visioning alternatives often feels solitary. And still, the subject's gaze opens up, reaches out: I see you, too.

I began the work that this book builds on as a queer of colour community organiser in Berlin in the early 2000s. It was a time when white queer and trans communities turned so racist that it became difficult to be in them. Meanwhile, people of colour were once again being divided, this time between the 'too queer' and the 'too homophobic'. As a person whom this changed terrain assigned new privileges on account of their 'sexually free' non-Muslim, non-Black Thai parentage, I am indebted to those who have taken risks with me while facing the brunt of racism.

Massive appreciations to all who have spoken up against gay imperialism, and inspired me to do the same. Many thanks to my comrades of the early days, Tamsila Tauqir, Jennifer Petzen and Koray Yılmaz-Günay – you will always be my role models. Over the years, I am proud to have joined shoulders in struggle with many fierce and brilliant queer, trans, straight and cis people of colour divesting from and building alternatives to racist and colonial regimes of gender and sexuality. A special thanks to Dzifa Afonu, Alexia Apolinario, Teht Ashmani, Laura Barker, Cengiz Barskanmaz, Sanchita Basu, Sokari Ekine, Meral El, Charlie Haddad, Rima Hussein, Nosh Khwaja, Mîran Newroz, Ashai Nichols, Raju Rage, Juli(a) Rivera, Aykan Safoğlu, Noah Sow, Danía Thaler, Anouchk Ibacka Valiente and Nika Zablotsky. I am grateful to Aren Aizura, Sara Ahmed, Sarah Bracke, Stacy Douglas, Craig Gilmore, Suhraiya Jivraj, Christian Klesse, Sarah Lamble, PG Macioti, Johanna Rothe and Gina Velasco for supporting this work at a time when it was embattled. Rachel Gorman, Noa Ha, Lu Lam, Olumide Popoola, Johanna Rothe, Salih Wolter, Koray Yılmaz-Günay and Nika Zablotsky have read and commented on chapters – thank you for giving me company and sharing your wisdoms, inspirations and expertise with me.

The penalties for doing antiracist, anti-colonial and anti-imperialist work on the intersections are high. Luckily, all the cool kids are already doing it anyway. I am fortunate to have collaborated with and learned from many brilliant minds, who each model ways of navigating oppressive systems and institutions with genius and grace. Thank you Anna Agathangelou, Paola Bacchetta, Sandeep Bakshi, Sirma Bilge, Karma Chavez, Kusha Dadui, Ena Dua, Fatima El-Tayeb, Esra Erdem, Umut Erel, Freda Fair, Chris Finley, Honor Ford Smith, Ruth Wilson Gilmore, Andil Gosine, Che Gossett, Noa Ha, Christina Hanhardt, Tobias Hübinette, Ren-yo Hwang, Adi Kuntsman, Gail Lewis, Chin-ju Lin, Martin Manalansan, Victor Mendoza, Angie Morrill, Chinyere Oparah, Silvia Posocco, Encarnación Gutiérrez Rodríguez, Humaira Saeed, Kiri Sailiata, Andrea Smith, Riley Snorton, Milena Solomun, Sunera Thobani, Lee Ann Wang and Pascal Yorks for imparting knowledge and support in the right times and places.

Amardeep Kaur has held my hand, soothed me and accepted me many times when I felt hopeless and overwhelmed – thank you for being here with me through these major life transitions.

Lu Lam has cheered me on during this last stretch and convinced me that I can thrive rather than just survive – that decolonial love can inform and transform our work entirely.

Universities are sites of institutional and interpersonal violence as well as places where many amazing people pass through. I have been lucky to have taught versions of these chapters in classrooms filled with smart and creative individuals, including at CUNY, Goldsmiths, Helsinki, Hamburg, Humboldt and Technical Universities Berlin, LSE, Kaohsiung Medical University, Basel, Northwestern, and in my current home, the Faculty of Environmental Studies at York. Among the (then) students who engaged with the ideas that ended up here are Babette Burrell, Samay Arcentales Cajas, Alvis Choi, Jessica Cook, Vero Diaz, Chelsea Fung, Tina Garnett, Ronak Ghorbani, Brandon Hay, Erin Howley, Anabel Khoo, Tamika Jarrett, Naila Lalji, Charmaine Lurch, Mosa Neshamá McNeilly, Melanie Patenaude, Princie Reza, Río Rodríguez, Boké Saisi, Negar Taymoorzadeh, Katie Ungard, Tess Vo and Jennisha Wilson, as well as Anu Radha Verma, who thoughtfully formatted several chapters of this book.

Words, however lonesome they may feel to string together, are never the creation of one individual alone. The ones in this book, too, have more co-authors than I can acknowledge or remember. I feel lucky to have moved in, through and alongside many groups and communities. *Queer Lovers and Hateful Others* is dedicated to the unsung heroes who gather informally at Berlin kitchen tables. At the same time, the book has been sustained and at times informed by several organisations, including Decolonizing Sexualities Network (fka Decolonize Queer), Next Genderation, SUSPECT and QEKON (Queer and Ethnicity Conference). The final touches to the book happened while I was co-organising the Critical Ethnic Studies conference in Toronto, alongside fabulous people such as Nadia Kanani, Kim Abis, Rachel Gorman, Shana Griffin, Sailaja Krishnamurti, Mona Oikawa, Syrus Marcus Ware and Krysta Williams. Being part of a collective that unapologetically centred queer and trans Black, Indigenous and people of colour leadership from the start was an incredibly positive experience. It has given me hope for what's to come, and what's possible.

This book, then, has sprung from many marvelous waves and grounds. May it return to them, and be at their service.

INTRODUCTION:
QUEER REGENERATIONS

Now, it is important for us to strengthen our very own structures and you know what? We do not want to be bothered by you. Do not enter our communities to destroy them. Our realities are not your realities! Part of our structures are the districts in which we live, our neighborhoods, in which we feel protected from racist attacks. You cannot even imagine that you might be part of the danger. You keep talking about fears concerning the move of Schwuz [a long-standing gay-male oriented venue] to Neukölln, but have you ever considered what Blacks and PoC [People of Colour] in Neukölln are afraid of? Rents are rising, police presence is increasing, drunk party guests pee in house entrances. And the neonazis are not far – whether they're bald or not. Our spaces get converted into your garbage dumps and become your fantasies of unmanned land with cheap rents. You consider yourself and your bourgeois squats to be 'pioneers' and you don't even realize how colonial your language is, you do not see the civilizing mission you are part of and that you prepare the ground for other white settlers to come. What do you think [Berlin-]Kreuzberg looked like 30 years ago? It was poor, run-down and at the margin of Westberlin. That is exactly why landlords allowed Blacks and PoC to live there. Have you ever noticed that there aren't any neighbours of color in your organic food stores and your queer bars? Do you prefer it this way? Stop investing money into anti-homophobia projects in [Berlin-]Wedding, [Berlin-]Schöneberg and [Berlin-]Neukölln that target us, the 'dangerous brown mass', and start dealing with homo-, and transphobia within the white society. (From the *Khalass!!! We're vex!* manifesto)

On Pride day in summer 2013, flyers rained down from a window onto a majority-white queer parade marching through the Berlin inner-city districts of Kreuzberg and Neukölln. The parade was part of the alternative Kreuzberg Pride or TCSD (Transgenial Christopher Street Day). The TCSD, which separated from the mainstream commercial Pride or CSD (Christopher Street Day) in 1997, gained currency in 2010, when Judith Butler mentioned it in her speech that would make 'homonationalism' a household term. She highlighted the TCSD as an alternative to the mainstream CSD, whose civil courage award she was refusing in protest against the CSD's complicities in racism (Crasshole 2010; SUSPECT 2010a). Ironically, three years later similar allegations are being

Figure 1   Hermannplatz Berlin-Neukölln, 22 June 2013: Banner with the writing 'CSD [Christopher Street Day] – [raised middle finger] – T*CSD [Transgenial Christopher Street Day]: **SPOT THE DIFFERENCE**'. Raining from the window, flyers with the *Khalass!!!* manifesto

Source: Photo by *Khalass!!!*

made against the TCSD itself, which identifies itself as anti-fascist, anti-racist and 'alternative', but to many queers of colour appears no less white.[1] As stated on the banner hanging from the window that rained flyers that day: '*CSD –* [raised middle finger] *– T*CSD: SPOT THE DIFFERENCE*'.

The *Khalass!!!* manifesto, written by anonymous authors who identify as 'queer_trans*_inter*_Black_Muslim*_Arab_Rromni*ja_mixedrace_Mizrahi _Refugee_Native_Kurdish_Armenian', and thereby already part of a coalition shot through with power and privilege, raises important questions, which have been the subject of queer of colour kitchen-table conversations in Berlin for years but have rarely reached a bigger public. This book engages these and other critical voices, which attest to a new critical mass of queers of colour who are ready to oppose racism and gentrification but as yet face a lack of real-life spaces where they could materialise into an outwardly visible community. These nascent queer of colour narratives challenge a colonial account of violence, space and safety that works to territorialise a singular notion of gay (or even queer) 'community'. Indeed, they gesture towards alternative goals and methods of placemaking that do not rely on privatisation, securitisation and eviction.

The 15 queers of colour whom I interviewed for this book echo the *Khalass!!!* manifesto's assessment that queer gentrification leaves imprints on the urban environment that deserve further inquiry (see also Decolonize Queer 2011; Hanhardt 2008; Manalansan 2005). In a context where 'queer space' is publicly carved out in ways that mark an area's recovery, and the displacement and policing of communities once confined to it, the kitchen table emerges as a key site of mobilising that is often unacknowledged in social movements. It is what and where remains in the wake of the racist backlash – and where most of the interviews conducted for this book took place. Interviewees described a shrinkage of environments where queers of colour can sustain themselves and build community that is not predicated on social death: from the neighbourhood, to 'queer' space that is accessible (enough), to the gendered and racialised body. I propose that we think of this as *queer regeneration*, a process that at once describes symbolic shifts in who or what is valued and vitalised, and inscribes actual places where people 'live, work, play and worship', in Bullard's (1994) famous formulation of environmental justice (see also Stein 2004; Teelucksingh 2002). Following McKittrick, I treat the queer and trans people of colour who participated in the interviews as 'geographic subjects', whose cognitive maps tell stories that are meaningful, in that they 'incite new, or different, and perhaps not just, more just, geographic stories' (McKittrick 2006: xix; see also Ingram et al. 1997; Jameson 1988). It is precisely because the queer of colour kitchen table does not reach the status of a social movement that it has lessons to impart to wider struggles against incarceration, dispossession and displacement.

Like the *Khalass!!!* manifesto, this book takes critical issue with figures of racialised homophobia and transphobia, which have become the defining drive of lesbian, gay, bisexual, transgender (LGBT), queer and trans organising transnationally. *Queer Lovers and Hateful Others* tracks the birth of the 'homophobic Muslim' as a new folk devil who joins an older archive of crime, violence, patriarchy, integration and segregation, in areas marked by racism, gentrification and neoliberal restructuring. It draws attention to what Povinelli (2008), commenting on the concurrency of 'state killing' and 'letting die' in Australia, describes as the *uneventful* occurences that accompany the production of events: from a drunken traffic altercation between drag kings and putatively racialised[2] people in Kreuzberg that arrives in the newspaper as 'Turks beating up lesbians', to the huge mobilisations over Proposition 8, the (now reversed) marriage ban in California, which was immediately ascribed to Black and Latino voters (see chapter 2 of this book). This book, in contrast, asks what happens if we enter via the unremarkable processes of policing, gentrification and social death that accompany these events.

I propose the term *queer regenerations* to describe the sometimes spectacular and often banal encounters, co-habitations, hauntings, mobilisations and reverberations that occur when formerly degenerate bodies, times and places come to life. To inquire about queer regenerations often means to foreground the uneventful. It involves asking, for instance, what else is going on, and who else is on the scene, as certain queer bodies become a lovely sight in the shadow of racialised Others; as transgender bodies, whose dehumanisation rarely gains the status of injustice, gain visibility as colourful subjects in revitalised areas that have let go of people of colour; and as assimilated rights-bearing subjects re/turn towards murderous times and places with queer nostalgia. It further involves asking who or what becomes legible as gay, queer and trans, and who gets run over on the intersections. To think of these processes as queer regeneration enables us to make sense of ascendancies that are uneven and contradictory, and leave scores behind.

Queer Lovers and Hateful Others traces these shifts in how gendered and racialised bodies are carved out, new populations are moulded, and older ones re-cast. For example, I ask how trans subjects, long excessive to 'LGB-fake-T' coalitions (Spade 2004), are becoming recognisable in an environment marked by gentrification, economic restructuring and racist backlash. These are the classic biopolitical and necropolitical questions over who gets to live, who must die, and who is let die (Foucault 2004 [1978]; Mbembe 2003). While Foucault highlights that it is often in the name of maximising life that 'improper' life gets taken, Mbembe draws our attention to the increasingly unabashed centrality of death in contemporary socialities. As Kuntsman, Posocco and I (Haritaworn et al. 2013, 2014) argue in the introductions to our collections Queer Necropolitics and 'Murderous Inclusions', the innocent and respectable queer subject who is worthy of intimacy, protection and safe space is born in 'topographies of cruelty' and against the backdrop of war, imperial rescue, violent borders, criminalisation, aid tying, urban regeneration, and other death-worlds (Mbembe 2003: 40). Queer ascendancies thus tend to bolster hegemonies of the state, the global North, the market, and the military, carceral and biomedical methodologies that bolster them through the punishment and reform of surplus populations, now with the help of LGBT experts.

At the same, queer regeneration often occurs in the spaces between and beyond, where life and death are symbiotic. In our introduction to Queer Necropolitics, we highlighted both literal and social death and graduated states of living and dying. Queer Lovers and Hateful Others adds to this attention to ambivalent and ambiguous times and spaces that are haunted by past and future deaths, while also being fertile grounds of revitalisation (see Ferreday and Kuntsman 2011). The queer regenerations examined here tend to stay close to what, following Sherene Razack (2002a, 2002b), I term 'degenerate' spaces associated with crime, disorder and dysfunction, such as the inner city, the prison and the asylum, which are segregated from 'respectable' spaces of 'proper' white middle-class life. Discussing colonial contexts, Razack describes the 'journey of transgression' between 'respectable' spaces where white settlers live, and 'degenerate' spaces where Indigenous people live, as foundational to the constitution of normative masculinities and femininities. In contrast, the transgressive mobilities of queers with race and class privileges into formerly degenerate areas do not perform straightforwardly respectable gender and sexual identities. They are nevertheless legitimated as transitional phenomena in transitioning areas that were hitherto considered ungentrifiable. Queer regeneration – whose echoes with urban regeneration I highlight on purpose – here takes the shape of encounters of formerly undesirable subjects with formerly undesirable spaces and the bodies that linger there.

Thus, it is telling that the drama of queer lovers and hateful Others has found its most fertile terrain in the former 'guest worker' district of Berlin Kreuzberg. If the authors of *Khalass!!! We're vex!* highlight Kreuzberg as a site of queer gentrification, it is important to note that the district has served as an exemplary setting for racialised pathology and criminality in German imaginaries of race and space. It was long a site of segregation for labour migrants, whose presence was planned to be just as temporary as the crumbling buildings containing them. In the 1960s and 1970s, the district was targeted for large-scale demolition. As a result of urban protest and changing planning fashions, the buildings stayed and underwent significant restoration, often led by queer and other 'alternative' collective living projects. Now objects of nostalgia, it is important to note that these counter-cultures never fully rid themselves of the trappings of their whiteness (see MacDougall 2011). At the conjuncture of 're'-unification and neoliberalism, the race and class divisions that have underlain the mythos Kreuzberg from the start were if anything intensified. While many of the former squatters have been able to buy houses or formalise their housing situation, racialised bodies, as degenerate residues in a regenerating space, are increasingly displaced as a result of rising rents and shrinking incomes. During the Cold War, West Berlin was relatively cheap to live in, not least as a result of federal subsidies for housing and industry that stemmed population decline in a city surrounded by the other, socialist, Germany. In the post-unification era, the city has become an ever harder place for poor people to remain in. Rents have risen most in inner-city areas like Kreuzberg, which moved from the 'shadow of the wall', as Jennifer Petzen (2008) puts it, to the heart of the city (see also Holm 2011). The removal of subsidies for housing and industry, the dismantling of services and benefits, and the marketing of the city and its 'neighbourhoods' to tourists and investors under an increasingly entrepreneurial city regime, have each made the inner city increasingly unaffordable (Ha 2013).

The ascendant queer subject thus stays close to deathly places, as well as times. These further include the Nazi past, the AIDS crisis, and the 'homophobic' geographies of the global South. To think of these proximities in terms of queer regenerations means to inquire into differential processes of valuation and devaluation. Thus, if gay, queer and transgender activists have stayed close to the prison and the asylum, these 'intimate investments' (Agathangelou et al. 2008) nevertheless produce real returns. Queer and trans prison abolitionists have sometimes assumed an inherent contradiction in fighting for hate crime laws that consolidate carceral and biomedical regimes that long criminalised and pathologised homosexuality and transgender. However, while the penal state remains one of the biggest perpetrators for (queer and straight) people of colour, especially those who are poor, gender non-conforming or disabled, the swift rise of a newly professionalising class of LGBT experts, who invest in institutions that expand white middle-class entitlement, demands that we acknowledge these contradictions as systemic rather than surprising (see chapter 3 of this book).

The pages ahead follow queer regenerations across various further sites, including the Nazi past, whose recovery has become a prolific source for queer art and activism, and the inner city, where the drama of queer lovers and hateful Others finds its evocative setting. They trace the displacement and dispossession of degenerate bodies alongside the arrival of transgressive subjects who, while not necessarily respectable, are tolerated as early-wave gentrifiers. Indeed, as gentrification theorists have long shown, it is in the regenerating inner city that capital is accumulated the fastest. Drawing on Neil Smith's (1979) theory of the rent gap, which accounts for the difference in a site's actual and potential value and is often used to explain how the poorest areas yield the highest investment returns, we can locate queer regeneration – a process that creates symbolic and material worth – in spaces where the value–pathology gap is especially large. People of colour communities, rendered disposable on account of both their 'inferior and deficient' cultural values and their decreased labour value in a post-Fordist regime of capital flight and restructuring, are nevertheless not without value. Indeed, they are raw material through which all kinds of valuations occur.

CORE VALUES, MORAL PANICS AND INVENTED TRADITIONS

I am an atheist who is friendly to religion. I don't believe in a god, but Christianity, Judaism or Buddhism do not bother me.

Except Islam disturbs me more and more. I'm disturbed by the highly disproportionate criminality of youth with Muslim origins. I'm disturbed by Islam's murderous contempt of women and homosexuals. I'm bothered by forced marriages, 'peace judges', 'honour crimes'. And anti-Semitic pogroms bother me more than half civilised words can tell.

Now I'm asking myself: Is religion a barrier to integration? My impression: not always. But with Islam, yes. This should explicitly be taken into account with asylum and immigration!

I don't need imported racism, and what Islam represents otherwise, I don't need either. (Fest 2014, my translation, bold in original)

Queer Lovers and Hateful Others argues that 'Muslim homophobia' has joined an older chain of criminalising and pathologising signifiers that must be understood within a longer history of racism and colonialism, which precedes the arrival of labour migrants from Turkey and North Africa in the 1960s and 1970s. Entitled 'Islam as barrier to integration', this lead commentary in *Bild*, the conservative German tabloid, places homophobia alongside crime, sexism, anti-Semitism, mal-integration and racism. This list of deficiencies is stabilised through repetition, even if the 'what' and the 'how far' it calls for are left open to personal and political preference. There is now a growing arsenal for how to deal with poor people of colour constructed as 'Muslim', regardless of how they identify themselves. On the soft end, this arsenal includes sexuality awareness, Holocaust awareness, anger management, and youth and social work; on the hardening end it includes psychiatric treatment and confinement, prison, border control, nationality law restrictions specifically for Muslims, and outright calls for deportation. Much of this focuses on young male-assigned people: the first generation of German-born individuals who officially have access to German nationality after the belated reform of the infamous *jus sanguinis* (law of the blood) in 2001, which restricted citizenship to those with German parentage. At the same time, never-ending moral panics about 'mal-integration' in apparently self-segregated Muslim 'parallel societies', measured in affective propensities to terror, crime and religion, as well as in failed genders and (hetero-)sexualities, have reversed these fragile claims to belonging on a substantive level.

One argument made by this book is that racism cannot be reduced to the work of isolated extremists or far-right movements. As many have pointed out, there is a dramatic increase in overt racism all across Europe and the settler colonies, which crosses political, gender, sexual and national identities (e.g. Lentin and Titley 2011; Fekete 2014). The transnational qualities of this surge became clear in January 2015 after the attack on *Charlie Hebdo*, the French satirical magazine specialising in making fun of Islam, which was quickly ascribed to Muslims. The global circulation of the attack through hashtags such as #jesuischarlie and through the magazine's cartoons serves to perform a West that comes into coherence through shared core values. Besides freedom of speech, these also include sexual freedom, as illustrated by a queer-themed cover of the magazine that encoded the bravery and innocence of the killed journalists (e.g. Fisher 2015). The cover, entitled 'L'Amour Plus Fort Que La Haine' (love is stronger than hate) features the kiss between a brown man stereotyped as Muslim and a white man with a 'Charlie Hebdo' caption on his T-shirt, glasses and a pencil behind his ear. The pencil, the 'more powerful weapon', has been a regular icon in the *Charlie Hebdo* debate, whose innocent connotation obfuscates the ideological work done by opinion makers. This is brought home by the increasing consent for globalised anti-Muslim racism, reflected in the simultaneous adoption of anti-'terror' policing and surveillance in countries ranging from Spain to the US, as well as the attacks by firebombs, gunfire, pig heads and grenades on 26 mosques in France, in the week following the attack alone (Stone 2015). They further include the pogrom-like anti-Muslim mobilisations that have raged across Europe in the same period. In Germany on 12 January 2015, the same day that an estimated 100,000 demonstrated across the country in solidarity with 'Charlie', 25,000 took to the streets in the East-German city of Dresden to 'defend' the country from immigrants. The demonstration was organised by Pegida (Patriotic Europeans against the Islamisation of the West), a new organisation founded in Dresden in 2014, whose name ironically references the transnational rather than national. Pegida is but the latest in a series of anti-Muslim movements and parties that have mushroomed across Europe in recent years (Paterson 2015). While mainstream politicians, progressives and LGBT organisations have condemned Pegida as an extremist movement, many Pegida followers describe themselves as regular citizens rather than neo-Nazis (Panorama 2014). Both Pegida and its 'mainstream' critics, meanwhile, share an orientation towards Islam as the constitutive outside of a Germany, Europe and West that are in danger and must be defended. When, on the evening of 12 January, Khaled Idris Bahray, an asylum seeker from Eritrea, was killed in Dresden, police ignored evidence connecting his death to the demonstration (Paterson 2015). To many observers, this recalled the recent scandal around another racist organisation, the National Socialist Underground (NSU), which enacted two bombings and nine murders in the 2000s, which again mostly targeted people racialised as Muslim. Not only were police and secret service complicit in ignoring and covering up evidence that the acts were perpetrated by NSU, they also actively criminalised the victims and their families themselves (Migrationsrat 2014a). While here, too, hate crime legislation was proposed as a solution to the violence, anti-racist activists have warned that, in a context that evades and naturalises racism and criminalises people of colour rather than white racists, such legislation would further punish the victims rather than the perpetrators. Indeed, this forecast is supported by the new discourse on reverse racism or 'hostility against Germans' – a moral panic that shares many ingredients of the 'Muslim homophobia' panic (see chapter 3, 'Hate').

Queer theorists have been slow to pick up on these confluences and complicities. If moral panics surrounding queer genders and sexualities, from sodomy to AIDS, might be considered the natural remit of queer theory, theorists of sexuality have barely begun to adjust their lenses to the queerly expanding borders of what constitutes a 'morality' that is worthy of protection (e.g. Herdt 2009; Weeks 2014). Indeed, theories of racism are more helpful in making sense of the figurative shift from the dangerous to the endangered queer. *Queer Lovers and Hateful Others* joins the renewed engagements with *Policing the Crisis*, the seminal text on neoliberalism and criminalisation by Stuart Hall and colleagues (1978). The authors sought to make sense of the birth of a new folk devil, the Black mugger, at the height of Thatcherism. They argued that the moral panic over the supposed increase in Black muggers served to manufacture consent for increasingly coercive state measures (1978: 221):

The 'mugger' was such a Folk Devil; his form and shape accurately reflected the content of the fears and anxieties of those who first imagined, and then actually discovered him: young, black, bred in, or arising from the 'breakdown of social order' in the city; threatening the traditional peace of the streets, the security of movement of the ordinary respectable citizen; motivated by naked gain, a reward he would come by, if possible, without a day's honest toil; his crime, the outcome of a thousand occasions when adults and parents had failed to correct, civilize and tutor his wilder impulses; impelled by an even more frightening need for 'gratuitous violence', an inevitable result of the weakening of moral fibre in family and society, and the general collapse of respect for discipline and authority. (Hall et al. 1978: 161–62)

The basic, long globalised, ingredients of the moral panic investigated in *Queer Lovers and Hateful Others* – failed heterosexuality, a disordered family tree, failed impulse control, and proneness to violence – are as hauntingly similar as the punitive paradigms and techniques that this panic ideologically justifies.

What has changed is that the 'morality' to be protected has expanded from a heteronormative vision of the family to queer intimacies that remain assimilable to it. In this new regime of diversity racism – which speaks the language of life while paving the way for death – homosexuality and transgender emerge as important, albeit not the only, symbols.[3] Women's rights, animal rights, and appreciation of racial mixing have each become features of a cosmopolitan, diversity-loving community whose Others are profiled by their patriarchal, homophobic, irrational, monocultural, backward or criminal dispositions (Grosfoguel et al. 2014; Haritaworn 2015; Jackson 2013; Melamed 2011). While these racial formations have long and brutal histories that predate the current encounter, the border is redrawn around 'core values' of women-and-gay-friendliness, philo-Semitism, post-Christian secularism, tolerance, and a care for peace and non-violence. This process nevertheless continues to follow the logics of racism, which Ruth Wilson Gilmore defines as 'the state-sanctioned or extralegal production and exploitation of group-differentiated vulnerability to premature death' (2007: 28).

In the never-ending repetitions of multiculturalism in crisis, the exceptional qualities in the above list are held up as core values that must be protected from Others. In contrast, I propose that we treat them as 'invented traditions', a term coined by Hobsbawm, the late theorist of the nation:

'Invented tradition' is taken to mean a set of practices, normally governed by overtly or tacitly accepted rules and of a ritual or symbolic nature, which seek to inculcate certain values and norms of behaviour by repetition, which automatically implies continuity with the past. (Hobsbawm 1983: 1–2)

Indeed, as queer of colour intellectual Koray Yılmaz-Günay comments, the author of the *Bild* editorial does not have a reputation of being 'a friend to gays or women' (Jakob 2014). Bodies and populations constructed as 'Muslim' become repositories for sexism, homophobia and anti-Semitism in ways that absolve white citizen subjects from responsibility for their violence and pave the way for more violence, now normalised as a social good.

I draw on the post-colonial notion of the constitutive outside to describe the process by which gender oppression is turned into an undesirable trait that is alienated and contained in racialised bodies (see Said 1978). It is against these constitutive Others that gays, queers and trans people are recruited as 'symbolic border guards' (Yuval-Davis 1997) for entities – from neighbourhood to nation to West – that are themselves undergoing rapid transformation. Such a view differs from a multicultural model that attempts to accommodate minoritised cultures while fixing 'their' values in a deficient and inferior position (Thobani 2007a). Indeed, as Yılmaz-Günay suggests, the claim that homophobia is imported reifies a biologistic understanding of Germanness as unhyphenable and white (Jakob 2014).

Queer Lovers and Hateful Others follows the spectacular and banal ways in which the alienation of gender oppression, and of the bodies that must bear it, occurs. For the purposes of this introduction, I will flag up two major landmarks: the Muslim Test and the Drag Festival. The so-called Muslim Test of German nationality was an administrative guideline introduced in 2006 by the German *land* of Baden-Württemberg, not long after the national reform of the *jus sanguinis*. As implied by the name, it was only applied to applicants whose prior nationality is with a so-called 'Muslim' country – which, in Germany, interpellates the majority of people of colour. Of 30 questions, half tested applicants' women-and-gay-friendliness, the other half their proneness to terrorism and 'undemocratic' beliefs and practices. Repeating globalised tropes of visibility and coming out (see Decena 2011), one question asked: 'Imagine your full-grown son comes to you and declares that he is homosexual and would like to live with another man. How do you react?' Another asked: 'In Germany various politicians have made themselves publicly known as homosexuals. What do you think about the fact that there are homosexuals in public office in Germany?' (see Courant 2006). Following public critique, the test was withdrawn in its blatantly discriminatory version. Nevertheless, the test's nationwide media career served to cement views of 'Muslims', then a relatively new racial formation, as intrinsically violent and homophobic and morally disentitled to citizenship and its benefits (Haritaworn and Petzen 2011).

By that time, the globalised terminology of religion had partially replaced earlier nationality-based terms such as 'foreigner', later replaced by the more polite 'migrants'.[4] As Yasemin Yıldız (2009) persuasively shows with regard to the shift from the 'abused Turkish woman' to the 'abused Muslim woman' in

Germany, gender is the central modality through which moulds of racialisation are currently globalised. Indeed, as Petzen and I (Haritaworn and Petzen 2011) have argued in our genealogy of the 'Muslim homophobia' discourse in Germany, the category Muslim, and the globalisation of gender-based tropes such as honour crime and homophobia, have rendered palpable a (unified) nation, Europe and West. These imagined entities have come to cohere against a common enemy and around a shared cultural origin and destiny, in the face of disparate histories of racism, colonialism, genocide, imperial competition and war. Invented traditions of women-and-gay-friendliness do significant work in infusing substance into these unstable realignments, whose borders become solidified in the process.

The Muslim Test may be read as a classic case of homonationalism – the concept coined by Jasbir Puar to describe 'how "acceptance" and "tolerance" for gay and lesbian subjects have become a barometer by which the right to and capacity for national sovereignty is evaluated' (Puar 2013: 366). While this concept has been used by activists in various contexts to scandalise racism and imperialism (e.g. SUSPECT 2010b), Puar herself has insisted that it be read closely with Lisa Duggan's (2004) seminal concept of homonormativity, which describes the depoliticisation of gay lifestyles under neoliberalism.

The second landmark that I will discuss here, however, gestures beyond both the 'homo' – a biopolitical standard that has haunted the post-identitarian strands of queer studies in particular ways – and the scale of the nation. The 'event' that ushered the 'hate crime' discourse into everyday German language took place in radical queer scenes that are highly critical of gay assimilationism and homonormativity. Notably, it found its first bodies in the genderqueer scene, during the Drag Festival, an internationally circulated event that took place in summer 2008 in Berlin Kreuzberg. Already in full circulation in the English-speaking world – where sexuality was a late-comer to a post-racial civil rights paradigm – the language of *Hasskriminalität* (hate crime) or *Hassgewalt* (hate violence) was barely known in Germany outside of policy circles. In fact, the criminal legal system was not the prime reference point for addressing homophobia and transphobia. Nevertheless, as chapter 3 ('Hate') discusses, 'hate crime' arrived in Germany on grounds that were already racialised through successive moral panics over crime, patriarchy and segregation. If critics of this paradigm in the US – one of its biggest exporters – have warned of the racist side effects of strengthening a criminal legal system that disproportionately targets Black, Indigenous and poor people of colour, it is these very capacities that made the paradigm instantly assimilable in Germany. The swift arrival of the 'hate crime' discourse in the late 2000s contrasts with its blocked arrival in the 1990s, when anti-racist activists tried to mobilise it to scandalise the racist pogroms in the wake of German re-unification. Chapter 2 ('Love') discusses the Drag Festival as the production of the first major event of 'hate crime' in left-wing queer and trans scenes, and its rapid spread to a national media and political public that was by then ready to protect even the most gender non-conforming queers from violent Turkified masculinities. I examine this ascendancy against the backdrop of Kreuzberg as a formerly degenerate, now gentrifying space. Indeed, such a view is reflected both in marches and other actions by radical queers to 'reclaim' Kreuzberg and Neukölln from their apparently increasing queerphobia, and in the queer-friendly actions of politicians eager to 'improve' these areas. Drawing on activist and media discourses, policy texts on hate crime and sexual diversity, studies of gentrification, and interviews with queer of colour participants, I argue that radical queers, while excessive to more respectable spaces (Razack 2002a), have become privileged symbols of a regenerating 'neighbourhood' that is figured as colourful even while it is letting go of the people of colour who were long confined to it.

Rendered in intensely local terms, the drama of queer lovers and hateful Others is nevertheless thoroughly globalised. Thus, both the hate/crime setting and the Muslim homophobe have crossed European borders. Marches to re/claim formerly poor and racialised inner-city areas for safer queer habitation have also occurred in the East End of London and in Grønland, the multicultural neighbourhood in Norway's capital Oslo (Decolonize Queer 2011; Lamble 2014; personal communication with Arnika Rodriguez in 2010; Safra Project 2011). The racialised hate crime discourse has a longer history in the Netherlands, and Dutch representatives have travelled to Germany to share their expertise with local organisations, politicians and policy makers (Bracke 2012; Çetin 2011; El-Tayeb 2012; Haritaworn 2010a; Haritaworn et al. 2008; Jivraj and de Jong 2011). Much work remains to trace these travels of capital, identities, ideologies and methodologies in ways that stay attentive to local histories and landscapes (see Grewal and Kaplan 1994).

LGBT expressions premised on murderous inclusions have thus expanded and crossed borders at an intense speed. This contrasts with the displacements and erasures that queers of colour have experienced in the wake of racism and gentrification. In this shrinking environment, the kitchen table is not only what remains, but also a good starting point to begin to tell better stories of gender and sexuality, which refuse to diversify the murderous status quo.

KITCHEN TABLES

> We become 'bilingual', fluent in both activist and scholarly cultures and language, and our research questions and intellectual concerns are shaped by our activist engagements. (Sudbury and Okazawa-Rey 2007: 8)

These pages began, and I hope will end up, on queer of colour kitchen tables, where I have been a regular participant since the late 1990s. Yet to switch codes and state this in front of an academic audience feels risky. How do I translate the kitchen table to readers who are not part of them, and how do I represent my role in these spaces, and in this translation? Should I describe myself as archivist of these conversations? Clearly, these knowledges existed and were passed on long before I began to record them. There are palpable dangers in sharing with a bigger public stories that were forged in the service of community. Besides the professionalising, institutionalising and depoliticising impulses to writing things that will make it into print (however precariously), such dangers include making the brilliant and often risky insights of community members vulnerable to extraction, appropriation and backlash. As someone who has spoken in both 'academic' and 'activist' vernaculars, I can confirm that speech acts that are not channelled through a disembodied, professional intellectual voice are far more vulnerable to punishment and pathologisation. This is illustrated by the responses to our chapter 'Gay imperialism' (Haritaworn et al. 2008), which was withdrawn from print after barely a year and then recirculated as an instance of sloppy scholarship and injury towards a well-known white gay male activist by the gay press, the activist, his allies and our publisher herself.[5] The experience taught me that intellectuals who cross organic-professional lines are especially vulnerable to backlash. In her insightful analysis of the *ad hominem* attacks on us as authors in the blogosphere and gay media, Johanna Rothe (forthcoming) documents how we were depicted as 'lunatics', 'fundamentalists' and impostors with 'computer-generated names' on the basis of our racialised and gender non-conforming names, phenotypes and precarious employment statuses, and rendered instantly unrespectable as academics. At the same time, we were evicted from an activist positionality, too. As the only author (barely) employed at a university at the time, I was targeted as the 'academic' attacking the 'activist', a location reserved for the 'innocent' white non-trans man, whom this identity served to inoculate from critique. In the meantime, our work was being plagiarised. We, too, became pre-theoretical raw material to which 'real' academics were able to help themselves, while depoliticising our messages and resourcing our labour for a sexy and newly respectable 'debate' whose cutting edge depended on culling the irrational and excessive margin. It is not a coincidence that repression occurs when our knowledges leave the kitchen table *as queer of colour knowledges*. The kitchen table, as the rare place where anti-racist queer critique can be shared in ways that evade surveillance and appropriation, must thus be accessed responsibly.

I also hesitated to do interviews because I worried about how traditional divisions of text into 'data' and 'analysis' can reinforce power differentials between the spoken and the written word, and between organic and professional intellectual labour. As a scholar attempting to be accountable to my communities,

I acknowledge that this book, published under my authorship, will both make me vulnerable and benefit me as someone who is employed as an academic. I appeal to you as readers to share responsibility for training yourself to perceive the kitchen table in ways that refrain from exploiting and objectifying it and its participants.

Furthermore, I have long refused pressures by white audiences to highlight 'real' queer of colour 'experiences'. These have been considerable. 'But what of queers of colour?' has been a frequent response to the lectures and presentations that have preceded this book. Not only are queers of colour constructed as ideally unadulterated by politics and education, they are implicitly reduced to an 'oppressed' standpoint whose legitimacy is equated with an ability and willingness to authenticate racism (see Haritaworn et al., 2008). In contrast, queer of colour speech acts that talk back at white supremacy are discredited as inauthentic. The queer of colour kitchen table in Berlin formed in response to growing anti-Muslim racism, and in solidarity with queer Muslims and others self-organising under various umbrellas (see SUSPECT 2011). The kitchen table constitutes a shifting coalition whose composites change all the time, depending who's at the table, and who's in town. Like the *Khalass!!!* manifesto, its existence reflects the necessity to discuss racisms as multiple, differential and relational. If participants have come together to counter the trope of the 'most homophobic', the next conjuncture may well reorganise this space, or dissolve it altogether. This also goes for identities such as 'queer of colour' (spelled 'colour' rather than 'color' on purpose), which at the time of writing is proliferating into 'QTIBPoC' (queer, trans, inter, Black and People of Colour), reflecting the changing and contingent nature of dis/identification in response to racism and gender violence, the dangers of essentialising social locations that do not automatically give rise to resistant and allied capacities but must be grown and nurtured with care, the ongoing conversations that occur about multiple forms of power and privilege, and the central importance of anti-Black racism in Germany and globally, alongside an insistence on self-determining how, with whom, and under what name we organise.

As I write this, I am hyper aware of the fragility of this emergent site, which all too often is attacked or dismissed as the 'p.c. that goes too far'. In the pages ahead, I will disappoint any ethnographic desires to measure and describe the kitchen table. To treat the important interventions that are happening there respectfully, we – as writers and readers attempting to form epistemic community accountably – can refuse to participate in the objectifying gaze. With this health warning in mind, I have nevertheless decided to cite fellow kitchen table organisers directly, as critics of the same forces that I have been writing about for a number of years. As this work is gaining an audience, it is increasingly important for me to acknowledge that the words that I am using are not (exclusively) my own, and that they reflect the collective wisdom and brilliance gleaned from building community by and for trans and queer people of colour. I have long taken care to credit insights gained from personal conversations. In this book, I am going a step further to highlight my interlocutors as important knowledge producers in their own right. Given the dangers of backlash that this also entails, this has meant running individual passages by participants, to ask which ones they preferred to be cited with their name, which with a chosen pseudonym, and which anonymously.

Encarnación Gutiérrez Rodríguez's (2000, 2010) characterisation of migrant feminists in Germany as organic intellectuals is inspiring here. Drawing on Antonio Gramsci, whose colonialist evasions and class reductionism she flags, Gutiérrez Rodríguez (2010) describes the embodied intellectual labour of migrant feminists as follows:

> It means to not delink representation from its material conditions. It means to not speak *about* the subaltern but to contextualize and situate one's speaking. It means to highlight the relations in which speaking becomes possible and representable.... And simultaneously, to be vigilant about the possibility that our forms of articulation are … instrumentalized. (Gutiérrez Rodríguez 2000)

The spectre of instrumentalisation that this quote ends on evokes Gramsci's other figure, the professional intellectual. While organic intellectuals originate in and theorise in the service of oppressed movements, professional intellectuals are often employed to work in the service of hegemonic projects (Gramsci 1996). Gutiérrez Rodríguez illustrates this with the demand for authentic expressions of Otherness in arts and academic industries. There, the labour of migrant feminists is not completely ignored. It even finds entry into the canon, but often disappears into it without credit and in ways that dilute and depoliticise its radical intentions and interventions (see also Bilge 2013; Sow 2014). Ironically, the appropriation of the political category 'migrant' that Gutiérrez Rodríguez warned of has since happened. Forged by anti-racist feminists in Germany in the 1980s, in coalitions that crossed generational and diasporic divisions, the 'migrant' has become a polite euphemism for the 'foreigner' and the 'Turk'. Furthermore, since the 2000s, massive media coverage has been given to 'migrant feminists' willing to authenticate discourses on their 'most patriarchal' and 'most homophobic' communities, such as Seyran Ateş, Necla Kelek and Güner Balcı (see Yıldız 2009).

In addition to warning against an essentialist understanding of location that evades its conditions of production and consumption, Gutiérrez Rodríguez (2010) cautions against interpreting the 'organic' in ways that naturalise the social. Similarly, my juxtaposition of 'organic intellectuals' at 'kitchen tables' with what I call the 'plastic' politics of homonormative non-governmental organisations (NGOs) should not be read as reifying correlationist hierarchies and technophobic distinctions between 'real' and 'fake'. In chapter 2 ('Love'), I describe the (post-)political methodology of the gay kiss as plastic activism: something that looks like a mass movement but is really the work of a small handful of paid functionaries and their graphic designer. Indeed, queers of colour are well represented in blogging and other media activisms that are high tech but accessible to individuals with little social capital.[6] At the same time, going viral means different things for different bodies. The awareness that for queer and trans people of colour, visibility often entails violence also informed the collective publishing attempts by SUSPECT, a trans/queer of colour anti-violence collective active in the late 2000s and early 2010s that intersects with both *Khalass!!!* and the kitchen-table snapshots presented in this book. The name SUSPECT, incidentally, references the surveillance of people of colour, including queer people of colour, in Germany, whose illegible unruly bodies could not be further removed from the script of the queer lover.

The following quote is from a SUSPECT piece that was published in 2010, in response to the Pride racism scandal. The piece interrogates the unequal relations involved in producing and consuming the 'event' of 'Butler's refusal', which happened after queers of colour and allies in Berlin had spent considerable time sharing their work and analyses with Butler (see Petzen 2011). Nevertheless, the 'event' that made the term 'homonationalism' go viral in a predominantly white European academy, became newsworthy in ways that centred academics from the US. Its virality did not contribute to a greater alliance with or engagement with local queer of colour struggles in Germany, which were thus once again reduced to pre-theoretical raw material from which value could be extracted for the packaging of 'real' theory.

> [D]iscussions have tended to focus on Butler as a person rather than the issues at hand, or at stake. This again threatens to sideline queer and trans people of colour in Germany, whose struggle may seem a little too far away for some to attend to in its own right.... As Angela Davis put it in her commentary on the situation (youtube.com/watch?v=T0BzKCRgnj8), the terrain of struggle has changed, yet the division of labour, risk, and gains is lagging far behind.... As queer and trans people of colour and allies, we are painfully aware of dominant hierarchies of political and intellectual labour, pervasive both in the academic, media and non-profit industrial complexes … and in less institutionalized and professionalized spaces. These are parasitic upon the bodies, experiences, and labour of those who are kept in the place of the deviant, developmental or exotic object of study, and who all too often are structurally excluded from formal education and employment. The claiming of a queer or trans of colour position is a complicated one, both demonized and desired, and often immediately dismissed for lack or excess

of intelligence or authenticity. While these injustices need to be named and redressed, especially by those who currently benefit from them, we believe that the politicization and democratization of knowledge production must go far beyond this. How can we begin to understand knowledge and skills as something that must end in radical struggle and transformation, rather than on a CV? How do we redistribute not only the credit, but also the risks of labour? (SUSPECT 2010a)

The blog entry cites an earlier, collectively authored, piece by SUSPECT whose title, 'Activist writings for organic intellectuals' directly rejects distinctions between academic and non-academic knowledge productions. The piece is a living archive that lists sources that the group read together in order to make sense of the moral panic over Muslim homophobia in Germany. Importantly, it asks readers to make connections to their own contexts, and to how techniques of punishment and pathologisation travel across borders.

Radical movements and individual acts of bravery or brilliance in speaking out against injustice do not come from nowhere but are the result of collective labour and local and transnational histories of organizing. SUSPECT was initially formed in order to monitor the arrival of the racist hate crimes debates in Germany. Recognizing the importance of emancipatory peer education outside the academic industrial complex, we started off as a reading group in the rooms of a local queer of colour NGO in Berlin. In this bibliography, we would like to share some of the resources which we managed to get hold of here. We felt we needed to learn from our siblings and allies in places where the punitive turn of LGBT organizing had already happened. The work of Incite!, the women/trans of colour anti-violence organization in the US, was a particular inspiration to us. We focused on German-speaking texts and texts dealing with the consequences of relying on a criminal 'justice' system which disproportionately incarcerates poor people, people of colour, people with mental health problems, and gender non-conforming people – but we know there is lots more out there. Please help us annotate this bibliography and list of resources, and send us further links and references including short descriptions! (SUSPECT 2010b)

Notably, the passage does not reference the US as an advanced geography whose superior socialities should be emulated in Germany, however likely such a comparative reading is in the current geopolitical context of activist and academic travel, including by radical women of colour and queers of colour themselves. On the contrary, queers of colour in Germany are aware that the US is the current centre of empire, which is built on conquest, slavery and imperial war and which, 'with 5% of the world's population, incarcerates

25% of the world's prisoners' (Braz et al. 2000). 'Progress' here amounts to the maximum exploitation, dehumanisation and erasure of Black, Indigenous and racialised populations that is rendered defensible under current moral regimes of rights and meritocracy (Davis 2011; Gilmore 2007; Smith 2005). This indeed makes the US a relevant reference point as an exporter of 'hate crime' and other punitive technologies, whose arrival in Germany must be closely monitored. Furthermore, movements that resist capital and the state and are relatively open to queer of colour and trans of colour participation have reached a bigger critical mass in the US than in Europe as a result of both scale and what they are up against.

At the same time, the conversations invoked here have many ancestors, some of whom are easily accessible to our memory, while others must be searched for and homed back into community. They include the Black German movement that has organised since the 1980s and been key to making speakable the whiteness pervading German culture and counter-cultures. Fatima El-Tayeb (2011) emphasises the forerunning role of Black women in this movement, many of whom have been queer, and in active conversation with queer women of colour movements in the US and other parts of Europe. El-Tayeb draws our attention to the tendency among US academics writing on Germany to repeat the conflation of Germanness and whiteness, and the erasure of non-white presences and histories in Germany. In contrast, she highlights the positive role that Audre Lorde played as an ally in Black German women's organising during her visits to Germany. Lorde used her writing classes in Berlin and her currency in white-dominated feminist circles to support Black German women's writing and publishing. An important product of these encounters is the first Black German collection, *Farbe bekennen* (English: *Showing our Colors*), whose editors included May Ayim (formerly known as Opitz) and Katharina Oguntoye (Opitz et al. 1992 [1986]). Rather than treat Afro-Germans as derivative of African American experiences, Lorde reached 'out to a black community that most African Americans still assumed to be nonexistent' (El-Tayeb 2011: 113).

Beyond the trans-Atlantic, it is important to highlight travels within Europe. El-Tayeb narrates the formation of a group of queer women of colour from Germany who congregated in the Netherlands, where they encountered an active presence of Black lesbian and queer women of colour organising. Two of these emigrées, Olumide Popoola and Beldan Sezen (1999), produced the first queer of colour collection *Talking Home: Heimat aus unserer eigenen Feder. Frauen of Color in Deutschland* (Home from Our Own Pen: Women of Colour in Germany), whose contributors claim various African, Asian and Latin American genealogies. The editors wrote in their prologue:

> Both of us considered anthologies/books by women/lesbians of colour important, a part of our everyday life. Both as possibilities for identification,

sources of energy, empowerment, inspiration, and as good literature that you can enjoy to the full. Audre Lorde, Barbara Smith, Alice Walker, Sonia Sanchez, Silva Makeda, Amy Tan, June Jordan, Kitty Tsui ... have each given us a lot. But we often wondered how there could be so little literature of this kind in Germany. We were tired of not having a voice. How could it be that we didn't exist? ... Like so many others we had to write the words that we would have desperately needed to read ourselves. (Popoola and Sezen 1999: 1)

It is no coincidence that the list of writers credited in this first queer of colour anthology begins with Audre Lorde. Lorde also appears on the back cover of *Queer Lovers and Hateful Others*; on the wall of a queer of colour kitchen that was photographed by kitchen-table participant Aykan Safoğlu, an artist whose own work has circulated in Turkey, Germany, other parts of Europe and North America. *Showing our Colors*, *Talking Home* and the writings of May Ayim and Audre Lorde have each passed through the Berlin kitchens and living rooms that gave birth to this book.

Moreover, there are axes of travel that completely decentre the US. The kitchen tables featured in this book include migrants from Turkey, Spain, France, Britain, North and South America, and other parts of Germany, whose trajectories were shaped by various histories of racism, colonialism, gender and sexual oppression, and organising (see, for example, Bacchetta 2014; Fekete 2006). Participants expressed a keen awareness of how regimes of oppression have long travelled too. For example, Anouchk Ibacka Valiente, who has lived in France, Spain and Cuba, discussed in an interview how the trope of the 'transphobic/homophobic Muslim' is globalised:

In France, these kinds of groups try to be integrated. [Mentions a queer Muslim group that] went to Israel, couldn't you be clearer with your position? We are the nice Muslims, we want to be integrated? And in [les Panthères roses, a group she was organizing with in France] it wasn't an immediate topic, but we were already like 'Homophobia exists everywhere, stop saying it's only in the banlieues [racialised and stigmatised suburbs]'.

Indeed, the kitchen table is itself a product of transnational, trans-temporal and trans-diasporic travels, even if this was not at the front of our minds when we started naming our spaces after it. It is important to highlight that queer of colour kitchen tables in Berlin do not conform to the celebrated mobility that remains the prerogative of queers with race and class privileges. On the contrary, they result from a contraction of the environment. They are where we ended up when the wider queer and trans scenes became so racist and so gentrified that it was no longer safe to participate in them. At the same time, they are embattled by these same forces: with rising rents, the kitchen table is no longer a space that we can take for granted.

The kitchen table has a long history in feminist and other struggles that do not rise to the status of a social movement. Writing about feminists in the US civil rights and South African national liberation movements, M. Bahati Kuumba (2001) argues that their contributions have been erased as they fall outside of dominant conceptions of the political, which locate 'social movements' in the public sphere and privilege visibility, numbers, legal reform, and other quantifiable, measurable outcomes (see also Reed 2005). This dovetails with critiques of the non-profit industrial complex for privileging sites and methods that favour those who already resemble 'citizens', and work to professionalise and institutionalise movements away from the grassroots, and into the state (Incite! 2007). Kuumba thus urges us to turn to the kitchen table and other informal spaces, networks of communication and action, where theory often emerges.

Alexis Pauline Gumbs, too, highlights the importance of investing in the 'undervalued energetic economy of the kitchen table' (2010: 466). She reminds us of the kitchen table's significance to Black feminist organising in the 1980s and to the contemporary queer of colour activisms that have stepped into its genealogy in order to forge 'counternarrative and poetic interruptions that not only threaten the reproduction of the narrative of heteropatriarchal capitalism, but also offer something else in its place' (2010: 57). To Gumbs, the anti-imperialist 'community of accountability' that the kitchen table gives rise to in the place of the market is illustrated by Kitchen Table: Woman of Color Press, the activist press conceived by Audre Lorde and Barbara Smith around 1980. Kitchen Table published many books and pamphlets that became pivotal to women and queer of colour movements transnationally, including the *Combahee River Collective Statement* (1977), *This Bridge Called My Back* (1981, edited by Cherríe Moraga and Gloria Anzaldúa) and *Home Girls: A Black Feminist Anthology* (2000 [1983], edited by Smith). Importantly, it was the underpaid and undervalued work of Black women that enabled the publication of many of the texts that have become foundational for transnational women and queer of colour movements, and that non-Black Third World Women, non-Black queers of colour, and Black gay men have benefited from substantially and in ways that remain to be reciprocated. Gumbs highlights the difficulties involved in sustaining the press for 15 years, and the toll that this took on the organisers (see also Ross 2003). As both Gumbs (2010) and Hong (2008) have pointed out, many Black women of this generation died prematurely.

While specific to its time and place, it is noteworthy that the kitchen table invoked by these publications did not arise out of a vacuum but reflected authors' and editors' involvement in many movements. As Barbara Smith put it in her interview with Loretta Ross:

I was involved, as you know, in political activism from high school on. And, of course, I was involved in the black civil rights movement and the anti-Vietnam War movement. There was a period of my early days in graduate school when I was not politically active and then I got pulled in, with a mighty sweep, into the black feminist movement, particularly or specifically because of attending the National Black Feminist Organization eastern regional conference in '73. (Ross 2003: 72)

Similarly, the individuals interviewed for this book have participated in many movements, including against police violence, racism, gentrification, borders and war. They indeed have organising histories in queer, transgender and feminist spaces, which are erased with each round of backlash proclaimed to defend people who 'have fought for this'. Just as their undervalued and appropriated labour disappears from view, queer of colour participants in these spaces go missing swiftly and are rarely remembered. One participant who identified as 'Meivi, Lautaro sisa [after the mapuche warrior and bartolina sisa wife of tupac katari], brown woman from the so-called global sur, and a non-academic' argued that white queer and left spaces rarely show accountability for excluding people of colour, who matter so little that they are ultimately interchangeable:

It's very funny to see that in these spaces, they pretend many times that 'Oh, someone says the word racism, it's the first time that this ever happened.' And how they are like collectively able to ally themselves to each other and wash out other people and other experiences.... For example, there is a super-queer friendly *wagenplatz* [formerly squatted trailer parks that emulate a Sinti and Rroma lifestyle]. *(JH: You're anonymising it ...)* Yeah, because also it's more than one, and it's happening the same way elsewhere, that's why. Most of the people living at this *wagenplatz* are white German or white non-German. I have a lot of friends there, I also had bad experiences there. But when something big happens, everybody pretends 'Oh, it's the first time, I can't believe it's happened here.' ... They often talk about how they can include people of colour in their spaces. Like Schwarzer Kanal [a prominent *wagenplatz* known for its international queer film festival *Entzaubert*] left leaflets in Babylonia [a left-wing language school] many times in many different languages, 'If you want to come here', even though Babylonia is another space that is just like that.

Rather than an alternative site to organising, then, the kitchen table is, for many, a place of visioning that can hold complicated bodies and histories without demanding that we rid ourselves of our excesses, fit ourselves into impossible moulds, and give away our labour and life blood without asking for something in return.

This does not mean that kitchen tables are always comfortable or that they are outside of power. While this book focuses on queer regenerations outside of the kitchen table, it is crucial to recognise that queer and trans people of colour in Berlin have faced some steep learning curves together, including about transphobia, disablism, anti-Black racism, anti-Rroma racism, and anti-Muslim racism. Training each other up, learning fast, and doing the footwork to reduce harm to each other has nevertheless followed a different economy than the one governing wider queer and left scenes. In contrast to a 'political correctness' that is not easily available to us on intersections that are excessive and devoid of value, these acts have often been grounded in the recognition that we are interdependent on each other, and that nobody, however badly they mess up, is disposable. Sometimes our kitchens are filled with laughter, at others the growing pains from strained and stretched resources are palpable. Critical moments called for alliance between trans and queer, and straight and non-trans people of colour, who as a result of the leadership of anti-racist queer and trans people of colour have begun to come out as allies. As our environments shrank, we realised that the kitchen table can be a site of transformation as well as critique. When friends got sick, we got a crash course in disability justice, and relocated to our living and bedrooms. Ironically, this made our organising more sustainable, less burnout driven, and more fun. In summer 2012, a queer of colour apartment with a long history of being inhabited by women of colour became a site of intervention into a feminist of colour conference that did not include trans people in its remit. Organising for this was prefigurative in that it resembled the kind of world we are trying to build. Between our friend's kitchen and living room, we shared food, films, long breaks and laughter. The result was historic: for the first time, a feminist of colour conference in Germany was actively conceived with trans and intersex people in mind.[7]

A launch pad and recharging place connected to broader mobilising, the kitchen table has also been a crucial site that many choose to invest in in its own right. Here, knowledge is produced in ways that decentre both the white logics of inclusion of wider queer scenes, and the competitive, privatising and commodifying logics of personal exceptionalism and brilliance that govern the academic, non-profit and arts industrial complexes. It is forged collectively, in ways that stay directly in the service of healing, visioning and community building. This is how Miran N. and Raju Rage (2013), two trans of colour organic intellectuals, refer to the kitchen table in their mutual interview:

> this kitchen-table discussion between two trans masculine-femme brown bears (of color) models healing justice through non-academic personal/ political narratives. this interview uses imaginative time travel dialogue as a tool for empowerment. mîran and raju talk to each other and their younger selves to create a transformative discussion about what it means to be us:

trans people of color in a world full of struggle and survival. this project embodies healing justice as a way through oppression, for our current and younger trans of color selves.

The kitchen table is thus not insulated from (other) social movements. Nor is it completely autonomous from the industrial complexes. Indeed, many queers of colour either work or try to find work in the arts, non-profit or academic industrial complexes, where their labour is again subjected to various forms of valuation and devaluation.

VALUE BEYOND CORE VALUES

Q: I have a feeling that white trans people are automatically treated as coalition partners by the anti-racist NGOs.

A: Sure, they're trans, so they must be anti-racist (laughs).

Q: Are they?

A: Oh please … but how else would you explain that [NGO X], a place that specifically works for women of colour and migrant women and foregrounds them as a target group, suddenly has so many white trans people on the team?

Q: Trans guys?

A: Of course, who else? And that they feel this is an alliance where both sides are in the same boat. That these are analogous experiences. And in the same breath disregard any form of trans femininity, as well as trans people of colour, so utterly and completely, by lumping together white trans people with the experience of queers of colour. This is happening a lot right now.

Q: How did trans become interesting?

A: I think particularly for organisations that have done lesbian and gay work forever, this became interesting as a result of the influx of interns from gender studies, who have theoretically dealt with things.… So that organisations that two, three, four years ago were transphobia incarnate, were oozing with gender essentialisms, are now specialists in trans lifestyles. […]

Q: But why white trans men?

A: This is not about a target group that needs advice, support and allies. It's not about trans women of colour. It's about a political claim and standard, the gender studies standard that these people are able to serve.… The study contents [these interns bring] are pre-digested and they're elitist, and formulated so beautifully that organisations jump at them. They have the language, they know the key words, that fit right in with these organisations and their agendas. And sex workers don't have this, don't use the right words, don't have the right things that are valuable for project funding.

The queer of colour kitchen table, a setting that does not rise to the status of a social movement, enables such radical critique. In this section, I will follow the lead of this participant, here anonymous, who argues that to understand queer regeneration we must first grasp the symbiotic relationship between various industries – sometimes referred to as the academic industrial complex (AIC), non-profit (NPIC), prison (PIC) and medical (MIC) industrial complexes (Incite! 2011; Smith 2007a). Each of these works to distinguish subjects who are able to pass as 'diverse' from those who are erased and managed *so that others can accumulate value.*

To enquire into queer regeneration thus means more than to include ever more diverse subjects into industries, institutions and fields of study, each of which is involved in extracting value from bodies assigned to the realms of risk, pathology and waste. Indeed, as the participant lays out, in these institutions diversity becomes a skill, a currency that can be performed by some but not others, who are capacitated mainly in their death. In the mode of difference that is valued in this context of professionalisation and institutionalisation, coalition becomes both a dodgy deal and a ground for extraction. While some emerge from these trade-offs – your race for my gender – as 'specialists', others, notably trans women of colour and sex workers, become a number to be added up, or a thing to be accumulated, on annual reviews and funding proposals.

The problem with this diversity economy is not simply that it renders some unintelligible – the political correctness that goes too far, the grammatical error that must be corrected. Rather, as anti-racist disability scholars such as Rachel Gorman (2013) and Nadia Kanani (2011) have also argued, racism and colonialism work by creating degenerate bodies whose main value lies in what can be extracted from them, through work, theft or warehousing, depending on what the current economic mode demands. These bodies can perform 'disabled' or 'queer' only at a great cost. They are *naturally* deficient and perverse: 'monocultural, irrational, regressive, patriarchal, or criminal' populations that are the constitutive Others of what Jodi Melamed (2011) refers to as the neoliberal multicultural subject, what I refer to as the respectable LGBT subject, and what Gorman (2013) refers to as the rights-bearing disabled subject.

Queer Lovers and Hateful Others interrogates how these ascendancies work precisely through the human raw material that is cycled through punitive, pathologising and diversity industries alike. The pages ahead explore how bodies that have become recognisable as gay, queer and transgender for the first time become a lovely sight in the shadow of criminalised and pathologised populations whose global production brings into coherence and imagined community geopolitical and biopolitical entities long considered unlike: nation, Europe and West, but also assimilated gays inside and radical queers outside the NPIC. These 'dodgy deals' serve to accrue value to each coalition partner. On the one hand, the migrant lesbian organisation receives further funding by adding 'trans*' to their remit, on the other, white trans-masculine bodies for the first time become worthy of inclusion into funded projects and positions as 'trans*'. This mobilisation across categories excludes trans people of colour, especially those who are male-to-female, trans women, trans feminine, poor or sex workers. They are less able to accrue value and more likely to remain resources for non-trans queers of colour and for trans people with race and class privileges. Their co-presence is not valuable; it does not add value to those who have already partnered with significant Others who possess matching capital and currency. It is precisely through this erasure that the coalition becomes productive and meaningful. This does not mean that trans people of colour are fully absent from the resulting politics and spaces. As Janet Mock (2013) argues in her discussion of why she did not go to Transgender Day of Remembrance, trans women of colour, unwanted and unintelligible as living breathing subjects, are often reintroduced into trans-designated spaces as dead or dying.

While lacking in moral value and exchange value, racialised bodies are not without value. *Queer Lovers and Hateful Others* highlights forms of work that occur outside formal markets. This includes anti-racist queer of colour interventions that remain excessive to non-profit and academic networks but are also often appropriated, resourced and surplussed by them. It further highlights capacitations that do not resemble work, but put the racially and sexually non-conforming body to work in ways that directly position it as a resource. Racialised bodies here become valuable not as labour (however hard they are working) but as raw material from which value is extracted for others' benefit.

Taking a leaf out of Beverley Skeggs' (1997, 2004) discussion of white working-class femininities, I propose that we view what is valued on a continuum with what is pathologised – a process whose disablist frames we must take care not to reify. Critical disability studies scholarship has challenged a biomedical framework that treats disabilities as deficiencies of the 'abnormal' body and mind. Most helpfully, anti-racist and anti-colonial scholars of disability have drawn our attention to the disabling workings and logics of racial and colonial capitalism (Erevelles 2010; Gorman 2013; Kanani 2011). Following Gorman, Kanani (forthcoming: 6) discusses the role of medical and psychiatric discourses in constructing Indigenous peoples as 'intellectually inferior and morally deficient'. However, while interpellated in the terms of disability, bodies that are racially pathologised are rarely able to pass as rights-bearing disabled subjects.

Drawing on Bourdieu's (1987) theory of social capital, Skeggs asks how bodies are classified as valuable or pathological, and how this mobilises them socially and spatially, 'to move in social space with ease and a sense of value, or to become fixed in positions and ascribed symptoms of pathology' (2004: 293). In particular, she is interested in mobilisations of style that cut across gender, race and class, accruing value to some while reinscribing others as pathological, but also as 'mobile resources' that can serve others' processes of valuation.

Thus, while straight men incorporate (certain) aspects of femininity in order to perform themselves as 'new managers' who are caring and friendly, women are expected to just be feminine without gaining value from this. Similarly, white men appropriate, attach and detach Black working-class masculinity in order to be 'cool', while Black men 'just are'.

> What operates as a resource for one person may fix, essentialize, and pathologize another, meaning that access and the relations of entitlement structure present relations of gender and sexuality. This process reveals how the cultural is put to use as an exchange value, as property, accrued and embodied. (Skeggs 2004: 296)

Mobilisation thus accrues exchange value to privileged bodies while reducing oppressed bodies to the status of resources that exist for others. In this book, I am similarly interested in mobilisations *across* categories that are classified differentially: the queer lover who becomes a lovely sight in the shadow of the hateful Other, the white drag artist who appropriates working-class Black, Latino and immigrant styles in order to perform an especially excessive masculinity and femininity, the white LGBT activist who specialises in the persecution of queers of colour and sexually and gender non-conforming people in the global South, and the queer subject with race and class privilege who participates in the regeneration of the formerly degenerate neighbourhood. These mobilisations are queer regenerations in that they describe shifts *within* as well as across categories.

The theme of racialised bodies as raw material threads itself through critical literatures on prisons, universities, mental health and anti-violence programmes, and other sites of post-industrial economic growth, which now also include an expanding gay, transgender and LGBT non-profit sector. In her interview with Avery Gordon, Angela Davis examines the post-Fordist context within which the PIC has become a key area of growth (Gordon 1999). She links the expansion of the PIC with a landscape of deindustrialisation and restructuring. Following the state-sanctioned departure of capital to regions where labour is considered more pliant, and the unfettered mobility paved for capital by international agreements such as NAFTA and G20, racialised bodies that were once workers have been turned into surplus populations. This coincides with the dismantling of a welfare state that, even in its heyday, created benefits and entitlements mainly for 'deserving' white working subjects – and indeed for middle-class ones (Kandaswamy 2008). Policing and warehousing are the prime political responses to the social problems that this creates for poor people, who have been abandoned on a mass scale.

If this sounds like a classic critique of neoliberalism, Davis does not subordinate race to capital. On the contrary, her political economy of prisons explains that the marriage between racism and capital long pre-dates neoliberal times. Thus, she highlights the continuities between slavery and punishment post-abolition, both in the reinstitution of slavery as a punishment for crime, and in the invention of successive laws that have criminalised Black people, who 'were divested of their status as slaves to be accorded a new status as criminals' (Gordon 1999: 151–52). In our current context of globalised capital, where most of the production process occurs outside the global North, racism and prisons work to disappear racialised bodies alongside the workings of racialised capitalism. Media and law enforcement collude in creating a culture of punitiveness that dehumanises Black and brown bodies, who appear as always already criminal. Thus, moral panics over dangerous dark strangers produce consent for forms of punishment that would otherwise not be tolerable, and target those who are 'basically no longer thought of as human' (1999: 154). Simultaneously, unemployed Black men and increasingly also Black women and trans people, 'dispensable within the "free world"', have become a major source of profit in the PIC (1999: 153). Disposable to manufacturers, their bodies are the raw material for an expanding punishment industry that has become a key site of investment, employment and economic growth.

While tracing how current shifts between welfare and neoliberal regimes impact racialised lives, it is important to acknowledge that extractive relations of valorisation pre-date neoliberalism. The racial capitalism that Davis articulates occurs in a genealogy of slavery as well as ongoing colonialism. It is no coincidence that the critique of extractivism is articulated most clearly by Indigenous thinkers. In her interview with Naomi Klein (2013) about Idle No More, the Indigenous resurgence movement in North America, Leanne Simpson argues that colonialism, from the hyper-extraction of resources from Indigenous lands, to the appropriation of Indigenous knowledges by environmentalists and other activists, is centrally built on extraction.

> Colonialism and capitalism are based on extracting and assimilating. My land is seen as a resource. My relatives in the plant and animal worlds are seen as resources. My culture and knowledge is a resource. My body is a resource and my children are a resource because they are the potential to grow, maintain, and uphold the extraction-assimilation system. The act of extraction removes all of the relationships that give whatever is being extracted meaning. Extracting is taking. Actually, extracting is stealing – it is taking without consent, without thought, care or even knowledge of the impacts that extraction has on the other living things in that environment. That's always been a part of colonialism and conquest. Colonialism has always extracted the indigenous – extraction of indigenous knowledge, indigenous women, indigenous peoples.

The extraction of value from Indigenous bodies and lands, as well as the theft of enslaved bodies, is the basis of wealth not only in the settler colonial societies of the Americas but also in the old empire. Much work remains to be done to explore how labour migration and anti-Muslim racism in Germany intersect with slavery and colonialism, regimes in which Germans also participated.

Davis's description of racialised bodies as the 'raw material' fuelling the punishment sector resonates with the German context, even if the privatisation of prisons and policing is still in its early stages there. While the dismantling of the German welfare state has proceeded at a slower pace, there is a noticeable shift from social welfare to social control. Labour migrants and their descendants are disproportionately affected by restructuring. Here, too, the very bodies that have been rendered disposable by global capital – through the departure of manufacturing and through gentrification – are the ones that are now targeted by accelerating practices of policing and incarceration (Eick 2003). And here, too, there is a tendency to move away from rehabilitative to repressive practices of 'throwing away entire populations [...] constructed and perceived – fixed, really – within the popular imagination as public enemies' (Gordon 1999: 155).

Queer Lovers and Hateful Others argues that gender and sexuality are key terrains on which this dehumanisation and disentitlement occurs. I propose that we view queer regeneration not merely as a culturalist discourse that serves to respectabilise formerly degenerate subjects and reinscribe racialised Others as deficient and inferior, but as a process that is highly productive and indeed lucrative. The queer subject comes to life in the proximity of the prison and other sites of social death, where the biggest symbolic and material resources now lie. Chapter 3 ('Hate') reads this in conjunction with the close proximity of 'hate', 'crime' and 'violence' – affects that always already 'stick', as Sara Ahmed (2004a) might put it, to racialised bodies. Through a close reading of media, activist and policy texts on hate crime and youth criminality, I argue that LGBT non-profit, criminal-legal and biomedical frameworks now directly serve each other by jointly moulding a perpetrator population consisting of young racialised men who are supposedly unable to control their hatred and anger. Disposable as labourers, low-income youth of colour are now capacitated mainly by the PIC, NPIC and MIC, where they are shuffled between warehousing, treatment and reform through a proliferating apparatus of anti-violence and anti-homophobia programmes.

In addition to the PIC, NPIC and MIC, we must acknowledge the AIC as an additional site where value is extracted from racialised bodies. This is rendered crucial by the massive expansion of knowledges on racialised and global South genders and sexualities, reflected in the rise of global LGBT and transnational sexuality studies, that coincides with the racialisation of queerphobia and the turn to 'murderous inclusions' by LGBT, queer and trans movements (see Arondekar 2004). Much work remains to be done to assess the extent to which these new disciplinary formations reflect a renewed desire to know not just the Orient – after Said – but an ever proliferating array of regions that constitute the 'rest' of the 'West' (Hall 1992).

Rather than treating the AIC and NPIC as innocent alternatives to the PIC, it is important to examine their symbiotic relationships (Sudbury 2007). Thus, 'the NPIC is the natural corollary to the [PIC. W]hereas the PIC overtly represses dissent, the NPIC manages and controls dissent by incorporating it into the state apparatus' (Smith 2007a: 42, drawing on Dylan Rodriguez). Similarly, Julia Chinyere Oparah (formerly known as Sudbury) identifies several ways in which the AIC supports the PIC: the production of carceral knowledges that naturalise the criminalisation of poor and racialised populations, the education of 'a global knowledge elite who will become the "prison wardens" [...] of the nonuniversitied majority', and the ways in which 'universities mine prisons as a source of data' (Sudbury 2007: 20, 23). Oparah points to the role of knowledge industries, including higher education, research, media and communications, in moulding two kinds of subjects: experts who 'are positioned as legitimate producers of knowledge and rewarded through salaried subjects', and human subjects who 'serve as the raw material for knowledge production, whether as experimental subjects, participants of social science research, or objects of mass media news stories' (2007: 23). This relationship between 'scientist and experimental subject, social scientist and research participant, journalist and news subject' is characterised by inescapable epistemic violence, including and especially where both share markers of oppression, as in the case of the feminist ethnographer mining the lives of women in prison (2007: 23). While Oparah's thoughts are especially important for researchers working directly on prisons, her reminder that academic work is deeply complicit with the structuring logic of the prison, and her analysis of research as an extractive relation that mirrors this logic, are highly relevant for all researchers of race and sexuality, especially those of us who work 'empirically' with social movements.

These critiques of the AIC, PIC and NPIC thus help us understand not only how value is extracted from surplus populations, but also how it is accumulated to valorise and respectabilise new subjects – including LGBT experts tasked with rescuing trans women of colour or studying transnational populations. As Neferti Tadiar (2012) discusses, this process of valorisation and distinction is magnified under finance capitalism, whose ideal citizen is the entrepreneur who manages hir life and makes it profitable. Like Davis and Oparah, she highlights the PIC as an exemplary site where value is extracted from life that has become surplus in a post-Fordist mode of capital accumulation, and becomes profitable 'not so much as labor' but 'as social waste' (Tadiar 2012: 789, 791). This occurs through finance capital's continual production and 'cycling through' of surplus populations that, once they have become disposable to capital as labour, are turned into 'life as waste – disposable material whose management has become an entire "province of accumulation", spawning proliferating industries of militarisation, security, policing, and control' (2012: 789). Tadiar thus describes valorisation as a process of distinction between lives worth living and lives worth expending. Her critique mirrors Davis's and Oparah's in that it grounds political economy in a thorough analysis of race, religion, nationality, gender and sexuality, which operate as biopolitical markers for these very distinctions.

Randy Martin (2007) similarly links valorisation and subjectivation in his discussion of finance capital and the war on terror. Finance capitalism has produced distinctions between 'risk-taking' investors and populations 'at risk', and between the self-managed and the unmanageable, which work to accumulate both moral and physical capital. The figure of the risk-taking investor represents a modification of the earlier ideal neoliberal subject of the consumer citizen. In hir place, the investor becomes the new model citizen who takes care of hir own futures, manages hir own affairs, and participates in the management of surplus populations. The latter category – often conflated with poor youth of colour – has a genealogy in successive wars on crime, drugs and terror. These bodies marked as 'bad risks' are nevertheless highly profitable:

> Those 'at risk' do not simply die or only suffer social death – although they may be subjected to death, they are also mined, managed, and materialized as a factor of production, just as Marx imagined for surplus populations that allow new social productivities to form. (2007: 166)

What distinctions, extractions and valorisations accompany the drama of queer lovers and hateful Others? How do queer ascendancies participate in divisions between lives worth living and lives worth expending? What is the role of the self-managed LGBT expert in the management of disposable bodies 'at risk'? *Queer Lovers and Hateful Others* explores how the birth of the respectable queer subject occurs against a proliferating array of racialised bodies whose 'risky' figuration calls forth a growing repertoire of techniques of rescue, punishment and reform. In the process, racialised bodies – whether nominally straight, cis,[8] queer or trans – are simultaneously erased and heavily put to work.

CHAPTER GUIDE

This book follows queer lovers and hateful Others around. In making sense of their multi-sited appearances and organising my – sometimes systematic, often coincidental – sightings of them in various political and geographic spaces and institutions, I am inspired by Sara Ahmed's (2012) 'ethnography of texts', which traces the circulation of 'diversity' through academic institutions, 'attentive to "where diversity goes (and where it does not), as well as in whom and in what diversity is deposited (as well as in whom or in what it is not)' (2012: 12). The texts through which I trace the drama of queer lovers and hateful Others are various and include media, arts, activism, policy and publicly funded scholarship, posters, newspaper reports, hate crime action plans, diversity plans, urban projects, crime reports, psychological studies, demonstrations, kiss-ins, political speeches and memorials, alongside practices of gentrification, policing and deportation.

Rather than starting with this overdetermined drama, the book begins by taking a closer look at its setting, whose spectacular scripting as a (crime) scene relegates its many other occurrences to the status of the uneventful. Chapter 1 ('Setting the scene') examines the making of the moral panic within architectures of gentrification and criminalisation, and with the help of the 'cognitive maps' of queer of colour interviewees (see Ingram et al. 1997). It reads local histories of urban development in the decades prior to and since the fall of the wall alongside current research into neighbourhood changes and mobilisations in LGBT, queer and trans scenes that mark certain neighbourhoods in Berlin – the former 'guest worker districts' of Kreuzberg and Neukölln, which are sites of queer gentrification, as well as Schöneberg, the older 'gaybourhood' – as dangerous areas that require increased protection for queer people.

The resulting picture adds further nuances to a queer space debate that has often foregrounded a critique of 'gay neighbourhoods' and homo-neoliberal accounts that interpellate gays as 'creative classers', who index a neighbour-hood's potential to gentrify (see Florida 2002). Adding a spatial analysis to Duggan's homonormativity concept, writers have linked gay assimilation, or the homogenisation of queer identities, to gentrification, or the homogenisation of inner-city spaces. It is indeed important to investigate gay villages as competitive features of global cities, which redevelop and brand inner-city areas into themed ethnic or sexual quarters whose main purpose is to attract tourists and investors (Bell and Binnie 2004; Kipfer and Keil 2002; Marcuse and van Kempen 2000). At the same time, the chapter argues that the 'mixed' neighbourhood, which commentators on queer space have at times celebrated as transgressive, has been a particularly fertile terrain for moral panicking. Indeed, the younger and more 'radical' queer and trans scenes that have settled there have been hailed as early-wave gentrifiers who break into areas considered ungentrifiable. This renders it important to critically map transgressive alongside homonormative geographies, as intersecting rather than contradictory sites of queer placemaking in the neoliberal city.

Indeed, it is in Kreuzberg that the drama of queer lovers and hateful Others found its first setting. The racialised inner city, where homophobia swiftly joins older scripts of violence, crime and patriarchy, emerges as an especially fertile ground for queer regeneration. The chapter thus goes beyond an analytic of neoliberalism that privileges distinctions between assimilated and transgressive spaces and identifications over other axes of investigation. Rather, it highlights the need to locate these processes in longer processes of racial capitalism and the spatial processes of migration and segregation that it produces. In the neoliberal city, older colonial notions of degenerate populations that fail to cultivate space and remain themselves uncultivable are remapped onto queerly regenerating spaces, whose recovery demands the expulsion of poor racialised bodies.

The rapid contraction of the environment for racialised, including queer of colour, bodies contrasts with the ways in which spaces, affects and visualities marked as queer and transgender are expanding. Chapter 2 explores this with regard to a changing public visual field, where positive images of queer intimacies, long confined to privatised, criminalised and pathologised spaces, are proliferating. From magazines to newspaper reports to billboards, queer kisses are now everywhere. They are placed in the formerly degenerate, now regenerating neighbourhoods, where they appear in the form of publicly funded trilingual posters that teach 'the migrants' that 'love deserves respect'. They accompany the media dissemination of a psychological study that scientifically proves that youth of 'Turkish' origin hold the most homophobic attitudes and are most likely to be repelled by gay kisses. These intimacies are homonormative in that they aesthetically and affectively reinscribe the values of a heteronormative neoliberal consumer culture. Again, understanding the conversion of the queer lover from criminal, diseased and repulsive to lovely and vulnerable requires an analysis of race and coloniality that is able to account for these uneven developments.

At the same time, not all queer bodies are visualised as lovely. The desirability of the queer subject follows familiar lines of whiteness, youth, ability and gender conformity. While transgender bodies, too, emerge as innocent and worthy of protection for the first time, their regeneration follows a different logic. As hyper-diverse bodies that add colour to areas from which bodies of colour are being displaced, they become desirable as an index of how far the LGBT-friendly society is willing to go. The chapter explores this with regard to the first extensively mediated 'case' of racialised queerphobia in Berlin, which ushered the term *Hasskriminalität* (hate crime) into policy and media discourse for the first time. Ironically, it was in the emerging genderqueer rather than the established gay male scene that the punitive turn found its first bodies in Germany.

The chapter takes issue with a reading of trans bodies as first and foremost victimised (see Snorton and Haritaworn 2013). Indeed, the emergence of the transgender subject follows the global rise of a hate crime activism that presents its constituents as victim populations that count and are made to count in their likelihood to be injured. It is on account of their lesser passability and greater vulnerability that gender non-conforming bodies become significant to an anti-violence politics that, as anti-racist feminist writers have shown with regard to an increasingly professionalised and institutionalised global anti-violence sector, needs processable bodies to accumulate value (Bumiller 2008; Kapur 2005). The victim subjectivities that emerge nevertheless differ from 'wounded attachments' or 'traumatised citizenship' in that their *ressentiment* is not towards the bourgeoisie, as charged by Wendy Brown (1993), but towards 'dangerous' racialised populations whose constitutive outsiderdom provides ascendant subjects with safer targets.

Trans people with race and class privileges have benefited especially from these victimologies. At the same time, trans of colour bodies have also found inclusion as the raw material for an expanding LGB (and newly)T non-profit sector. In fact, the new tendency in queer, trans and LGBT organising to include those deemed precarious often reinscribes their killability while securing a newly professionalising class of experts in the realm of life. As Riley Snorton and I (2013) suggest in our essay on transnormativity, it is in the moment of their death that those most in need of survival become valuable, as experts, allies and funders become literate and numerate in hate crime paradigms whose main function is to secure further funding (see also Bhanji 2013). Most starkly, this is illustrated by the globalisation of Transgender Day of Remembrance (TDOR), whose travels from the US to the rest of the world again call for a bio-, necro- as well as geopolitical lens that explores how populations are moulded and fostered for life and discarded for death in ways that are intrinsically spatialised (see Haritaworn et al. 2014; Mbembe 2003). Thus, TDOR events from Toronto to London to Berlin enable mainly white trans people from the global North to commune by reading out the names and looking at the photos of dead people, mainly poor, trans feminine, Black and/or from the global South, who most likely had little access to trans communities while alive (see Lamble 2008). This illustrates how queer and trans vitality, besides symbiotically enhancing the death-making capacities of the market and the state, is often cannibalistic on the lives and deaths of the very people it claims to represent.

While those whose multiple vulnerabilities lend the moral panic its spectacularly violated bodies are continually reinscribed as degenerate, the same process also secures a newly professionalising class of experts in the realm of life. This forces us to examine the rise of a global trans movement against the globalisation of various intersecting industrial complexes: the PIC, NPIC and, increasingly also, the AIC. How do the deaths, both social and actual, of trans-feminine people of colour provide the fuel and the raw material for these regenerations?

For trans and queer people of colour, these modes of coalition impose impossible choices between complicity and complete and utter isolation. Interviewees rarely narrated their selves, communities and surroundings in the registers of love or injury, whose 'structures of feeling' they were unable to participate in (Muñoz 2000). They became 'affect aliens', as Sara Ahmed (2008) might say, to both the homonormative affect of love and the transnormative affect of injury. Failed queers, they were more likely to be interpellated by the 'bad' feelings ascribed to the failed straight populations from which they refused to seek rescue. Drawing on the vibrant queer of colour scholarship that has emerged in critique of gay marriage, the chapter argues that anti-racist queers of colour perform different kinds of care that are unfamiliar to dominant structures of queer love and trans injury.

Chapter 3 ('Hate') attends to the hateful Other who enables these structures of feeling to emerge and become recognisable – in whose shadow the queer lover becomes a lovely sight. It traces some of the techniques, again thoroughly globalised, through which poor people of colour, especially young people of the generation that is ostensibly included post-*jus sanguinis*, are prepared for social death. Through a range of media, activist and policy texts, the chapter traces the birth of the hateful homophobe alongside that of another folk devil, the *Intensivtäter* (repeat offender), which in public debates has been claimed by right-wing politicians rather than the progressive actors of the hate crime debate. Nevertheless, in LGBT activist texts, hate crime action plans, the infamous Pfeiffer study and other studies on criminalised racialised youth, and psychiatric, criminological and social work research on chronic delinquents, the personality profiles of 'homophobes' and of 'chronic delinquents' starkly resemble each other. The two moral panics share a setting in the gentrifying inner city, a psy profile, an arsenal of techniques of punishment and reform, and a bio- and geopolitical horizon and orientation towards degenerate bodies and spaces as, crucially, sites from which value is extracted. Their shared violent family background and inability to come to terms with bad experiences of racism and poverty make them equally prone to hate, crime and violence. Indeed, as suggested in the *Bild* editorial discussed above, the criminal, patriarchal and homophobic 'Muslim' shares the same cultural and familial genealogy.

This has implications beyond what kinds of languages we choose to use. The chapter questions the uninterrogated role of hate as the hegemonic paradigm for understanding and organising against violence globally. While we have at our disposal a range of analytics – from affect studies to feminism to homonormativity – to make sense of dominant figurations of queer love and the neoliberal multicultural publics and carceral landscapes that they render palpable, hate has not undergone similar challenges. I propose that hate is a risky diagnostic to organise around, in that it always already sticks to racialised bodies. The chapter calls for an abolitionist imagination that goes beyond the prison and extends to institutional and other sites more often considered caring and benevolent, including the communities we wish to build ourselves.

The hateful figure that is carved out in these sexual, carceral and biomedical personality profiles is haunted by bio- and necropolitical moulds of deficiency and inferiority whose genocidal logics apparently belong to the past. Chapter

4, 'Queer Nostalgia', examines this script in its temporality. In activations of LGBT movement histories, the past is periodised teleologically and parochially: as atrocities that happened in Berlin from 1933 to 1945, and that must be appropriately remembered. At the same time, the *Never Again!* that practices of remembrance call for serves to repeat the sticking of hate, crime, violence and terror to racialised bodies. The chapter examines this with regard to the Memorial to the Homosexuals Persecuted Under National Socialism, an artistic and activist production that rediscovers the German past as a fertile terrain on which to vitalise current agendas of marriage, visibility and hate crime. Far from something that we must get away from, as dominant queer temporalities often assume, the traumatic past here emerges as a site of queer nostalgia: an active investment in murderous times and places that the nostalgic subject ostensibly seeks to overcome.

In asking what is the time of LGBT inclusion, we arrive, as so often, at a bigger picture. The conclusion takes its cue from Reddy's (2011) proposal that we view gay marriage as a 'hybrid' between the welfare state and the neoliberal security state. In the German context, where the infamous *jus sanguinis* was reformed belatedly, extending citizenship benefits and privileges as they are being shrunk to a pittance, we can take this further. Drawing on Winnicott (1953), I propose to think of the queer lover as a transitional object that eases the shift from a welfare to a neoliberal regime, and ushers us into consent with techniques and horizons that would not otherwise be palatable. The drama of queer lovers and hateful Others accompanies changes in the borders between bodies and communities, publics and counter-publics. In making new worlds that are big enough for some queer subjects, it performs a community that sees itself as colourful and diverse while increasingly letting go of its people of colour. It leads us over from one state to another: from the racialised to the gentrifying neighbourhood; from a multiculturalist politics to an assimilationist one; from a homophobic and transphobic to an LGBT-friendly community; from a welfare regime to a neoliberal one. It eases these transitions, rendering them palpable within older structures of feeling. And yet, to begin this timeline with neoliberalism would be to evade the *longue durée* of racial and colonial capitalism, antiblackness and settler colonialism. The epilogue revisits the themes of the book by placing the figure of the 'most homophobic' alongside other failed genders and sexualities, including those that are constructed as 'too queer'.

1

SETTING THE SCENE[1]

In the introduction, I argued that the queer lover comes to life in formerly undesirable spaces that are discovered for regeneration and prepared for 'proper' (middle-class, white or whitening) habitation. This chapter explores the setting of the drama of queer lovers and hateful Others by enquiring into the uneventful occurrences that accompany the production of degenerate bodies whose disappearance is a condition for the formerly degenerate area's 'recovery'. To set the scene and enter into the urban setting within which queers have become a lovely sight, it is useful to go back to the *Khalass!!!* manifesto, written by queer of colour activists in Berlin, with which this book began:

> You consider yourself and your bourgeois squats to be 'pioneers' and you don't even realize how colonial your language is, you do not see the civilizing mission you are part of and that you prepare the ground for other white settlers to come.

What are the stakes of bringing an analysis of racism and colonialism to a space where the history of colonialism has been successfully repressed, where racism is remembered only as a 1933–1945 phenomenon, and where mentioning the continuities with what came before and what has come since entails penalties (see Barskanmaz 2011; El-Tayeb 1999; Samour 2012)?

The evasion of racism and colonialism in discussions of queer space is not an exclusively German phenomenon. The literature on queer space, much of which has focused on the US, contains similar raced and classed omissions that the *Khalass!!!* manifesto and other queer of colour analyses usefully address. The chapter begins by revisiting discussions of queer space with regard to the rare entries that racialised and colonised subjects make into them. Through a close reading of seminal social movement theorist's Manuel Castells' (1983) famous study of the Castro, an early gay neighbourhood in San Francisco that has become foundational in global imaginaries of queer space, I illustrate how the assertion of the queer need for space has left in place a colonial paradigm that reinscribes the erasure of those who were there before. While a sustained focus on the policing and displacement of degenerate bodies from regenerating areas is missing, these early accounts already contain the seeds for later hate crime discourses that treat subjects of colour in areas of queer settlement as violent, queerphobic, and in need of targeted policing (see Hanhardt 2013).

The cognitive maps of queers of colour further provide an important corrective to accounts of the neoliberal city that focus on the homogenisation of spaces and identities that accompanies the branding of gay villages (see *Fenced Out* 2001; FIERCE 2008). Such maps have not only resisted the way LGBT subjects with race and class privileges have been incorporated into neoliberal visions of the creative class (Florida 2002), they are also able to account for differences within LGBT, queer and trans populations. This contrasts with a wider queer space debate that treats the most salient distinctions as those between 'assimilated' gays and 'radical' queers, and between homonormative 'gaybourhoods' and transgressive 'mixed' areas. While the former crystallise everything deemed wrong with LGBT communities – from racism to commercialism – the latter are presumably less affected by these wrongs.

The shortcomings of this spatial dichotomy are illustrated by the Berlin district of Kreuzberg, whose 'mixedness' is reflected in its ambivalent place in queer imaginaries as a counter-cultural paradise but also as a degenerate space that is rife with violence, crime and hate crime. Through an iterative reading of local histories of Kreuzberg, demographic studies of household changes in the district, activist and media productions of Kreuzberg as a degenerate space rife with violence, crime and patriarchy, and queer of colour interview accounts of the district as a place where it was long possible to be both queer and racialised, I argue that queer gentrification has been an important but often overlooked dynamic in the district's development. Besides providing a corrective to this, the chapter suggests that the queer space of Kreuzberg must be understood in relation to its neighbouring districts: to its south-east, the district of Neukölln, which was long considered ungentrifiable; to its south-west, the 'gaybourhood' in Schöneberg, which is home to the homonormative organisations. While the three districts have long held opposing spatial meanings – as the transgressive multicultural neighbourhood, the 'ghetto' and the 'assimilated' gay village – these distinctions are nevertheless complicated by the ways in which each has been mobilised as a setting for the moral panic, with various degrees of success: scripted in the homonormative NGOs in Schöneberg, it is in the intensely racialised space of Kreuzberg, and in the genderqueer scene, that the hate crime panic finds its first setting. It is in the shadows of degenerate bodies, and the architectures of formerly degenerate spaces that queer regeneration occurs. As the old trope of the degenerate 'ghetto' converges with the new trope of the 'recovering' inner city, where the properly alive like to live, eat and party, a recognisable queer subject worthy of protection and visibility comes to life.

Given these omissions, convergences and complicities, it becomes necessary to revisit queer space through currents of thought and action that are able to explain racism and colonialism and account for queers of colour as placemaking subjects (El-Tayeb 2012; *Fenced Out* 2001; FIERCE 2008; Hanhardt 2008; Manalansan 2005; McKittrick 2006; Razack 2002a, 2002b; Teelucksingh 2002). Drawing on environmental justice principles, I propose to treat queer regeneration as a cultural as well as material process that inscribes actual places where people 'live, work, play and worship' (Bullard 1994; Teelucksingh 2002). In other words, urban spaces are not transparent or static (see Lefebvre 1991 [1974]), yet they are more than just figures, as the unequal chances of life and death in the inner city bring home (see McKittrick 2006). This renders it necessary to attend to 'the alternative geographic formulations that subaltern communities advance [...] that can incite new, or different, and perhaps not just, more just, geographic stories', as Katherine McKittrick (2006: xix) maintains with regard to Black diasporic interrogations of white Canada. Indeed, the queer of colour interviewees who lived in Kreuzberg and Neukölln mapped the changing areas around them as sites where queer of colour survival and collectivity, however embattled, was long possible but now increasingly precarious. In these alternative maps, a different picture emerges that contests the celebration of queer vitality that pervades both neoliberal and alternative accounts of the city. For queers of colour, the environments featured in the mythos Kreuzberg have rapidly contracted at various scales – from the body to its physical and social surroundings, which are fast becoming inaccessible as a result of racism and gentrification.

'GHETTOS', 'COLONIES' AND 'MIXED NEIGHBOURHOODS'

> In order publicly to express themselves, gays have always met together – in modern times in night bars and coded places. When they became conscious enough and strong enough to 'come out' collectively, they have earmarked places where they could be safe together and could develop new life styles. But this time they selected cities, and within the cities they traced boundaries and created their territory. These boundaries were to expand with the increasing capacity of gay people to defend themselves and to build up a series of autonomous institutions. (Castells 1983: 138–39)

In the over three decades since Castells wrote about the Castro in San Francisco, a substantial amount has been written on queer space, yet attempts to theorise it in relation to race and class are fairly recent (see Gieseking 2013: 178; Nash 2013: 199 fn 8; Nash and Catungal 2013: 188). As Manalansan argues, the debate has tended to foreground 'struggles to claim spaces by various gays, lesbians, and other queers' (2005: 144). In contrast, scholars have variously ignored queer gentrification and racial profiling or actively participated in constructing homo/transphobic hate crime as a problem of racialised bodies and spaces (for a notable exception, see Hanhardt 2008, 2013). An example for this was the Urban Laboratory workshop 'Backlash? The Resurgence of Homophobia in Contemporary Cities', an event organised at University College London in 2010, the very time that a moral panic raged through London, culminating in the East End Gay Pride, a pink washing march organised by the far-right English Defence League (see Decolonize Queer 2011). The invite stated: 'Recent attacks in London and other cities have brought homophobia to the surface of urban life, alongside other forms of hate crime and lines of social and cultural division.' The programme featured several queer researchers and activists alongside a speaker from the London Metropolitan Police (UCL 2010).

In comparison, Castells' discussion of the Castro was decidedly benign. It evaluated the area's transition into a gay neighbourhood in remarkably positive terms, as it allowed gay men to claim an urban terrain where they could enter into visibility, autonomy and community. Castells went to great lengths to imagine the effects of discrimination and invisibility as a 'major obstacle to finding sexual partners, discovering friends and leading an unharassed, open life' (1983: 145). Since then, a burgeoning literature, which has been in fertile engagement with queer theory, has mapped various sexual urban formations. Investigators have often focused on the factors motivating non-heterosexuals to move to the city and form 'gaybourhoods' and other, increasingly dispersed, sexual spaces, which, besides gay men, soon also included lesbians and self-identified queers (Ingram et al. 1997; Nash and Catungal 2013; Rubin 1984; Weston 1995). While the tenet of the early texts was distinctly celebratory, more recently critical attention has been paid to the ways in which such 'queer migrations' are informed by a 'metronormative' binary between 'progressive city' and 'backward country' (Halberstam 2005; Tongson 2007). In addition, the emphasis on territorialisation and property ownership in the Castellian 'neighbourhood' paradigm has been critiqued as masculinist (Gieseking 2013). Fewer questions have been asked about the racial and colonial assumptions embedded in discourses on queer and other urban spaces, including the 'gay ghetto', the 'ethnic model' and the 'urban frontier' (but see Petzen 2008).

In many queer and allied writings, the association of queers and the city has been decidedly celebratory. Early queer writings assert an undifferentiated queer need for safe spaces in the city that recalls Castells' highly sympathetic account. Cities are described as havens from a small-minded, homophobic country and suburb, and as important grounds for community development. Many of these early writings focus on North America, particularly San Francisco and later the rest of the Bay Area and New York. In Gayle Rubin's foundational essay 'Thinking sex', young queers used all kinds of routes (including the armed forces) 'to get out of intolerable hometown situations and closer to functional gay communities' in San Francisco (1984: 24). A decade later, Kath Weston (1995) questioned this 'Get thee to a big city' narrative of urban exceptionalism. Not only are city and country relational concepts, but we must examine the role played by 'the urban/ rural contrasts in *constituting* lesbian and gay subjects' (Weston 1995: 255). Drawing on interviews with a heterogeneous sample of gay and lesbian migrants to the Bay Area, Weston shed a critical light on the biopolitical and geopolitical imaginaries that inform gay migration: 'How did "we" come to believe that others like ourselves existed? Even more puzzling, what led us to conjecture that those "like" others were to be found in urban centers?' (1995: 258). While treating the biographies that propel queer migration respectfully, she asked us to question a sexual geography in which 'the city represents a beacon of tolerance and gay community, the country a locus of persecution and gay absence' (1995: 282). In the light of current events, we can go further, by interrogating how queer migration, both nationally and transnationally, assumes a mobility that is often denied to racialised people. As Fatima El-Tayeb (2012) shows with regard to the German figure of the eternal migrant, the latter are hindered or pathologised in their mobility as a result of racial profiling, gentrification and border control. Thus, in the panics over 'dangerous places' in queerly gentrifying cities such as London or Berlin, queers from all over the global north become residents the minute they arrive, while those who have been there for generations are erased from dominant multicultural maps (Decolonize Queer 2011).

Ten years after Weston, Jack Halberstam (2005) coined the term 'metronormativity', also taken up in Karen Tongson's (2007) discussion of queer of colour socialities in suburban LA, in order to highlight the dislocation of the countryside from neoliberal imaginings of queer life. The concept takes issue with 'the conflation of "urban" and "visible" in many normalising narratives of gay/lesbian subjectivities':

> [T]he metronormative story of migration from 'country' to 'town' is a spatial narrative within which the subject moves to a place of tolerance after enduring life in a place of suspicion, persecution, and secrecy. (Halberstam 2005: 36–37)

This chimes with an older literature (d'Emilio 1993 [1983]) that explored queer movement building in conjunction with capitalism, urbanisation and, we must add, colonialism. If queer spaces have arisen in the architecture of the city, the rise of the city, long a dystopic spectre of upheaval, was itself far from straightforward. As Mortimer-Sandilands and Erickson (2010) remind us, the link between queers and the city was long decidedly negative. Queers, along with immigrants and communists, embodied eugenicist anxieties about an industrialising society turned unnatural and immoral. These anxieties went hand in hand with the invention of the wilderness as the place where the natural order of things was preserved: the artificial city caused its inhabitants to become degenerate, while the country was the place where (white) men could still be men (Mortimer-Sandilands and Erickson 2010: 14–15).

These critical spatial imaginaries can be extended in three directions. First, how has the mutual constitution between queer subjects and the city shaped not only queer movements and subjectivities, but also the very urban spaces where queers have settled? I will examine this by revisiting the earlier literature on gay gentrification which, while largely anti-intersectional, at times paid greater attention to racialisation than later writings on queer urban space. Second, how can we extend this analysis to scales other than the city? The rural–urban dichotomy, which posits the urban as where queer and transgender people come to life, and the rural as where diversity dies, has arguably been transposed onto a bigger global map. I argue that the global north – still epitomised by its cities, but cast through larger scales of nation, Europe and 'West' – now figures as the prime site of queer life, while the south and the east have come into relief as terrains of queer death. Third, it is time to unpack the racial and colonial metaphors that thread themselves through queer and other alternative urban imaginaries – from the 'gay ghetto' (or, ironically, considering our rampantly anti-Muslim climate, the 'queer mecca', see Petzen 2008), to its critique as an 'ethnic model' (Epstein 1987), to the metaphor of the 'colony', where 'pioneers' open up hitherto uncultivable territory.[2]

Writers on queer urban spaces go some way towards addressing these questions. This includes reflections on the rise and fall of 'gay neighbourhoods' (e.g. Ghaziani 2010; Gieseking 2013), and on the nostalgic mobilisations against their perceived decline in places like Toronto (Catungal 2010). One important area of investigation is the recasting of queer space in the neoliberal city, and the ways in which gay assimilation, or the homogenisation of queer spaces, coincides with gentrification, or the homogenisation of inner city spaces (Binnie 1995; Doan and Higgins 2011; Schulman 2012). Bell and Binnie (2004) explore this with regard to the emergence of gay 'neighbourhoods' in the global city (see also Brenner and Keil 2006; Marcuse and van Kempen 2000). As cities begin to compete for tourists and investors, the local state turns from 'an agent of redistribution to a promoter of enterprise' (Bell and Binnie 2004: 1809). In order to ease the mobility of capital, the entrepreneurial city rebrands itself and homogenises its areas. This leads to the formation of cloned spaces, as each city requires its own gay village, ethnic towns and other themed quarters. Existing queer spaces, in turn, become internally homogenised and are desexualised in order to make straight visitors and consumers comfortable (Binnie and Skeggs 2004). As a result, 'the "gay public sphere" [is reduced] to consumption spaces and gentrified neighbourhoods only' (2004: 1811). The authors show how this homogenised concept of queer space has entered into dominant policy models such as Richard Florida's (2002) creative class. In a thesis that has been highly influential among urban policy makers globally, Florida claims that the spatial concentration of gays, called the 'gay index', along with other 'creative classers', like 'people in design, education, arts, music and entertainment, whose economic function is to create new ideas, new technology and/or creative content', correlates with an area's potential for gentrification (2002: 8).[3] Queer counter-publics and public sex scenes, meanwhile, which do not fit sanitised ideals of gay space, are pushed out: 'For many assimilationist gays ... gay male sex zones are seen as an embarrassment that must be cleaned up' (Bell and Binnie 2004: 1815).

A similar observation is made by Sarah Schulman (2012), who places the gentrification of parts of Manhattan, including by gay men with race and class privileges, into a context where previous queer formations have been erased as a result of the AIDS crisis. Rather than in the homogeneous gay neighbourhood, Schulman sees promise in the mixed neighbourhood, which revalues 'multiculturalism [sic], gender non-conformity and individuated behavior', as well as '[i]nnovative aesthetics, diverse food traditions [and] ease with mixed race and mixed religious communities, free sexual expression and political radicalism' (Schulman 2012: 25). Schulman makes serious attempts to discuss how queers are impacted differentially by gentrification, yet her distinction between queer victims and beneficiaries of gentrification foregrounds age, political beliefs and consumption habits over more salient factors such as race and class.[4] For example, she differentiates an older radical generation of queers who have suffered from the effects of the AIDS crisis from a younger conformist generation who do not appreciate what it is to suffer; authentic community leaders who are into '[h]ustl[ing], unsafe sex, masochism, phone sex, enemas, and endless tricking' from homonormative gays who are into marriage and monogamy (2012: 120), and 'bohemians' who prefer 'authentic, neighborhood-based ethnic cooking' and 'lived among our neighbors as they did' (2012: 30–31, citing artist Penny Arcade) from 'bourgeois' who eat at chains that are 'homogenous, corporate, boring and destroying cultural complexity' (2012: 33). However, the mixed neighbourhood traits that she highlights – dynamism, tolerance, freedom, diversity, individualism, creative ideas, innovation (2012: 27) – chime with cosmopolitan spatial frames that have long informed neoliberal city planning, including the creative city and its sister concept, the social mix.[5] The ideal of the social mix, which, as some have pointed out (see Holm 2009; Lees 2008) is regularly applied to areas with a high concentration of low-income and racialised people but rarely to areas with a high concentration of wealthy white people, has its origins in nineteenth-century urban planning paradigms that were forged in response to class struggle. Designed to dilute the revolutionary threat posed by a critical mass of workers, it has since become transposed to racialised populations who, from the US 'cultures of poverty' thesis to its German equivalent in the 'parallel societies' paradigm, are pathologised for their apparent desire to self-segregate and their concomitant *failure to mix* (see also Ahmed 2004a). In the era of gentrification, as Lees (2008) and Holm (2009) each argue, the 'good social mix' often means displacement.

More nuanced discussions of queer gentrification are coming out of Toronto. Catherine Nash (2013), drawing on Merrick Pilling (2011), draws our attention to the formation of an alternative queer community in Parkdale, the long abandoned but now rapidly gentrifying area of Toronto that has been unofficially renamed 'Queer West' as a result of this queer migration. The research participants, whom she describes as predominantly white and middle-class, distinguish themselves from the assimilated, consumerist landscape of Church and Wellesley. In contrast to the Village, the 'Queer West' is claimed as 'queer' not because of its sexual attributes, but because of its raced and classed marginality. Ironically, this marginality vitalises 'transgressive' identities even as the bodies marked as 'marginal' disappear from the area. Nash's analysis describes the subjectivities and socialities that flourish in Parkdale as complicit with gentrification. The landscape that becomes imaginable this way is, she states, particular to her sample. Indeed, the Village/Queer West distinction may well work differently for queer and trans people of colour, whose sense of place is situated in different relationships to mobility, marginality and transgression (see El-Tayeb 2012). What would it mean to treat queers of colour as spatial subjects in their own right, who draw our attention to multiple oppressions, multi-issue agendas and multiple sites, and who complicate dominant maps of sexuality, race and place?

The tendency in the literature on queer space to foreground the experiences of bodies that are recognisable as queer – assimilated or transgressive, depending on authors' own political positionalities – and unmarked in terms of race and also often class, is compounded by a lack of discussion of the fate of those who inhabited these spaces before they were re-territorialised as queer neighbourhoods. Where writers mention race, this is often analogical: the gay or queer neighbourhood is regularly described as a 'ghetto' or 'colony' (see Petzen 2008). And where writers have mentioned displacement, they have still tended to focus on the liberating potential of these 'colonisations' for gays or queers who, in the absence or understatement of other markers, are often reified as white, middle-class and gender conforming (Castells 1983: 156). In the remainder of this section, I will illustrate some of the problems associated with this approach through a detailed reading of Castells' iconic treatise on the Castro.[6]

As already stated, Castells' (1983) essay strongly advocates for gays' (explicated as male but largely unquestioned in terms of race and class) need for their own space.[7] This space is described in state-like terms: the gay neighbourhood has its own territory, population, culture, defence mechanisms, and institutions. What I'm interested in here are the ways in which bodies that are excessive to this spatial profile of the gay community appear or disappear from this map. Castells paints a non-intersectional landscape where 'gays' (white) exist alongside racialised populations (straight) who only appear by the way and are excessive to the newly forming gay community. On the one hand, the two 'minorities' are alike: gays need their own 'ghetto' for their 'everyday survival', just like 'Jewish people in Europe, black people in America and oppressed ethnic minorities all over the world' (1983: 158).[8] Besides analogy, however, there is contestation. While gays emerge as the spatial heirs to the Irish, who have abandoned the Castro for the suburbs, Latinos and Blacks in the bordering Mission and Bayview-Hunter's Point areas are described in the terms of 'interests that were not always easy to reconcile' (1983: 165). Castells explicitly states: '[g]ays' desire for urban restoration was viewed by blacks as a threat of intensified gentrification. Police control of anti-gay violence was often considered as a potential source of a crackdown on Latino youth' (1983: 165). Given the more legitimate needs and superior spatial uses by gay incomers, the erasure of people of colour from the same spaces seems unfortunate but inevitable. This is also reflected in the following statement:

> So there has been little urban improvement for the black families forced to move out of Hayes Valley, or help for the Latinos suffering high rents along the Dolores corridor because of real estate speculation from the increasing influx of gays. These hardships have been at the root of the hostility of ethnic minorities against gay people, a hostility often translated into violence. Class hate, ethnic rage, and fear of displacement by the invaders have clearly held greater sway than prejudices from family traditions of machismo ideology. (1983: 167)

This early account of queer space, while not calling for criminalisation, nevertheless already displays the major tropes of the hate crime framework: hateful Others whose own experiences of race and class oppression and backward cultures and inferior gendered intimacies make them prone to prejudice, violence and hostility; a gay community that needs space for its safety, protection and self-expression; and (as discussed earlier in the chapter) a largely benevolent police who may overreact at times, but whose 'consultation with the gay community' is celebrated as a major achievement (1983: 138). As Hanhardt's (2013) historiography of gay organising in San Francisco and New York confirms, this convergence between gay anti-violence activism, private developers, urban planners and police has since been institutionalised'.

Castells' chapter, written from a white and presumably straight perspective, figures gay and racialised populations anti-intersectionally and competitively. This occurs through two related comparisons. First, gay men are described as adding value to their environment *in contrast to racialised peoples*: 'Unlike other oppressed communities, gay people have raised the physical standards and economic value of the space they have occupied' (1983: 160).

Every incoming urban group has an impact on its housing and physical space. The gays of San Francisco definitely improved the quality of housing through repairs, remodeling, and excellent maintenance. Most gay households established themselves by renting or buying houses in middle-level neighbourhoods, worked on them, and upgraded both the buildings and the surrounding environment. The process of urban renovation in San Francisco has been largely, although not exclusively, triggered by gay people. As a result, property values in gay residential areas have been considerably improved, far above the already impressive average for the entire city. The aesthetic quality of most houses renovated by gays has greatly helped San Francisco to preserve its historical heritage of beautiful old Victorian buildings ... (1983: 158)

In a foreshadowing of the contemporary creative class paradigm, gays here emerge as the model urban regenerators. Their artistic 'talents as renovators and ... their care as urban dwellers', which constitute 'an invaluable resource in the preservation of urban beauty', have 'accounted for one of the most beautiful urban renovations known in American cities' (1983: 166). The argument that 'other oppressed communities', who are clearly legible as racialised, fail to add value to their environment resuscitates the colonial trope of space that accompanied the conquest of the Americas, in whose 'architecture', as Thobani (2014) puts it, later forms of oppression have arisen.[9] Andrea Smith (2005) describes how the displacement of Indigenous peoples from their land was justified by the view that they failed to properly cultivate it. On the contrary, many Indigenous cultures did not draw strict hierarchies between human and non-human beings. In a European capitalist frame, this made them undeserving of resources and space.

Besides failing to display hierarchical distinctions between human and non-human, colonised peoples in the Americas and elsewhere also failed to display proper gender binaries and patriarchal distinctions, and frequently shocked colonisers with their non-heterosexual and gender non-conforming behaviours (Morgensen 2011; Smith 2005). Castells' discussion prefigures the later reversal of this colonial taxonomy of gender and sexuality, which locates racialised inferiority not in excessive homosexuality and gender non-conformity, but in excessive homophobia and adherence to gendered extremes. In fact, gay men emerge as model urban regenerators on account of their unique and enriching combination of female and male qualities, which contrasts with the failed 'macho' masculinities of the displaced. A whole section in Castells is dedicated to the special relationship of gay men to the built environment, which he attributes, in an interesting spin on sexological inversion theory, to their mix of a male socialisation (exchange value, or 'power, conquest and self-affirma- tion') and a penchant for 'women's culture' (use value, or 'solidarity', 'tenderness', a 'special sensitiveness' and 'a desire for communication') (1983: 166).

The unique affective traits of non-trans white gay men are reflected in the almost metaphysical transformation they induce in their houses. Once restored and occupied by a gay man, a building becomes 'distinctive and valuable': 'it has beauty, comfort, and sensuality, and it is saying something to the city while expressing something to its own dwellers' (1983: 167). These 'gay' qualities imprint themselves not only on individual houses but on the whole city:

> The development of a gay community ... has been a major factor of urban change in San Francisco during the 1970s. Most of the changes triggered by the expansion of gay culture have been major contributions to the improvement of the city's quality of life. New gay households account for a significant proportion of the renovation of old buildings, for the repair and maintenance of many sections of the city, for the upgrading of property values, and for the dynamism of the real estate market. Although gay people have operated in a very attractive urban environment, they have also been pioneers in taking unusual risks to live in decaying areas ... (1983: 166)

Castells is not the only urban commentator to invoke the figure of the 'pioneer' for race- and class-privileged incomers who dare to venture into uncivilised lands (see Smith 1996). In Castells, the 'gay pioneer', whose entrepreneurial spirit is enhanced by his exclusion from other opportunities, is personified by the politician and entrepreneur Harvey Milk.[10] This celebratory figure is devoid of any connotations with either gentrification or the settler colonialism in whose architecture displacement and dispossession occur. Rather than gentrify, Castells argued, gays 'make enormous economic sacrifices in order to be able to live autonomously and safely as gays' (1983: 160). They are 'moral refugees', whose willingness to seize opportunities is not only commendable but also contributes to the greater good by improving the entire community's quality of life.

The figure of the gay pioneer makes another early appearance in Gayle Rubin's essay from the same period. In a section containing the same analogies of race and sexuality, she argued that '[g]ay pioneers occupied neighborhoods that were centrally located but run down' (1984: 24). Like Castells, Rubin warned of competition between gays and 'low-income groups' over housing which she – more dramatically – described as 'one source of the epidemic of street violence against homosexuals' (1984: 24). Rubin's essay, which is foundational to queer theory, thus features a key building block of the racialised hate crime discourse.

In contrast to these power-evasive discussions of queer space, Lawrence Knopp (1990) clearly identified gay gentrification as a problem. 'Interestingly', he commented on Castells' work, 'there is little in the way of economic or class analysis in the study. He does not discuss displacement at all, emphasising instead how the most heavily gay community developed in a neighborhood (Castro

Valley) that "was being abandoned by its Irish working class'" (Knopp 1990: 338–39). Based on interviews with gay newcomers, estate agents, architects and speculators in Marigny, a formerly working-class area in New Orleans, Knopp argued that gays in the 1970s and 1980s, partly inspired by the Castro, claim space and profit from the land market by mobilising social and cultural capital. Like Castells', this discussion is analogical and comparative, and does not take into account queer positionalities that are not white, middle-class and non-trans male. It nevertheless helpfully highlights Castells' evasion of class:

> Rather than constituting an oppressed community's collective strategy for coping with discrimination or a 'tough' housing market, as Castells' study suggests, this type of gay involvement in a land market can be seen primarily as an alternative strategy for accumulation. It is a strategy that happens to include the development of gay community resources. (1983: 348)

The critique of Castells' figure of the dynamic self-made gay entrepreneur who breaks into hitherto ungentrifiable territory in order to take risks that will benefit us all deserves further analysis in the light of its more recent incorporation by neoliberal urban experts. Told by a left-winger and recent settler – Castells, born in Spain, moved to Berkeley in 1979, a mere four years before *The City and the Grassroots* was published – it chimes comfortably with a capitalism and a settler colonialism that have each been foundational to American nationalism and multiculturalism. Indeed, Castells traces the queer origins of San Francisco all the way back to the heydays of the gold fields, which he reclaims as an incipient gay-friendly terrain on account of their 'easy moral standards' (1983: 140).

In narratives of queer gentrification, multiple scales – from the queer body to the transitioning home and neighbourhood – reverberate through each other. Besides Castells' and Knopp's, we can examine this in more critical accounts such as the documentary *Flag Wars* (2003) about the gentrification of Olde Towne East, a low-income Black neighbourhood in Columbus, Ohio, and the gentrification of the Christopher Street piers highlighted in the activism of the queer of colour youth group FIERCE (2008) and the scholarship of Martin Manalansan (2005) and Christina Hanhardt (2008). From the ascendant (white male) bodies of enterprising gay men, to the decaying houses that they occupy, renovate and 'save', to the regenerating neighbourhood, which 'recovers' the moment its prior inhabitants leave and gays arrive to 'coloniz[e]' it (Castells 1983: 156), this cross-scale imaginary renders the vitalisation of the queer lover palpable through the revitalisation of formerly racialised architectures. Knopp cites the example of a New Orleans architect who made an 'inventory of properties that "needed saving", determining who their owners were, and then making "marriages of building and people"' (Knopp 1990: 343). In the gay gentrification narrative documented in *Flag Wars* (2003), 'poor houses' must be saved from the unproductive and degenerative in/actions of their impoverished occupants. Meanwhile, gay buyers and estate agents crack jokes about when the next homeowner will die. In both Ohio and New Orleans, gay gentrifiers, however 'unpopular' socially, have been able to ally themselves with local leaders eager to promote their own 'economic self-interest' (Knopp 1990: 338), by inscribing themselves into historic preservation and quality-of-life discourses. In New Orleans, this involved an active decision to ally with churches, local government, business communities and other conservative institutions. In Ohio and New York, this further included the police. As *Flag Wars* filmmaker Linda Goode Bryant describes, newcomers would call the police on their neighbours, limit their use of public space by reporting young people's gatherings in the community park and Black elders' annual drumming, and criminalise economic activities such as a young man's provision of grass-cutting and other informal services to his neighbours.

> Many of the older residents became irate at this, given that their own efforts (starting in the late 60s and early 70s) to get the police to be more responsive to criminal activity the residents considered far more threatening than any risk posed by [the young man] had been in vain. (Bryant 2006: 721)

New residents were also able to appeal to local government by invoking historic preservation district legislation that not only raised the costs older homeowners faced in maintaining their homes but was also differentially enforced by courts.

> [L]ong-term residents of Olde Towne East had for years been painting their homes various shades of pinks, purples, and blues; the idea that they would have to get permission before they repainted their houses again was shocking and insulting to them. More problematic was the fact that historic designations restricted those residents from painting their homes purple or pink at all, although we never quite discovered why it was that a single white male resident had no trouble painting the trim on the exterior of his renovated home in a varied palate of bold, colorful hues. [A]pparently, such trim was a feature of Victorian houses. (2006: 717)

In the Olde Towne East, the line between gentrifier and gentrified is clearly cast in terms of race and sexuality: on the one hand, Black people (assumed to be heterosexual), on the other, gay and lesbian gentrifiers (who in *Flag Wars* all appear to be white). This picture gets complicated when we consider urban spaces whose queer formations were not from the start figured as white. A legendary site that was long associated with low-income queer and trans people of colour are the piers in Greenwich Village in New York. These are close to the Stonewall Inn on Christopher Street, home to the 1969 riot that is annually celebrated as the birth of the LGBT community in Pride parades all over the world.[11] As the area is rapidly gaining value, the very groups associated with the riots (poor, of colour, gender non-conforming), are being displaced by police and private security guards – whose remit now includes the protection of gay business owners and wealthy residents who are presumably drawn to the area because of its queer culture and history. The violence of this process was brought home most clearly by the redevelopment of the Christopher Street piers by the Hudson River. Like Kreuzberg, the piers have been a paradoxical site of perceived degeneracy, regeneration and resistance. The bodies that have used and inhabited them have been pathologised and criminalised but also mined for their transgressive habitus, which adds value to edgy cultural producers and music industries (see hooks 1992). This is reflected in the continuing mass circulation of Jenny Livingston's documentary *Paris is Burning* (1990), and the discovery and commodification of voguing and other aspects of Black and Latin@ queer house/ball cultures by Madonna and other artists. The piers and the subjects who long inhabited them have thus been a site of cultural appropriation and value extraction.[12] At the same time, they long remained a place where people could find shelter, community and a good time without spending much money (*Fenced Out* 2001). They are also one of the sites shared by Stonewall veterans Sylvia Rivera and Marsha P. Johnson. Randolfe Wicker's documentary (*Sylvia Rivera: Trans Movement Founder* 2011) shows Rivera discussing her relationship with Johnson, trans organising, and collective struggles to survive, against the backdrop of the piers.[13] The piers' redevelopment from, in Manalansan's (2005: 149) terms, 'cruising and socializing areas [that] occupy an important place in the memories and imaginaries of queers, particularly queers of color' into a manicured park catering to 'residents' has provoked one of the biggest queer of colour-led mobilisations that, even if it failed to prevent gentrification and surveillance, succeeded in raising awareness of the fact that low-income trans and queer of colour youth, who are most in need of safer spaces, are also most vulnerable to being erased. This was beautifully brought home in the film *Fenced Out* (2001), made by activists from FIERCE, the queer of colour youth group that assumed leadership in the campaign to defend the piers:

> [Caption:] Do you like being able to come to the only queer youth hang-out area in the city? ... Well guess what, the pier is already fenced off and soon the pier, as we know it, will be gone.
> [Voiceover:] Under the leadership of Governor Pataki and Mayor Giuliani 5 miles of the river bank from Battery Park to 59th Street is under construction to become Hudson River Park. It's gonna be transformed into a 'green and blue oasis, for all of New York to enjoy' – *(laughing)* except for us of course.
> [Voiceover:] Imagine you finally find a place where you feel comfortable.... Imagine that your place, the place where you feel is your second home is

now, is now being bombarded by gay bashers who are harassing, beating and murdering you and your friends. Imagine that the police, who are supposed to protect you, are no better than the criminals they have sworn to take off the street.

Some of the police and private security employed to criminalise and 'move along' illegitimate users of the space work for the condominium buildings that have mushroomed along the Hudson and often target a gay market (see Manalansan 2005).[14] The active role of race and class-privileged gay and gay-friendly residents and business owners in the "'clean-up" of places where sexual minorities of colour, many of whom identify as lesbian, gay, bisexual or transgender, have long socialized', is also documented by Christina Hanhardt (2008: 62). Hanhardt's incisive historiography of gay enclaves in New York and San Francisco points to a long relationship between racialised anti-violence narratives, policing and gentrification:

> Overwhelmingly, residents, gay and straight alike, demand policing and zoning changes with a focus on securing 'safety', citing the quality-of-life laws that target low-level offenses (such as public drinking and loitering) first instituted by the former mayor Rudolph Giuliani. (Hanhardt 2008: 62)

While grounding their discussion in a homonormativity framework, Manalansan and Hanhardt go beyond a simple neoliberalism critique. In explaining queer gentrification, an analysis of neoliberalism, which highlights the conformity of some queer subjects to capital, goes a long way. The ability of socially and spatially mobile queers to exercise consumer rights and citizenship in order to mobilise the state to protect their property and claim space or, as Knopp put it, perform 'gay in-migration [as] responsible middle-class in-migration' (1990: 344), is an important starting point. Nevertheless, collapsing gentrification with homonormativity entirely would miss some important points. First, queers participate in and are impacted by gentrification very differently. Our ability to claim and retain space, both materially and symbolically, differs greatly according to our access to class, race and gender privilege, and our proximity or distance vis-à-vis the degenerate bodies and spaces that are targeted for erasure, dispossession or 'recovery'. Some queers are able to perform themselves as valuable; others are expendable. While this is not a one-to-one function of our positionalities, these differences clearly matter. Thus, I will argue that some trans people and queers of colour in Berlin have been celebrated as 'victim subjects' (Kapur 2005) and/or transgressive subjects who embody colourful neighbourhoods in need of defence (see chapter 2). If a blunt distinction between 'gentrifying queers' and 'displaced queers' is insufficient, in that no positionality is automatically outside of gentrification, our proximities and distances from the good multicultural subject on the one hand, and the degenerate disposable non-citizen on the other, shape the kind of invitations we get, and the performances we must make, to become or stay part of queer spaces forming in gentrifying areas.

Second, reducing gentrification to neoliberalism is insufficient in that it only addresses half of the equation. The matching of undesirable populations with undesirable locations (Knopp 1990: 342) is highly productive not just in preparing an area for regeneration, but in carving out a terrain whose 'development' enables formerly degenerate subjects to revitalise as well. In state contexts that are or were colonised or colonising, this requires an analysis of racism and colonialism. Sherene Razack (2002a: 13) provides such an analysis by drawing attention to the centrality of journeys from 'respectable to degenerate space' for the formation of white gender identities. It is in the 'liminal space' between respectability and degeneracy, where colonisers encounter colonised subjects through (often sexualised) violence, that hegemonic gender identities are formed. Her focus is on hegemonic settler masculinities in Regina, Canada, where white middle-class boys become men by venturing out of 'respectable' urban areas and having sex with Indigenous women.[15]

> Moving from respectable space to degenerate space and back again is an adventure that confirms that they are indeed white men in control who can survive a dangerous encounter with the racial Other and who have an unquestioned right to go anywhere and do anything. (Razack 2002b: 127)

While grounding her analysis in contemporary Canadian colonialism, Razack maps similar 'journeys of transgression' in other biopolitical, geopolitical and historical contexts, including contemporary development work in the global south. Drawing on analyses of early Victorian adventure stories, she argues that, for white girls, journeys into liminal space 'required a gender transgression' (Razack 2002a: 14). In contrast, the same journeys matured white boys into gender-conforming men.[16]

We can apply Razack's account of gender and sexual transgression in the colonial terrain to the gentrifying area. This can also help us make sense of the appearance of the queer 'pioneer' in the German context – an apparently deracialised figure who must be understood in the same genealogy as the disavowed history of German colonialism. Similarly, Neil Smith (1996) pointed to a globalising imaginary of gentrification that is shot through with colonial references. Smith traced the 'discovery' of Manhattan's Lower East Side in the 1980s as the new 'urban frontier', whose wild, dangerous landscapes must be tamed, cleansed and regenerated. He documented this in real estate advertising strategies; in arrival narratives by newcomers who fantasise themselves as '"urban pioneers", presumably going where, in the words of *Star Trek*, no (white) man has ever gone before'; in film narratives such as *Crocodile Dundee* and *Bright Lights, Big City,* which make 'of urban life a cowboy fable replete with dangerous environments, hostile natives and self-discovery at the margins of civilization'; and in the revival of cowboy styles, 'nature idolatry' and primitivism in art, food and clothing markets (Smith 1996: 11, 12, 14–17). He further traced the recurrence of frontier ideology in media and political reactions to anti-gentrification struggles that likened the Lower East Side to a 'Wild Wild West' that must be reconquered.

> Insofar as gentrification infects working-class communities, displaces poor households, and converts whole neighborhoods into bourgeois enclaves, the frontier ideology rationalizes social differentiation and exclusion as natural, inevitable. The poor and working class are all too easily defined as 'uncivil', on the wrong side of a heroic dividing line, as savages and communists. The substance and consequence of the frontier imagery is to tame the wild city, to socialize a wholly new and therefore challenging set of processes into safe ideological focus. As such, the frontier ideology justifies monstrous incivility in the heart of the city. (1996: 16)

In making sense of the coloniality of gentrification and anti-gentrification discourses, we must take care not to reduce Indigeneity to a metaphor (see Tuck and Yang 2012). At the same time, it is important to interrogate how gentrification, as a process that often involves racially privileged subjects replacing racially subordinated ones, remains shaped by colonialism. This is, if anything, more obvious in contexts that are still occupied. In the settler colonial space of Canada, past and present technologies of dispossession and displacement, from forcing Indigenous peoples off their lands and into reservations, and now from their remaining land bases into the cities, are obviously related (see Coulthard 2013; Lawrence 2004). For scholars working in these contexts, the question thus becomes how different modes of emplacement and displacement occur, not after but *in the architecture of* settler colonialism, as Thobani (2014) states insightfully.[17] For those working on the old centres of Empire, which are now often recipients rather than producers of social, economic and spatial paradigms, two sets of questions arise: first, how colonial desires and modalities of control shape the outlook and behaviours of those who never left and, second, how they 'return' in ways that reify or contest local regimes of power. For example, the figure of the *'pioneer'* – sometimes in opposition to, sometimes interchangeable with that of the *'autochton'* (originary or native person, which in Germany is interpreted as white) – has found eager reception in German anti-gentrification debates (for example, Holm n.d.; Trudelfisch 2010). There, left-wing activists, who are often first-wave gentrifiers themselves, use both as positive self-descriptors, without a trace of irony.[18] How do discourses travel (back) to places such as Germany, which disavow any participation in colonial projects – both in the Americas and Australia, where Germans have been settlers, in Asia, which Germans have avidly consumed in the form of tourism, colonial adventure writings and expatriate settlement, and in Africa and the Pacific, where Germans were colonisers (El-Tayeb 1999; Sailiata 2014)?

If the scholarship on queer space has largely ignored the colonial and racial logics undergirding urban landscapes, activist approaches to the urban environment have actively mobilised them. The following sections explore this with regard to homonormative activism in Schöneberg and queer and trans activism in Kreuzberg and Neukölln. While often understood to be disparate paradigms of queer space, I suggest that these are in fact unified by a tendency to reinscribe the spaces in which queers settle, and the subjects who continue to inhabit them, as degenerate and disposable. In fact, the moral panic over the 'dangerous area' can be traced from the gaybourhood, where it was slow to stick at first, to the 'ghetto' in Kreuzberg and Neukölln, where it found a much more fertile terrain, and from there back to the gaybourhood, where it eventually became institutionalised as part of the neoliberal, revanchist city (see Smith 1996).

FROM THE GAYBOURHOOD …

The three Berlin districts that have been salient settings and (hate) crime scenes in the drama of queer lovers and hateful Others map neatly onto the assimilation/transgression binary. Schöneberg is home to a gaybourhood that, in many ways, could be described as homonormative; Kreuzberg is a gentrifying 'mixed' neighbourhood that invokes a transgressive unassimilated space but was long considered the 'Turkish ghetto', a reputation later inherited by Neukölln, its poorer neighbour that soon began to rapidly gentrify itself. True to what might be expected, the moral panic began in 'homonormative' Schöneberg (see also Petzen 2008). Nevertheless, as I trace in the remaining sections, it took a detour via Kreuzberg and then Neukölln to successfully perform Schöneberg as an embattled neighbourhood that deserves protection. Attempts to mark the district as such go back to at least the late 1990s (Haritaworn and Petzen 2011). An early example is an article by Jan Feddersen (2003), a journalist close to the big gay organisations, in the left-wing paper *Tageszeitung*. Feddersen invokes a Schöneberg that is under threat and 'in danger of becoming a no-go area for gay men' (2003, my translations). The article opens with a graphic hate crime scene on a bus, whose perpetrators are described as linguistically and culturally deficient youth 'with a migration background'. Their inability to understand the 'laws applying in Germany, that homosexuality is not punishable, and that bashing gays is actually considered prohibited' is reflected in their failed mimicry of German. This is highlighted by quotes from the verbal exchange preceding the attack ('You gay or wha'?'), as well as the title of the article itself, which generically frames the problem as 'Whatcha looking at? You a fag?' As experts, the author cites three gaybourhood institutions, two of which (the big gay organisation LSVD [Lesbian and Gay Association Germany] and the anti-violence hotline Maneo) frequently appear together in discussions of 'Muslim homophobia'.

> Café PositHiv in Berlin's district Schöneberg will have to close, as the windows are increasingly smeared by kids whose appearance, one hears very cautiously, indicates a Turkish or Arab background. The federal headquarters of the Lesbian and Gay Association Germany (LSVD) on Willmanndamm in the same district is an equally popular target of aggressive taunting. (Feddersen 2003)

Feddersen further cites Bastian Finke, head of gay anti-violence hotline Maneo, as stating:

> Thirty-nine per cent of these violent acts are perpetrated by young men who, in the broadest sense, can be counted as part of the Muslim culture, whether or not they have a German passport or one from Turkey. A major cause of public danger for gay men is youth of Turkish or generally Islamic coinage. (Feddersen 2003)[19]

The article follows a dominant paradigm of representing people of colour that Ann Phoenix (1987) describes as 'generalized absence, pathologized presence'. While employing an anti-intersectional concept of gay identity (as white and generally unmarked), it also cites two activists from the queer of colour NGO GLADT (Gays and Lesbians from Turkey). After slating them for failing to dialogue with 'their' ethnic communities, Feddersen concludes that collaboration between various gay organisations 'is the best recipe to continue the civilization of the pre-modern' (see also Petzen 2008). Even though the drama of queer lovers and hateful Others is not yet fully fledged at that time, early traces are already present. Displaying signs of what Gloria Wekker (2009) terms homonostalgia for a white benevolent nation free from 'homophobic' people of colour, Feddersen wonders if gay men are vulnerable because they wrongly assume that homosexuality can now be freely expressed in Germany: 'It is this very matter-of-factness in showing love and affection also among men that many interpret as encouragement for impulsive intervention' (Feddersen 2003).

These early attempts at moral panicking were awkward in their blunt use of stereotypes. It would take several years, and several re-stagings of the same 'conflict' in more densely racialised spaces, before policy and opinion makers would respond in the demanded way, and give visibility and protection to a 'gaybourhood' that is essentially in decline (see Wolter 2011). The first of these stagings, in 2007, was not in Berlin but in the Hamburg district of St Georg. Like Schöneberg, St Georg contains 'the gaybourhood' alongside streets that are racialised as 'Muslim' (Hieronymus 2011 [2009]). Even though no cases of homophobic violence had been documented, the local gay magazine *Hinnerk* featured a five-month debate that described St Georg as the dangerous setting of a war against gay men. *Hinnerk* headlines included 'Expulsion from Paradise' and 'Nicer without [German: *Schöner ohne*] Döner? Gays and Muslims: struggle over St Georg'. 'Nicer without Döner?' was on the front cover of the September issue and accompanied by an illustration by popular gay comic writer Ralph König (*Hinnerk* 2007, my translations). The cartoon leaves no uncertainty over who is being discursively expelled. It features a scene in a kebab shop, where a white man in drag (appearing to wear a hijab) submissively waits for his döner kebab sandwich while a hunky hairy Middle Eastern server wields his knife against a giant meat skewer. Readers' letters printed in *Hinnerk* called for a boycott of Muslim shops and stated that Muslims who were unwilling to integrate into an overly tolerant Germany and a human rights-abiding European Union (EU) should get lost. As one put it: 'Something must be done against this religion and its effect on the lives of enlightened people!' (cited by Petzen 2008: 178). The 'debate' reached a bigger public. The daily newspaper *Hamburger Morgenpost* (2007) drew attention to the embattled plight of gay men with the headline 'Powderkeg St Georg: Muslims against gays'. Anticipating a performance of queer love in the face of religious hate that, as the next chapter discusses, would soon become all-too common, the cover featured a kiss-in in front of the local mosque, which was accused of refusing dialogue (Figure 4, p. 102).[20]

While invoking intensely local sensibilities, these spatial tropes are not at all parochial. On the contrary, they are intertextual and transposable. Two years after the *Hinnerk* debate, the November issue of the Berlin gay magazine *Siegessäule* revived all its major ingredients. Invoking the military theme more directly, the issue's cover, entitled 'Defend yourselves! Fear-free through the village', sports a group of butch white men in military outfits. The lead article describes Schöneberg as an embattled 'homo paradise' – 'one of the most tolerant neighbourhoods in the world', an 'island of bliss' (Fertig and Salka 2009: 12, 16, my translations). The same ambivalence shines through the headline 'Fearsome space Schöneberg: Site of escalating violence – or tolerant, cosmopolitan homo quarter?' (2009: 12). This tension is clearly mapped out: 'our cosy Motzstraße' – also known as the village – directly meets 'Pallasstraße, Bülowstraße or Alvenslebenstraße' – also known as some of the poorest post codes in Berlin, where many racialised people live (2009: 13).

There is no doubt over which streets are valuable and which pathological. In this 'creative city'-inspired landscape, poor people of colour are dangerous

Figure 2   'Defend yourselves! Fear-free through the village'
Source: November 2009 issue of *Siegessäule*.

threats to efforts to 'boost the neighbourhood's attractiveness' and make stronger use of 'existing potentials of the quarter' (Fertig and Salka 2009: 16). This occurs by invoking the transnational criminalising trope of the 'gang':

> 'But there, two streets ahead, begins the parallel society' [an interviewee states pointing towards Bülowstraße]. The situation on Hauptstraße is 'especially awful' … 'I wouldn't hold my boy-friend's hand there as there's numerous gangs of Turks making trouble.' (2009: 12)

The issue interestingly oscillates between numbers and feelings as measures for the dangerousness of the area. Numbers, or rather their lack, are repeatedly invoked to legitimate this assessment: 'No number confirms that homophobic violence has risen in Berlin in the last years', the opening sentence of the lead article states (2009: 12). Despite its absence, statistical knowledge here comes to reify 'our' feelings about what is happening in 'our' neighbourhood. The interview with the city's foreigners' affairs deputy in the same issue similarly expresses uncertainty about the level of threat:

> Schöneberg is the liberal neighbourhood where gays and lesbians actually can move without fear. This makes for the quality of the district, and that's where a certain insecurity has spread in the last few years as a result of attacks. One does not know how big the real threat is. People who are often out and about in Schöneberg tell me folks often walk around in the neighbourhood with a queasy feeling. One could say that a space of fear is arising in Schöneberg, at a very high level for sure, but it is a space of fear. We cannot let this happen. We must defend the openness of the neighbourhood. (2009: 13)

As Hall et al. (1978) argued, numbers are vital ingredients in moral panics. Citing numbers, or indeed their absence, is highly productive in the economy of fear. The felt increase in violence may be a 'real threat' or indeed a result of racist media representations. Either way, it presents cause for action. In the issue, the stated feeling of insecurity contrasts with the tight and confident manner in which the 'facts' are presented, by an arsenal of experts who all sing from the same songsheet. In addition to Maneo and the LSVD, who already appeared in the 2003 article, they include gay businesses and 'regular' gay people in the neighbourhood. The stated feeling of insecurity is further belied by the playful and pleasurable tone of the war scenes enacted in the accompanying photos. We are even assured that everybody who participated in these photos had fun, including a 'young Turk' who 'absolutely wanted to be in the picture' (Hall et al. 1978: 17). Fun is also signalled by the pink feathers and tiny green water pistols worn by the 'soldier' models, whose look is decidedly mischievous and sponsored, the acknowledgement says, by Military-Stores.de. If military gear has long been a part of queer communities, subversive performances (Yeğenoğlu 1998) such as the Village People's have in a context of homo-neoliberalism, gay imperialism and war on terror turned into what I have called loyal repetitions of the nation (Haritaworn 2008b). It is necessary to 'hit back sometimes', (Fertig and Salka 2009: 12) the lead article suggests, merging protectionist and militaristic discourses on queer space. This reimagination of queer safer space inscribes its constituents across multiple scales of neighbourhood, nation and West. As the need for war becomes palpable locally, globalised notions of terror and security become relevant to the local neighbourhood.

… TO THE 'GHETTO' …

No area underlines this like Kreuzberg, the district that has born the heaviest weight of the 'ghetto' label in Germany. It is here that the drama of queer lovers and hateful Others has found its most fertile ground. Scripted in the offices of gay functionaries in Schöneberg, it took a detour via first Kreuzberg and then Neukölln, the similarly racialised neighbourhood that inherited the 'ghetto' identity as Kreuzberg gentrified, to lend the moral panic its currency and intelligibility. It is noteworthy that, besides their starker racialisation, these areas have given rise to different sexual and gender formations than Schöneberg. Thus, the queers who have settled in and claimed Kreuzberg and Neukölln as 'their neighbourhood' have tended to be younger and radical (but no less white). Many of them have arrived more recently but have nevertheless been able to mark these areas as a 'queer' neighbourhood. The particular ways in which radical performances of gender and sexuality have entered into the drama of queer lovers and hateful Others will be the subject of the next chapter. Here it should suffice to point to the productive proximity between 'queer' Kreuzberg and 'gay' Schöneberg in the figuration of the hate crime scene. This complicates any binary opposition between 'assimilationist' gay gentrifiers on the one hand and 'transgressive' queer victims of gentrification on the other. Iterating between historical accounts of a changing urban development and official data on gentrification on the one hand, and interviews with queer and trans people of colour living in Kreuzberg and Neukölln on the other, this section departs from the more discursive approach to queer space taken so far and considers Kreuzberg as an actual urban environment where racialised populations and those who are recognisably queer are differentially sorted for life and death, opening up resources and life chances for some while foreclosing them for others. In making sense of these tensions I cite analyses co-produced with the interviewees. Unable or unwilling to pass as colourful queers who brand Kreuzberg as multicultural in the face of racialised displacement, interviewees described a shrinking environment where queers of colour have become disposable alongside other people of colour.

Traditionally working-class, Kreuzberg underwent a massive population exchange in the 1960s and 1970s, when upwardly mobile white working-class people, the winners of the post-war economic boom, were encouraged to move to newly built apartment blocks in other areas, which conformed more closely to city planners' fantasies of a modern, functionalist society. As Carla MacDougall (2011) reminds us in her historiography of urban struggles in Kreuzberg, the district's old Wilhelmine buildings were then decidedly unfashionable, and left to crumble by developers waiting for funds to realise their tabula rasa fantasies of urban renewal by demolition. To planners and landlords alike, the temporary houses became an ideal site for segregating the temporary bodies of the so-called guest workers from Turkey, North Africa and southern Europe, who were excluded from the housing market due to economic exploitation and racist discrimination. This local history was studied by one of the interviewees, who presented it to me as follows:

Kreuzberg was a district where nobody wanted to live at first. Where the living situation was bad, where there wasn't any hot water, where there was only coal oven heating, damp flats, mould, etc. Large parts of Friedrichshain and Neukölln were derelict, too, because they weren't attended to. Kreuzberg and Neukölln were border regions after all and not city centre, which is why houses were rotting away. At the time there were plans to restructure Kreuzberg population wise. So Zentrum Kreuzberg was intended for business people, so were Dresdener Straße und Adalbertstraße – and Oranienplatz – a motorway junction was planned there. So that's important as context information. Then, as nobody really wanted to do business in Kreuzberg, since the houses were in such bad shape, people couldn't imagine that people with money would move there. So they just rented the houses out till their demolition – there was supposed to be large-scale demolition in the area. And what happened is that the first generation of people of colour who'd come for work and making money put up with these conditions as temporary tenants.

MacDougall (2011) similarly argues that the labour migrants who arrived in the 1960s were ideal placeholders in houses planned to remain as temporarily as them. They were also ideal distractors from this planning disaster when the tide changed in the 1980s and a large part of Kreuzberg was declared a 'careful urban renewal area', following prolonged left-wing resistance and an oil-crisis-induced household slump. As a result of changing planning fashions and their own resistance and tenacity, migrants and their children and grandchildren were able to stay and made Kreuzberg their home.

Marked by segregation, hyper-exploitation and neglect, the multiracial inner city nevertheless offered something that was never achieved at the scale of the nation. If Germanness has remained white and unhyphenable, Kreuzberg for a long time was not (see also El-Tayeb 2012). Efforts to build community were tightly controlled, and between 1975 and 1990 'foreigners' were banned from moving to Kreuzberg and other inner-city areas following racist fear mongering about an 'alien' takeover (Çağlar 2001). Nevertheless, Kreuzberg became home to racialised communities that, contrary to the later ambivalent mapping of a (white) queer Kreuzberg versus a (homophobic) Turkish Kreuzberg, always already included sexually and gender non-conforming people. This is illustrated by Frida, a queer of colour interviewee who remembers a 1970s and 1980s Kreuzberg where intellectuals, workers and artists, queer, trans and straight, shared a space that was socially and politically mixed:

The scene at the time, I know it from my mother, was not an explicitly gay or queer scene but a large circle of intellectuals, artists as well as workers. For example, my mother had a friend, she was a trans woman, but that wasn't an issue. I was eight and I remember her long blonde hair *(laughs)* and also how she had surgery. She always asked my mother 'Abla [Turkish: older sister], am I pretty?' My mother affirmed: 'Yes, you're pretty!' I remember these dialogues (laughs). Or my mother's hippie friend, Turkish background, with his giant wooden necklace. I liked him a lot. He always looked chilled. My mom asked him not to smoke weed in our presence.

These accounts of conviviality and solidarity differ from the pathologising images of Kreuzberg that for decades determined mainstream media and political debates. They also differ from the blue-eyed picture painted in many progressive accounts, where squatters, draft dodgers, migrants, artists and queers (all non-overlapping) live side by side in perfect harmony. Rather, the described relationships are shot through with power and the result of sustained investment and collective care. In these alternative historical landscapes, people arrived with unequal privileges and capacities to lay claim to the terrain and its resources. Frida described how, as children, they often had to run from old white people who let their German shepherd dogs loose on them. She was equally critical of the well-meaning white lefties who arrived from West Germany to escape the draft, or help 'poor Turkish women and children':

> The first arrivals were white wessis [Berlin slang for people from West Germany]. Berlin didn't have the military draft after all. Then there was the social worker fraction, or alternatives, who found it cool to occupy houses. Wessis you know (laughs). We couldn't really take them seriously, those social workers.

This contrasts with urban justice discourses that uncritically juxtapose a bad state and market on the one hand, and good social movements on the other. MacDougall (2011), too, observes that 'depictions and discussions of Kreuzberg as a district consisting mainly of two distinct subcultures, one political and one ethnic, rarely address the inequality between the two subcultures and the subsequent unequal access to political decision-making and models of participation' (2011: 102). Her historiography complicates a narrative of heroic activists (from squatters to social workers) who fight power and oppression and lead the way to a progressive future. Even before the onslaught of neoliberalism, newcomers with race and class privileges and spatial mobility were able to accumulate political value and become sovereign subjects by reducing racialised bodies to raw material that must be helped, liberated and acted upon. The nativised population, then still constructed as Turkish, were treated as apolitical objects. This is also suggested by MacDougall's observation that conservative and alternative media in the 1970s and 1980s tended to construct Kreuzberg in parallel terms, as an overcrowded 'ghetto' left to decay by its backward, mal-integrated, rapidly reproducing inhabitants (2011: 196–202, 208ff). While white housing activists saw themselves as advocates, they still treated their racialised neighbours as 'passive victims' whose 'side by side' lifestyle was a problem. One left-wing tenants' newsletter, *Südost Express*, sought to address this by encouraging 'seniors to reach out to their Turkish neighbors and offer babysitting or after school services such as helping migrant children with their homework' (MacDougall 2011: 216). Benevolent discourses, as so often, coexisted with pathologising ones. Overall, MacDougall concludes, left-wing positions on race and space were not far removed from the dominant discourse. Leaving behind a celebratory or power-evasive view of the white left, then, we should examine the formation of social movements in Berlin and elsewhere within processes of acquisition and accumulation, professionalisation and institutionalisation, in an environment shaped and contested between groups with uneven access to power and resources.

Well-meaning white 'helpers' thus participated in the making of a 'Turkish ghetto in Kreuzberg' that constitutes the natural scene for successive moral panics, both uncanny microcosm of what's wrong with society, and prophetic looking glass of what's to come if 'we don't put a stop to this': be it immigration or segregation, crime and disorder, mal-integration and parallel societies, terror and insecurity, or violence against women or queers (MacDougall 2011; Stehle 2006). Kreuzberg and later Neukölln became the natural habitat of an ever growing array of dangerous and undesirable figures, including gangs, drugs, patriarchs, school drop outs and women wearing headscarves, who were later joined by terrorists, honour killers and homophobes. Like other spaces where racialised populations have been concentrated across Western Europe and trans-Atlantically, the label 'ghetto' has been productive in that it culturalises the conscious segregation, neglect and decline of these areas as the migrants' own fault, a testimony to 'their' lack of responsibility and integration (see also Wacquant 2008). As elsewhere, the figure of the 'ghetto' has served to depoliticise and normalise gender, race and class divisions as a function of 'their' inherent degeneracy and deficiency and 'our' failure to discipline and control them.

The figure of the ghetto demands further attention, especially in Germany. The compulsion to treat the effects of racism as self-inflicted is part of broader efforts to insulate it in the Nazi past. As Chapter 4 discusses in greater detail, this demands a clear de-linking of spatial and other techniques of controlling racialised populations before, during, and after 1933–45. What follows is an erasure of racist presents as well as pasts. As Petzen notes:

> It was shocking to hear the word ghetto being used in Berlin to describe, with definite distaste, a Turkish or Arabic neighborhood. Not that there had been a Jewish ghetto in Berlin – there was not – but because the word was uttered as though Jewish ghettos had not been part of European life for hundreds of years. (Petzen 2008: 163)

Drawing on Stehle's (2006) analysis of German media reports on the Paris riots, Petzen highlights that the blueprint of today's 'ghetto', in public, academic and everyday discourse alike, is Harlem and the Parisian banlieues, rather than Warsaw.

The spatial imaginary of the 'ghetto' has material effects in that it constructs its inhabitants as a surplus population fit for punishment, exploitation and neglect and disentitled to benefits and care. Besides the urban development practices examined above, Kreuzberg has served as a test tube for policing and surveillance. The district has long been a hub of left-wing activism, from workers' in the nineteenth and twentieth centuries to anarchists' and squatters' movements since the 1970s. With the fall of the Eastern bloc, however, the target of surveillance has shifted to people of colour.[21] Berlin as a whole is exceptionally well policed – Eick (2003) counted twice as many police officers to inhabitants as in the rest of the country. Yet Kreuzberg presents a particular focal point for the German versions of the wars on terror, immigration, drugs and poverty. Instruments used for racial profiling have proliferated and included special units that target different types of crime, differently racialised populations (such as the 'Working Group "Arabs"' or the 'Task Force "Black Africans"'), and different places (Eick 2003).[22] The latter – the designation of 'dangerous places' – is especially powerful in that it allows for the suspension of legal rights in particular places. The poorer part of Kreuzberg is officially considered such a 'dangerous place' where anyone, without specific grounds for suspicion, can be stopped, searched, arrested and expelled. According to Eick (2003), Kreuzberg has its own 'operative group' which, according to numbers from 2003, arrested a thousand people every year.[23]

Racial profiling has if anything increased since, and follows in the footsteps of gentrification.[24] At the time of writing, Görlitzer Park, a park in Kreuzberg that was long a free hang-out used by all kinds of people, has become a regular target of aggressive drug raids that profile and segregate Black masculinities.[25] The raids accompany a successive whitening and straightening (at least for people of colour) of this public space. More analysis is needed into the antiblackness and coloniality through which the current changes in this environment are normalised, including in benevolent counter-publics, with headlines such as 'Working the African bushes' (Werntz 2012). Such analysis requires a queer of colour lens that is currently missing from accounts of urban and racial justice. Thus, an interviewee who is Black and gender non-conforming shared not only being criminalised while using the park but also experiencing transphobia when seeking support from an anti-racist victim support organisation. They subsequently chose to deal with the incident on their own.

In contrast, white feminist, gay, queer and trans discourses have long invested in the policing of Kreuzberg as a natural crime scene. The next chapter contains a detailed account of the kind of trans activism that has become possible through 'queer punitiveness' (Lamble 2014). In comparison to the older left-wing stance of rescue, recent gay, queer and trans activisms have laid claim to a Kreuzberg that is already marked by the thorough disenfranchisement of racialised communities, under such logics of neoliberalism, backlash against multiculturalism and securitisation against terror and crime. What is more, queer claims to Kreuzberg have less often figured people of colour as poor victims in need of support (though queer Muslims sometimes become interesting objects of rescue). More often, they have treated people of colour as vehicles and competitors for resources and publicity. In a special *Siegessäule* issue entitled 'Turks out!' the apparent impossibility of 'coming out in two cultures' is metonymically linked to the closed space of Turkish neighbourhoods. According to the author of the lead article:

> The woman is under house arrest, cut off from the outside world, inaccessible to everyone. In school, the daughters are allowed neither to go to gym class nor on class trips, and are prepared for their roles as housewives. Whoever chews gum on the street or even smokes is considered an impure slut. In contrast, the sons, teeming with power, scratch their balls ostentatiously and put their potency on display. The identities of people of other orientations are repressed or hidden. (Winter 2003: 13, cited in and translated by Petzen 2008: 183)

With its provocative title, reminiscent of neo-Nazi slogans like 'Foreigners out!', the issue was met with considerable protest both by queers of colour and allies, first and foremost the self-organisation GLADT (Gays and Lesbians from Turkey) (see also Polzer 2004). In contrast, virtually no debate happened when the moral panic, which had till then taken the form of mediatic fear mongering, found its first bodies five years later. This may be because the first flesh-and-blood 'victims' were radical queer and gender non-conforming people. The setting of the 'event' that would launch the odd neologism *Hasskriminalität* (hate crime) into the German vocabulary was the Drag Festival, an internationally publicised gender/queer performance event, which culminated in an altercation during which several festival visitors and performers were beaten up. Dovetailing with a decade-long moral panic over 'homophobic Muslims', and set in the heart of Kreuzberg, the incident, which was highly contested in its 'truth' content, instantly became an 'event' that circulated rapidly through a queer and trans community that was increasingly formed around stories of racialised hate and violence. As discussed in the next chapter, the resulting mediations were highly ambivalent towards gender non-conforming subjects, who nevertheless for the first time emerged as bodies worthy of both protection and celebration. Trans and queer people became important symbols of a diverse neighbourhood that can be colourful even while its older poor and racialised inhabitants are ghosted from it through gentrification and policing.

Danía, an interviewee and kitchen-table participant, similarly identified 'the supposed attack on a group of queers' at the Drag Festival in 2008 as the starting point for a new queer presence that marks its claim to the 'dangerous migrant neighbourhood' through marching.

> For me it started that year [2008] that queer spaces gained more prominence. That Dyke Trans March that marched through Kreuzberg with the warning that we are located in an unsafe area and should all walk close, not walk by ourselves. I coincidentally walked past there and heard this announcement, woah.... There's this intense link between the LSVD and other white gay [homornormative] associations that white [radical] queers normally distance themselves from. At the same time they join forces to agree that white queers in Kreuzberg are suffering and in danger. Exactly, white queers that differentiate themselves from [white gay men] and anything that's conservative, and still use the same machinery. At the same time they fancy themselves as the alternative bearers of culture, in contrast to conservative, patriarchal people of colour who are great at selling vegetables but not in charge of culture. And that's what Kreuzberg stands for, alternative culture – and who can be its bearers? This entitlement, this feeling of having always already been here.

Queer community building here emerges as a raced and classed form of sociality. Danía's account echoes longer-standing feminist practices of space and safety, including Take Back the Night marches through poor racialised areas whose 'dangerousness' has at times been similarly marked through race and class (Bhavnani and Coulson 1986). It further troubles the assimilationist gays versus transgressive queers binary of the queer space literature. Especially in Germany, where there was no trans-of-colour-led Stonewall that can be reclaimed as our 'real' origin before the gays turned problematic, the distinction between corporate *racist gays* and radical *anti-racist queers* does not hold. Rather, Danía's analysis highlights the salience of other distinctions, between those who become the symbolic bearers of a place and those who emerge as superfluous to or even in the way of this colourful community. I am reminded of Jodi Melamed's thoughts on neoliberal multiculturalism, which 'scripts its beneficiaries as worthy multicultural global citizens' who get to signify post-race and post-gender values of freedom, choice and equality, and 'its losers as doomed by their own monoculturalism, deviance, inflexibility, criminality, and other attributes' (2011: 87). While class is crucial here, the activisms critiqued by Danía and other interviewees complicate a notion of homonationalism as a problem that is mainly about neoliberalism. Rather, queers with race and class privileges have actively participated in marking Kreuzberg as a degenerate space.

They have also participated in its gentrification. Political economy theorists usefully highlight the centrality of capital in the gentrification process. With German unification, the inner city moved from 'the shadows of the wall' to the heart of the city (MacDougall 2011). By then, new demographic and cultural trends had replaced the family home in the white suburb as a model of the good life. Its place is taken by single, couple, or for the more alternative, shared dwelling in the multicultural city centre (see Holm 2008). Kreuzberg, with its beautiful old buildings (once awaiting demolition, now symbols of vitality), its numerous ethnic eateries and bohemian cafes, and its rebellious counter-cultural flair, is becoming ever more popular with newcomers from West Germany, North America, and other parts of Europe and the global north. Unlike inner-city areas in the former East, such as Prenzlauer Berg (Holm 2006), the hip neighbourhood where the bulk of the population was exchanged within a few years of unification, gentrification was slower in Kreuzberg. The influx of big capital was delayed by its special status as a careful urban renewal area, which aimed to preserve the historic and social structure of the neighbourhood by controlling rents and modernisation, and giving inhabitants rights of occupancy and participation (Holm 2006). In the mid 2000s, however, the 20-year subsidy contracts ended, resulting in a massive rent gap (Smith 1979) that both smaller and bigger capitalists have been able to exploit. Houses are being sold and converted into private condominiums. Many others are being upgraded and re-rented at a much higher price. Already, the district has the most expensive rents for new tenancies, and is treated as the biggest ascendant on the property market (GSW 2010: 1; Holm 2010a).

This intersects with a neoliberal city politics that increasingly abandons low-income people. In the 1990s, the city began to privatise its social housing stock[26] and public utilities such as water, gas and electricity (Holm 2011). Coupled with economic restructuring, mass unemployment and the drying up of subsidies after the fall of the wall, the result has been a sharp increase in poverty, which is concentrated in the inner cities. Poverty statistics have 'improved' in some areas, including Kreuzberg, giving social democratic city experts grounds for optimism that these areas are catching up (Häußermann et al. 2007).[27] Nevertheless, unemployment statistics and poverty rates are still among the highest in Berlin: fewer than half of all people of employable age have regular employment, and it is estimated that every fourth or fifth person lives in poverty (TOPOS 2008: 13, 21). This affects poor racialised people disproportionately. According to a study by TOPOS city planning, which was commissioned by the local government, there is a growing polarisation between those who have been in the area since before 1990, who are predominantly old white working-class people and what the study refers to as 'migrant' families, and those who have arrived since the 1990s, who include high-earning individuals and young families and upwardly mobile young people: 'Of all poor households, 57 per cent are migrant households. Of all poor people, 73 per cent are migrants. Of all poor children and youth, 82 per cent are migrants' (TOPOS 2008: 50–52). Any 'improvement' in statistics must thus be understood in conjunction with the arrival of wealthy newcomers who are displacing poor racialised residents who were there before (see Holm 2010a).[28]

Sexuality and gender identity are not measured in the TOPOS study. The data set nevertheless allows for an interesting comparison between the access to housing enjoyed by younger single people who are not classified as migrants and by families who are. Many queer living arrangements match the profile of the average newcomer more closely than those of most migrant families: according to TOPOS, the typical incoming household consists of one or two people and is child-less, on a good income or upwardly mobile (TOPOS 2008: 59). This contrasts with larger households with children more typical of migrant families, who often have difficulty finding affordable flats and are forced to move away.[29] While rent is already one-third of the average household income,[30] large, family-friendly flats in particular have seen huge rent increases (TOPOS 2008: 60). With a medium income of just over €2000, the average four-, five- or more-person household has a smaller total income than the average Kreuzberg two-person household (TOPOS 2008: 18). Many middle-class flat-shares and collective living arrangements are in a better position to rent in Kreuzberg than racialised families with whom they compete for these larger flats, and who, as is now widely documented, are discriminated against by racist landlords (Kiliç 2008; Yiğit et al. 2010).

In Germany, gentrification became regarded as a public problem relatively recently.[31] Even then, it took a while before racialised people became visible as its primary targets. Anti-gentrification activism, which has strong continuities with the squatters' movement, has tended to focus on more recent waves of gentrification that directly impact the spaces that white alternative people have claimed for themselves. According to the kitchen-table participants, these spaces have stayed predominantly white, despite successive attempts by people of colour to intervene in them. The following interviewee, who migrated to Germany as a young adult, describes their first-hand experience of alternative living projects:

A: In the beginning when I moved here I was living in [the district] Mitte, in a very big so-called *hausprojekt* or ex squat…. At first I was just watching, because I couldn't communicate that much, but I have to say, when I started to speak more English, I start to also have more trouble, for sure. Because I guess a lot of people, some people consider me very nice, as long as I don't talk. And for me it was very shocking, in this house, the majority of people were like white, German, middle-class students. There were like two people of colour without papers. That was an unbelievable, disgusting, manipulative situation. Only one day after I'd moved into the house, three different people told me that these people are actually not paying rent. Information that for sure I didn't ask for, and I don't need and I don't care about it. It was very funny also for me to see, these two people were a heterosexual couple. Like most of the people in the house. But apparently this guy was the only so-called macho around. [They describe being labelled as aggressive, too.]

Q: Was this to do with your race as well as your queerness?

A: My queerness was welcome for sure, my race was not welcome. And everything else I am, it was not welcome. I moved out, after a very tragic house meeting *(we laugh)*, where I was really happy, because I could express myself and tell all of them to just fuck off. I have some other friends who had the same experience in this house, who also had confrontations with the same people, over the same topics. And these people are still there, seven years later. So who are these spaces for? For me it's very clear. It's very funny also to see that many of them, in these spaces, they often pretend that 'Oh, someone says the word racism, it's the first time that this ever happened.' And how they are like collectively able to ally themselves to each other.

At the time of writing, racialised people for the first time have become the face of the anti-gentrification struggle. In May 2012, residents of one of the biggest social housing complexes in Kreuzberg, 80 per cent of whose population have migration histories in Turkey, occupied a public square (Kotti Camp 2012). As Cold War subsidies to the property owner are phased out, rents are expected to increase exponentially. Job centres are refusing to raise housing benefits in line with the increase and tell benefit recipients to move to Marzahn and other districts at the margins of Berlin that are not only predominantly white but also known for their big neo-Nazi presence. The protest, named Kotti Camp after its iconic location by Kottbusser Tor, the subway stop at the heart of Kreuzberg, has been highly successful in organising mass protests that have gained considerable media attention (Kotti Camp n.d.). Queers of colour, too, have actively supported the camp. One interviewee compares the camp, whose everyday organisation is run by older women of colour, with the older white-dominated anti-gentrification movement.

Q: This is the first time that POCs [people of colour] have become central in the anti-gentrification movement, right?

A: Earlier, not even two years ago, demonstrations against rent increases were extremely white.… I remember. A friend and I were the only POCs *(laughs)*. We joined the march and then just dropped out again. It's not that inviting, the autonomous block. Which auntie of Turkish origin would join that?

(Laughs) The demonstrations are still very white.… Then there's the racist comments by the white guy [involved in Kotti Camp], microphone in hand, very sensational and loud. He goes: 'This newspaper *BZ* is reporting on us. When are you finally gonna learn German so that you can understand it and boycott the paper?' I asked, twice: 'I beg your pardon?' That night I wrote an email to the organisation as I couldn't let go of it. The response – he does a lot of good for the camp – didn't satisfy me, so I decided to drop out of the discussion rounds. I'm doing my night shifts, I'm organising, I go to the demos, I distribute posters and flyers. I listen to the women, they have a big need to talk. It's not about giving advice but about listening. This is my role and I feel good with it.

Q: There's a lot of media reports about this right?

A: Yes. I recently got a request from a journalist. She wanted an interview. I wrote her that I'd like to introduce her to the women who have initiated the whole thing. I find it important to keep naming this. This is not about Tom, Dick and Harry, or about me. We are parts of a whole and not exceptional individuals. I also need to mention how the media report on 'those poor people on benefits'. Those articles are so tawdry and turgid, so disgustingly sentimental. I wonder if it's possible to report objectively on the topic of 'migrant women'. [Discusses several attempts by white lefties to hijack the camp, including picking fights with the cops in a derailing manner and getting themselves arrested.] My first night shift was with a white leftie woman. She was at the demo as well and then in front of the prison. And she came and introduced herself and I'm like 'Hey, we're doing night shift together.' There was a table with women of Turkish origin, some were passing by on their way from a wedding, and there was lively chitchat. I'm like 'Come join us'. She goes *(crosses her arms)*: 'I'm feeling really excluded right now, I don't understand anything.' I go: 'They will leave soon.'

Q: Woah! Why should they leave?

A: She replied: 'I don't feel like they will leave soon.' I got impatient and said 'Well, now you know what it long felt like for us.' She then sat in a corner with her puzzle mag. At some stage I asked her how she felt about the whole camp. She said she'd just been thinking for two hours if she wants to support it. That it's no longer the old movement where you support each other and wait in front of the jail. I said to her 'It's not what the camp gives to you but what you give the camp.'

The following interviewee, who did night shifts for Kotti Camp with a group of queers of colour, similarly expressed support for the camp, and contrasted it positively with the wider anti-gentrification scene:

It's a nice change, this POC-organised Kotti Camp, with actual neighbours who are sitting there and doing night shifts. With folks who, when they can't live here any more due to rent increases, will lose their whole history, that they have built here in the last 50 years. And to see how existential this is, and that the basic idea is not 'Yay, we're doing something fun and occupying this house, or it's my political duty' or what white middle-class kids are thinking when they move into occupied houses without water and electricity.[32]

Besides allying themselves to anti-gentrification spaces where racialised people, however tenuously, play leadership roles, the trans and queer people of colour whom I interviewed described how their own environments were shrinking, too. Dania nostalgically remembered a Kreuzberg where queer and trans people of colour were a recognisable part of the local landscape. With gentrification, this space is now being eroded.

> There was a community of shops owned by people of colour who also happened to be queer, where folks would congregate. And all that's now gone. The only businesses that made it have catered to an audience of white middle-class yuppies from the start. All others have gone bust. The feeling of walking through Kreuzberg and ... it may sound funny but being legible to neighbours, as part of a group, that meant a lot to me. Even if it was a group that wasn't immediately respected. QPoCs were simply part of the landscape, we hadn't just moved here but we'd always been here. Today I walk through the streets and as a result of all the tourists I am turned into a tourist again. Neighbours now talk to me in English.

Besides rapid changes in who is able to physically and symbolically occupy Kreuzberg, Dania attributed the loss of queer of colour space and visibility to cultural appropriation. As several other interviewees also noted, early-wave gentrifiers – who included white queers and other 'alternatives' – appropriated racialised styles and made them 'cool' to the 'hipsters' who followed in later waves of gentrification. While racialised styles were now everywhere, the subjects who had invented them for collective survival were finding it hard to stay. This shrinkage of the environment extended to multiple scales, of housing, accessible queer spaces and the body. Thus, Dania had decided to stop wearing their favourite Afro-punk hairstyle, now resignified as white, queer and hipster, as they didn't want their Middle Eastern neighbours to think they were a gentrifier. And vice versa, white queer somatic norms – from thin white vegan bodies wearing black sportswear 'as if they're about to go camping' to asymmetrical haircuts – became a frequent butt of queer of colour jokes. Beyond their status for queer of colour solidarities, it is important to recognise these somatic norms as profiling techniques that serve to further whiten the queer and trans spaces developing in the gentrifying inner city. As this trans of colour activist explained:

I nearly wasn't let into the party by TriQ [the major trans organisation]. Only when this white queer person said hi to me did they realise I was queer. As I was approaching security already watched me closely. The guy starts coming at me with a face that says 'You're not getting in here', when this white person with an asymmetrical haircut comes up to me and the guy's facial expression changes from one second to the other. Haha.

For trans people of colour, who have few places to go and are rarely missed from even the most radical coalition, losing access to trans spaces, which serve as gatekeepers for vital resources such as information about doctors who are less abusive, can have serious repercussions. Misster Raju Rage described how the increased racism in trans spaces had made transitioning much harder:

Accessing certain spaces is personally hard. In order to access those spaces you need to feel safe and they often aren't. You would need to access them to get certain resources and I don't even feel comfortable or necessarily safe going into them to access them. I feel like I can't access those spaces anonymously, there's so much connection and engagement I'd need to have with people, and that's unsafe. I can't just go in, get what I need or want and leave them, with myself intact. There's so much I've seen in those spaces and so much I have experienced that is problematic and downright traumatising.... I don't even want to be part of them any more. I don't feel like the resources I'm getting are gonna be beneficial for me or worth the trauma involved in getting them. But it's not easy to not have access to resources either and I need them. I see certain individuals and groups accessing them with no issues and that leaves me enraged. Resources should be reaching those people who need them, not just those privileged enough to receive them.

Ironically, as the next chapter further explores, trans-designated spaces have mushroomed in this densely racialised space. However, even spaces that long catered to queers of colour or had a sizeable non-white clientele in the past have become harder for queer and trans people of colour to access. An oft-mentioned example for this is the long-standing club night Gayhane, which is advertised on the venue's website as a 'Belly Gogos, Midnight Show and HomoOriental Dancefloor' (Gayhane n.d.). The authors of *Khalass!!!* polemically highlight the contested and changing meanings of this space:

Some of us think: places like the Gayhane bear a political meaning, which is constantly being denied, distracted from and questioned by you. When white masses appear there, exoticizing us and gazing at us, it drains these spaces of their political potential. These locations should be empowering to us, you already have enough white spaces. Our bodies are not screens to project your orientalist fantasies, your exotification and sexualization. We do not want to be the white people's entertainment at Gayhane and simultaneously get lectured on how music by PoC and Blacks is generally being 'homophobic', 'transphobic' and 'sexist'. You must be joking! (*Khalass!!!* 2013)

While non-trans gay male bodies read as Turkish continue to symbolise this flagship event, there was a sense among several of the interviewees that the white straight bouncers at the door can no longer distinguish these very bodies from the 'homophobic hordes' who must be warded off in order to protect the 'real partygoers'. Several directly linked this to gentrification. As venues follow the new opportunities that open up in the changing environment, their target audience shifts. One interviewee put it thus:

A: SO 36 [the big alternative venue where Gayhane is held]: White cis guys stand in front of the door and decide who is queer enough to get in. They don't even take note of POCs even if the party is explicitly POC or uses POC music and resources to attract the audience. And they decide what real queers should look like leaving cis guys of colour out of the question.

Q: Can you describe what happened in Roses [the long-standing bar next door]?

A: Roses has bouncers now, too, and of course they won't let cis men of colour in either. The perverse thing is, they used to have a Black bouncer to keep out the group of Black men who met up there for a while without attracting racism allegations. And this is now a 'really safe place' where tourists can check out the 'authentic Berlin'.

As Kreuzberg is restructured to cater to white consumption needs, old ambivalences give rise to new distinctions between those racialised subjects, styles and products that are valuable – desirable, palatable, easily digestible, in bell hooks' (1992) much-cited terms – and those that are pathological and disposable. This has drastic effects on queer of colour communities. Interviewees critically reflected on the rise of a new industry in QPoC-themed parties, awareness-raising workshops and other services that ironically worked to lend further resources to white queer spaces while rendering queers of colour who critiqued queer racism excessive. I, too, have found that queers of colour who try to name the contradictory convergence of gentrification, racism and economic opportunity often go missing, either silently or with a bang. One interviewee described what happened when they tried to open up dialogue over racist door policies with an event organiser, who responded by marginalising them from their networks:

I was quite depressed for a long time. I had crying fits, I couldn't leave my flat for a while, I was quite depressed. My whole friendship circle changed. The people who knew about it positioned themselves against me. I had to quit my job, as I worked with this NGO [that worked with the venue]. I had to give up my position there.

What can we learn from these conversations on queer gentrification? Even as queer of colour topics gain currency, the environment for many queers of colour is shrinking, at various scales: from the body, which loses access to technologies of self-determination (from hormones to hairstyles), to the neighbourhood, where queers of colour are turned into tourists, and displaced alongside other POCs, to queer and trans spaces, to the queer of colour community itself.

Besides shrinking the space that queers of colour are able to move in and access, the influx of white people arriving with gentrification and touristification has rendered people of colour more vulnerable to racist violence in the very areas in which they were once confined. Rima Hussein, who grew up in an inner-city district close to Kreuzberg, argued that spaces where people of colour would stand up for each other across diasporic divisions were lost:

There are few people of colour spaces that are protected from Nazis where POCs are still the majority. And that is a massive loss, that this is now all disappearing with gentrification. When I was 18, I was nearly beaten up in Kreuzberg 36 by Nazis, right on Adalbertstraße, they called me an N slut. And this classic BMW stops, the window rolls down, the guy opens his glove compartment, gets out a gun, and goes: 'You can't do that here, this is our district.' First, I don't feel like various communities still show this kind of solidarity with each other any more and, second, this isn't our Kreuzberg 36 any more.

The cognitive maps described here differ both from the Kreuzberg of the racist media panics and from the idealised multicultural fantasies of the wider left. The queer of colour Kreuzberg that emerges in these accounts was no paradise but a fragile terrain that demands mutual care. It was a place where you could be queer and of colour, where neo-Nazis and even police were afraid to go, and where community infrastructures existed, even for such impossible subjects as trans and queer people of colour.

As Kreuzberg is becoming less and less affordable, the queer scene, along with other newcomers, has moved to Neukölln, the district just across the canal. At the same time, Neukölln, too, has been discovered for development, leading to a dramatic population exchange. To newcomers the two districts would look almost identical. However, until recently Neukölln was considered too bad to gentrify. Ruled by violence, crime and 'Turks and Arabs', who, by definition, prefer to live in parallel societies and disrespect white Germans and their 'lead culture', it still embodies the mobile figure of the ghetto, which has dominated European public spheres since multiculturalism was declared 'in crisis' in the late 1990s. Neukölln's central location, its attractive turn-of-the-century architecture, a massive rent gap and a district government that makes no secret of their desire to exchange the current population for more valuable inhabitants, have nevertheless made it an ideal candidate for gentrification (Smith et al. 2007). Since the late 2000s, Neukölln has been among the districts with the highest rises in prices of investment objects, and its northern part, home to 'more and more students, intellectuals, artists' as well as cafes, pubs and restaurants, has become the next Kreuzberg and Prenzlauer Berg (GSW 2010: 5, 16; Holm 2010b). Change has been fast and cruel in this post-social housing context, which is as neoliberal as it is 'revanchist' (see Smith 2002).[33] While sexuality has not thus far made it into any urban plans, queers with race and class privileges nevertheless present relatively attractive newcomers, at least in the medium term. Indeed, the mayor of Neukölln Heinz Buschkowsky has stated in an interview with the queer magazine *Siegessäule* that the problem of the district is that it doesn't attract the right kind of people (*Siegessäule* 2008).

According to kitchen-table participants, queers with race and class privileges have actively stepped into this role. In the interviews, Neukölln emerges as the site where queer gentrification is felt most painfully. Rima Hussein contextualised this with the rapid pace of gentrification in Neukölln, which she compared to the slower pace of development in Kreuzberg 61, the less poor part of Kreuzberg, in less neoliberal times.

> In Kreuzberg 61 I had a feeling that things work more in a hippie-green politics kind of way. That people have discussions where the district should be going. While in Neukölln I had a much stronger feeling that this wave [of often queer-identified people] is arriving with this quite aggressive attitude already, often from very privileged families.... And that this is a very academic thing, they're already assuming somehow that they will be greeted with hostility, by the brutal homophobic mass ...

Danía's memory of the recent 'discovery' of Neukölln resonates with Neil Smith's account of the Lower East Side described above:

> People who can't afford rent already moved to Neukölln five years ago. 'Really, you live in Friedelstraße? That's so far away.' There was nothing there then. Today 'Nord-Neukölln' it's a new amusement quarter that's been raised out of thin air. It far supersedes O-Straße and Kreuzberg, simply because Neukölln was far poorer, far cheaper, there was no infrastructure. The ideal place for

an art gallery. Whole streets were redeveloped, with boutiques, galleries, second-hand shops, cycle shops.

Dania's is an excellent translation of Smith's (1979) theory of the rent gap, one of the key concepts in gentrification theories. The rent gap measures the difference in a site's actual value and its potential value at 'best use' once stigma and other obstacles for development are removed. Shedding a very different light on the gay gentrification literature discussed above, Dania's account underlines the possibilities for queer and trans community development in this changing environment. Several interviewees echoed this by pointing to the many queer businesses and organisations that have sprung up in Neukölln in recent years. Even more than with the gradually grown structures in Kreuzberg, these have largely remained in the hands of white people who often move within virtually segregated infrastructures. Interviewees highlighted that many newcomers manage to live a life that is completely insulated from and indifferent to the area's older inhabitants. In contrast to the dominant anti-gentrification discourse circulating in the wider (whiter) left, interviewees did not theorise gentrification as a problem of political economy alone. They actively contested a disembodied view of gentrification as something that affects us all alike, as tenants who are equally displaced. Rather, the revitalisation of Kreuzberg, and especially Neukölln, coincides with a new vitality for queer and trans subjects and communities that is cannibalistic upon bodies and spaces that are treated as degenerate. Thus, queer formations that gained visibility in these neighbourhoods and were able to participate in branding them did so in ways that normalised the displacement, and actively contributed to the criminalisation, of those who were there before.

Examples of this included the sudden expansion of the TCSD, the alternative 'Kreuzberg Pride', into Neukölln in the late 2000s. In 2010, the year that the event was mentioned in Butler's now famous refusal speech, the starting point of the Kreuzberg Pride suddenly shifted across district borders to Neukölln. No explanation was given for this by the organisers. On Berlin queer of colour kitchen tables, however, this altered map was clearly identified as a symptom of gentrification that reflected the expansion of the radical queer scene across district lines. To make things worse, this enlarged terrain was immediately marked as a dangerous space in need of intervention by some TCSD organisers. Several interviewees reported that individual queers of colour had invested time and energy to intervene in majority-white planning meetings in order to prevent worse racism from happening. For example, they were able to prevent a clearly racialised TCSD motto to 'Reclaim Neukölln' from being passed. Protectionist themes have nevertheless repeatedly entered TCSD communications. The TCSD motto in 2008 highlighted 'homophobic, transphobic and sexist assaults in Neukölln and Kreuzberg' alongside a call to resist 'fascism', 'commercial shit' and 'displacement' (presumably directed against queers) from 'our neighbourhood' (TCSD 2008). Through public statements such as this, kitchen-table participants felt that the radical queer scene was evading its responsibility for gentrification and participating in the pathologisation and criminalisation of a neighbourhood to which they had more rights and access than the people who had long lived and survived there.

Kitchen-table participants also critiqued territorialising practices in the queer scene and the wider white left that symbolically or physically displaced people of colour. Thus, some of the leftist establishments mushrooming in Neukölln displayed Israeli symbols and banned Palestinian or 'anti-Zionist' symbols, which effectively served to render these spaces off limits to Palestinians and other Arabs living in Neukölln.[34] When prompted for examples, Rima Hussein, who is of Palestinian origin, linked her family's experiences of Israeli settler colonialism with the displacement of people of colour from Neukölln, among them Arabs, by gentrifiers, among them white queers with pro-Israel attitudes.

> For example, I go to *Silver Future* and am stared at and think 'You assholes, this by the way is my city and *you* are the guests here.' And maybe that's not politically correct, but to continually have your home taken away from you through colonialism and experience displacement is re-traumatising. And I feel like it's white entitlement. They just imagine that this is a land full of empty flats that cost little, and that's exactly the imaginary that underlies colonial projects.

The queer of colour kitchen table is a rare space where conversations that interrogate the colonial logic of this supposedly non-colonial space are possible. Again, this contrasts with a white anti-gentrification discourse that frequently references 'pioneers' and other colonial figures without enquiring into the coloniality of the setting in which it seeks to intervene. Like that of the Lower East Side discussed by Neil Smith (1996), the development of Kreuzberg and Neukölln repeats the colonial logic of an exotic and transgressive contact zone whose violent and dangerous excesses must be cleared out and civilised. If Kreuzberg and Neukölln have been the most fertile soil for moral panicking, this nevertheless enabled the moral panic – now consolidated – to swiftly travel back to Schöneberg.

… AND BACK TO THE GAYBOURHOOD

In preparing the gaybourhood for securitisation, new constituencies – including trans people, sex workers and queers of colour, who had not thus far been considered interesting coalition partners or even fellow occupants of queer space – became highly salient, even if this did not always translate into direct clout. Some of the organisations representing these constituencies had previously assumed an ambivalent and at times outright critical stance towards assimilationist, homonormative organisations. Nevertheless, in putting new queer bodies on the map – as 'victim subjects' (Kapur 2005) who would not have been interesting without the detour via 'genderqueer' Kreuzberg – these mobilisations ultimately served to consolidate a homonormative brand of Schöneberg as a gay neighbourhood.

Years after the first attempts to paint it as homophobic terrain, Schöneberg finally earned this reputation in summer 2009. Significantly, the district is home to both the gaybourhood and to Frobenstraße, a street whose 'queer' uses differ greatly from the former's infrastructure. One of the poorest streets in Berlin and long completely neglected by state and queer interests alike, Frobenstraße was that summer discovered as a highly evocative hate crime scene. Recent migrants from Bulgaria and Romania, many of whom are Rroma and/or from the Turkish-speaking minority in these countries, live, work and socialise in the street amid other racialised people with longer histories in the area. The area has long been a site of trans street sex work, and many new migrants, including trans women, trans-feminine people, non-trans women, and gay- and other-wise-identified non-trans men, use it to sell sex. Of course migrant sex workers of all gender and sexual identities have experienced all kinds of violence for a long time: from residents who blame them for littered condoms and other signs of chronic disinvestment, from police and other authorities who variously target and exclude them as under-documented migrants and sex workers, and from the utterly unremarkable and uneventful neglect and exploitation to which poor racialised people and sex workers are regularly subjected. Nevertheless, with the exception of a programme for sex workers (which has since lost funding) offered by queer of colour NGO GLADT, the lives of sex workers, let alone migrant trans sex workers, were long of absolutely no interest to queer and trans activists in Berlin. It is arguable that, beyond their short-term capacitation as injured victims of hate crime, they have largely remained so. Archived as trans women being beaten up by migrant youth gangs, this 'event' of violence both fed the moral panic over criminal and violent Muslim youth and accrued value and visibility to more powerful queer and trans positionalities. In September 2009, a coalition of trans (mainly white), queer of colour (mainly non-trans), and sex work (mainly white and non-trans) activists organised a 'Smash Transphobia' demo at Frobenstraße (Siegessäule TV 2009, author's field notes). Most of the queer and trans demonstrators were white; most were visiting Frobenstraße presumably for the first time; and for most it would remain the only time. The speeches, slogans and posters interpellated a transnormative, protectionist victim subject of 'violence against trans people (or trans women)' and called for policy attention to this hitherto neglected group. While sex work occasionally made it into the speeches, slogans and placards, the local context was barely mentioned. And where it was, this again occurred in highly racialised and classed ways:

> You may be unemployed but this is no excuse! (Call through the loudspeaker into the open windows of random residents)
> Transphobic people go to hell. (Placard held by a white and presumably secular/Christian organiser)
> This is our street, too! (Slogan at the demo)

The gaybourhood institutions that were the original authors of the protectionist gaybourhood discourse were not directly involved in either the Drag Festival or the Frobenstraße event. Indeed, organisations such as the LSVD and Maneo continue to show little interest in trans people, let alone migrant trans sex workers. However, their long-standing investment in Schöneberg and ample expertise in racialising homophobia enabled them to swiftly capitalise once the panic had taken root. In many ways, the policy attention that resulted from these two spectacles of transphobia fulfilled these organisations' long-standing attempts to spatialise Schöneberg as a dangerous area where (white) gay men live in constant fear of Muslim youth. Even if the bodies that were injured, first in Kreuzberg and then in Frobenstraße, less than a kilometre away from the office of the LSVD, radically exceeded this binary, the events nevertheless served to consolidate a homonormative constituency and to insert it firmly into urban policies of gentrification, securitisation and touristification.

Projects that became possible in their wake include the 'Rainbow Protection Circle', which arrived hand in hand with an increased police presence in the area specifically for the protection of LGBT people. An association of local businesses and NGOs, it was founded in February 2010 by the LSVD, half a year after the Frobenstraße mobilisations and three months after the above-cited *Siegessäule* issue on the embattled gaybourhood. It was inaugurated in a grandiose manner in the town hall of Schöneberg by the district mayor, who allocated additional police in the area specifically for the protection of LGBT people (author's field notes, February 2010). By then, the perpetrators no longer needed to be directly racially marked. In fact, any accusations of racism were pre-empted by including anti-racism alongside homophobia in the remit of the Rainbow Protection Circle.

Besides branding Schöneberg as a queer area with the help of a diversity policing that *de facto* increased racial profiling in the city, these spatial panics served to inscribe a homonormative agenda into neoliberal city politics. They also expanded the remit of individual organisations such as Maneo, which underwent a remarkable ascent from a small local anti-violence hotline accused of forging racialised perpetrator statistics (see Blech 2009; Petzen 2008; Ruder

2011) to a queer representative of the global city. The organisation first inserted itself in the public arena through forensic-style press releases that selectively highlighted cases of homophobic violence perpetrated by men of 'southern appearance' or 'with migration background' (e.g. Maneo 2008a). These early performances of queer victim subjectivity and racialised criminality already served to inscribe a queer urban discourse into an entrepreneurial city that had long begun to brand itself as a safe and clean destination for tourists and entrepreneurs (Ha 2013). Mimicking the city's own 'Be Berlin!' advertising campaign, Maneo's press releases not only inscribed a homonormative politics into neoliberal multicultural values of 'tolerance' and 'respect'. They also volunteered to brand Berlin as a global city willing to say 'No to hate violence against homosexuals in Berlin!', and to 'Protect every kiss – for love is the future of Berlin!' (Maneo 2008b: 2, emphasis in original, author's translations). These attempts to inscribe queer love into the global city proved successful precisely following the mobilisation of first Kreuzberg and then Schöneberg as dangerous places where the properly alive require protection, and new subjects may come to life in revitalising streets and buildings.

In 2011, Maneo hosted a big international conference called 'Building a Queer and Tolerant Neighbourhood'. Introduced by Berlin's former mayor Klaus Wowereit, who prior to his election came out with the words 'I'm gay, and that is a good thing', the conference programme had all the trappings of the global creative city. Its remit was to explore the 'potential benefits and development possibilities' of 'rainbow neighborhoods' like Schöneberg, whose 'importance lies in the signal that they can give to city managers that the city is socially open and tolerant' (Maneo 2011). The queer media announced the conference in a distinctly homonormative cadence. In the *Siegessäule*, the capital is painted as an idyll that is unalloyed but must nevertheless be protected:

> Queer life is visible here: a gay café joins the next lesbian-managed bar, most of the city's LGBT community live in the neighbourhood. Rainbow neighbourhoods increase the visibility of diverse queer life and create a pleasant climate of societal openness, that besides locals is also appreciated by tourists. Economically this bears great potential. [...] But where homosexuality is lived openly, there are conflicts too. Violent attacks occur not infrequently. (*Siegessäule* 2011, my translation)

The workshop titles listed on the conference programme, too, bear all the hallmarks of the neoliberal city, from touristification to securitisation: 'History: Remembrance and Memory – Preservation of Cultural Heritage', 'Tourism: LGBT* Marketing and Correlations', 'Media, Networking, Marketing, Events', 'Partnership of Queer Neighbourhoods', 'Security and Policing: Safety in Queer Neighbourhood', 'Economic Development – Queer Economy', 'Urban

Governance – Neighbourhood Development' (Maneo 2011). The programme included visitors from 'metropolitan cities from across the world' and presentations on key global 'gaybourhoods', including Chicago's Boystown, San Francisco's Castro, Sydney's Oxford Street, Montreal's Gay Village and Cape Town's Green Point. According to one report by a Chicago visitor, attendees included law enforcement officers, international diversity officials, entrepreneurs and NGO representatives (*Windy City Times* 2011). At the same time, the conference's reach went beyond a purely homonormative constituency. For example, it included attendees from earlier, more radical generations of queer space scholarship (Gordon Brent Ingram, personal communication, 22 November 2011). It also found unproblematic circulation in left-leaning urban studies forums (Noa Ha, personal communication, 21 October 2011). A queer rendition of the neoliberal city, it seems, is insulated from critique, even (or maybe especially) in left-wing, gay-friendly Berlin.

There have been, then, various travels and circulations of queer vulnerability, visibility and vitality that have crossed identitarian borders along with district ones. This increasingly has material equivalents. After becoming the target of Butler's critique in 2010, the mainstream Pride parade followed its alternative defector by rerouting through Kreuzberg in subsequent years. The alternative 'Kreuzberg' Pride or TCSD in turn has begun to include Neukölln. Meanwhile, the SchwuZ ('Gay Centre'), which has traditionally been a bastion of white cis-gay masculinity, is moving from the wealthier part of Kreuzberg to Neukölln. On its Facebook page (SchwuZ n.d.), updates announcing the decision received both positive and negative comments, including statements such as the following:

> You should only go there in a group, I wouldn't being [sic] alone at night while bumping into fellow citizens in whose country homosexuals are stigmatised, persecuted or murdered ... (11 July 2013 at 12:48)
> Off to Neukölln where the trannies will throw bottles at homophobes from southern [countries]. (26 June 2013 at 10:07)
> Schwuz goes Burka (30 April 2013 at 11:14)
> By day as a gay you're repeatedly spat at for holding hands on a bench in front of Neukölln Town Hall (my own experience).... Now at night partying there. That I call adventure! (30 April 2013 at 18:30)
> I'm definitely not coming to Neukölln. Too many foreigners ... (1 May 2013 at 01:53).

According to the moderators of the SchwuZ page, several comments had already been deleted because of their racist content (19 July 2013 at 07:30). While not everyone shared in these fantasies of violence and racism, there was almost no discussion of what the impact of the move to Neukölln might be on those who had lived there longer. The *Khalass!!!* manifesto sums this up succinctly:

You keep talking about fears concerning the move of Schwuz to Neukölln, but have you ever considered what Blacks and PoC in Neukölln are afraid of? (*Khalass!!!* 2013)

Indeed, the manifesto mentions homonormative and radical queer scenes, and Kreuzberg, Neukölln and Schöneberg, in one breath, as spaces that are similarly regenerating at the expense of poor people of colour. For, unlike the latter, the bodies, businesses and scenes that are legible as queer have long begun to cross lines, of district as well as identity, in ways that fundamentally challenge binaries of gay versus queer, or 'assimilationist' versus 'transgressive'.

CONCLUSION: SETTING THE SCENE FOR THE QUEER LOVER

In this chapter, I have treated queers of colour as 'geographic subjects' (McKittrick 2006) whose nascent spatial narratives, while not rising to the status of a social movement, challenge a colonial account of queer space and safety, and propose alternative methods of placemaking that do not rely on territorialisation, securitisation, displacement and dispossession. In these alternative maps, queer regeneration becomes perceptible as the confluence of formerly undesirable bodies with formerly undesirable spaces, whose recovery coincides with and is predicated on the expulsion of racialised populations, whose inhabitation of space can only ever be uncultivated and pathological.[35] This concept, first, allows us to think through the ways in which queers with race and class privileges have, according to *Khalass!!!* and queer of colour kitchen-table participants, participated in gentrification. Second, it enables us to link the biopolitical and geopolitical processes through which subjects are vitalised in material and symbolic environments whose symbolic and material delineations cannot be reduced to neoliberalism. To think of the modes of emplacement and displacement examined here as queer regeneration thus also means to complicate distinctions between homonormative and transgressive politics, identities and spaces – a distinction that has, if anything, become more important with the proliferation of a homonationalism debate which, in its circulation through white-dominated queer communities in Europe, has produced a new need to project racism elsewhere.[36] In contrast, the queer of colour narratives discussed here map the 'gaybourhood' in Berlin-Schöneberg as overlapping with, rather than distinct from, Kreuzberg and Neukölln. As these areas are 'recovering' (read: whitening) – a process that coincides with the arrival of queer and trans people with race and class privileges – their boundaries with more respectable terrains such as Schöneberg, which (a stone's throw from Kreuzberg) was long socially distant, are palpably thinning. Indeed, the transposability of the queer neighbourhood as the (hate) crime scene *par excellence* is accelerated by the mobile spatial scripts of the 'war on terror' and the crisis in multiculturalism (Lentin and Titley 2011). In the epilogue, I will think further through the apparent 'coincidence' that the drama of queer lovers and hateful Others has made similar appearances in other north-west European inner cities, including London's East End and Grønland, the multicultural neighbourhood in the Norwegian capital of Oslo (Decolonize Queer 2011; Lamble 2014).

I began and ended this chapter with the *Khalass!!!* manifesto because its analysis of queer regeneration as a process that follows a colonial logic is insightful and, given the German erasure of colonial histories and racialised presences, brave (see El-Tayeb 1999; Opitz et al. 1992 [1986]). Its polemic recounting of inner-city development through the arrival of queer 'pioneers' bearing a 'civilizing mission' and preparing 'the ground for other white settlers to come' is mirrored by the interviews, reports, activist texts and other data presented in this chapter. In dominant publics and queer counter-publics, the inner city emerges as an ideal setting of revitalisation, for formerly degenerate subjects as much as for the formerly degenerate spaces within which they come to life. This phenomenon, which I have called queer regeneration, involves two intersecting processes each of which requires attention: of the built environment, which recovers the moment racialised people leave; and of the queer subject who, freshly decriminalised and depathologised, prepares the ground for a progressive whitening and straightening of this environment and, as we shall explore next, deserves protection in return. In this, it matters little that not all of the newcomers are straight. Explorers with race and class privileges, including people with transgressive bodies and identities, become residents *the minute they arrive*, while those who have been there longer, first under conditions of confinement, now under conditions of displacement, lose all right to place. Theories of gender and coloniality are helpful here, as they remind us that the 'pioneers' who prepare a terrain for civilised habitation – a figure that recurs in both the gentrification and the anti-gentrification discourse – were not necessarily bearers of respectability and domesticity. On the contrary, they were often transgressive in terms of their gender, sexuality, class, and wider place in the world (see again Razack 2002a).

My theorising of queer regenerations is intended to supplement rather than replace a political economy and ecology framework that rightly insists that no one can escape participating in gentrification, and that nurturing possibilities for queer of colour survival and community must necessarily be part of a bigger picture of urban and environmental justice. In naming queer gentrification, participants of the kitchen table did not describe gentrification as reducible to any particular populations, either 'gentrifying' or 'displaced'. Nevertheless, as we will explore next with regard to the figures of the queer lover and hateful Other, the fact that it occurs in a queer register is important. Thus, the simultaneous arrival of queers and of gentrification, and the queering of existing regimes of pathologisation and criminalisation, do crucial work in ushering even well-meaning people into consent.

My queer of colour interlocutors did not propose a voluntaristic view of gentrification as something that we can opt out of by making better consumption choices. Neither did they assume that all gentrifiers are white and that other axes, especially class, do not matter. At the same time, their accounts differed from an economically determinist view where we are all equally affected as tenants, or where we do not have any agency in how we arrive and act upon a terrain marked by social death. On the contrary, they cited multiple instances where queer gentrifiers exerted agency in ways that clearly exceeded their need to pay their rent.

> I don't know, where is the end of gentrification. So now we are forced to live in museum cities, where everything is very nice, with nice colours, nice atmospheres, and when I say nice colours it's about skin colours too. Where the only thing that counts is economic power. And the only way you could be a PoC living in these fancy spaces is if you are an artist or if you have a partner who is in an important position. And you have to be ready to answer when people challenge you. What are you doing here? It's not the space for you. And to forget who was here before, you know. (AnouchK Ibacka Valiente)

AnouchK, who had moved to Berlin a few years ago, and chosen Neukölln because she wanted to live close to other people of colour, argued that she, too, was a participant in rising rents. At the same time, she had a wider transnational analysis of gentrification as a phenomenon whose workings and outcomes are deeply raced as well as classed. While further research into this is needed, tracing queer of colour migrations into gentrifying areas may give just as much insight as documenting queer of colour displacements from them. This is because it may help us explore alternative modes of arrival that are not exclusively predicated on dispossession, acquisition and securitisation. While taking care not to conflate various geopolitical and biopolitical contexts, theories of decolonisation – from Andrea Smith's (2011) thoughts on land as something that must be outside ownership to coalition politics in Canada where non-Indigenous people of colour work to become allies against settler colonialism – could present important sources of inspiration for such a project.

To thus enquire about queer regeneration would mean to push the scholarship on queer space beyond a celebration of gay or even queer or trans territories. While acknowledging the important contribution of homonormativity critiques to debates on queer space, this chapter has complicated the oft-made distinction between homonormative and transgressive spaces by highlighting the travels and cross-fertilisations between 'queer and trans' Kreuzberg and Neukölln on the one hand, and 'gay' Schöneberg on the other. In the next chapter, I extend this spatial project to a biopolitical one, by tackling another distinction, between homonormative and transgressive subjects. For just like the transgressive space of the 'mixed' inner city, the transgressive body of the trans or genderqueer subject has been a particularly productive ground for moral panicking.

2

LOVE[1]

What kinds of queer regenerations are possible within the rapidly changing environment of the gentrifying inner city? What bodies and intimacies are vitalised in the drama of queer lovers and hateful Others? Breaking with a western tradition of punishing, pathologising and concealing queer intimacy, same-sex kisses have recently begun to come out in public. This chapter takes a closer look at the kisses that have gained sudden visibility and publicity. Drawing on Ahmed's (2004a) cultural politics of emotion, I suggest that queer lovers and hateful Others travel as part of a shared economy where meaning and value accrue to a narrow range of feelings, bodies, values and objects, which gain currency, familiarity and intelligibility through their joint circulation. In the course of these circulations, new intimate publics become imaginable (Cvetkovich 2004). While promising to make room for queer intimacies, I will argue that these nevertheless take shape within familiar modes of emplacement and displacement.

The coming outs that become possible in the fertile terrain of the inner city are neither universal nor incidental. While some queer bodies emerge as deserving of protection, others are rendered unrecognisable and out of place. This is a function of homonormativity – the newly visible intimacies appear desirable and familiar precisely because they are inscribed in the values and aesthetics of heteronormative consumer culture (see Duggan 2004). Besides an analysis of neoliberalism, the regeneration of (some) queer bodies as lovely rather than criminal and diseased also requires an analysis of race and place that is able to grasp how chances of life and death are distributed in urban and other environments (see Gilmore 2007; Povinelli 2008; Teelucksingh 2002). The chapter examines how queer subjects come to life in the proximity of racialised Others, and in formerly degenerate places that revitalise in tandem with the eviction of bodies whose morbidity is hardly spectacular, but a natural outflow of their intrinsic degeneracy (see Razack 2002a, 2002b).

The coincidence between valuable queerness and racism is far from random. The bodies that circulate follow scripts and share authors and trajectories with the racialised homophobia panic. They accompany newspaper reports about an academic study comparing homophobic attitudes in 'migrant' and 'German' school children. They adorn articles that warn of increased homophobic violence in Turkish and Arab neighbourhoods. Gay kisses cite and follow each other around: from the websites of LGBT NGOs to state-sponsored poster campaigns, from the billboards to the street. They appear in activist and policy documents that translate the languages of international LGBT rights and protections into German, which until recently did not use terms like 'hate' or 'crime' to describe homophobia (let alone transphobia). The term *Hasskriminalität* – hate crime – rolls off German tongues awkwardly; its enunciation requires effort and expertise.

Besides as kissing, queer bodies are visibilised and valorised as injured. While the romantic, innocent kiss performs the respectable gay subject as human, this humanisation nevertheless requires the performance of spectacular vulnerability. Drawing on anti-racist feminist accounts of anti-violence movements, the chapter identifies the queer subject that is invited into visibility as a victim subject (Bumiller 2008; Kapur 2005). The circulated performances of victim subjectivity nevertheless complicate accounts of 'wounded attachments' that posit a unitary subject of suffering whose primary target of resentment is the white middle class (see Brown 1993). Queer intimacy deserves protection precisely because it is under attack from hateful Others who form the constitutive outside of the newly gay-friendly community.

This also has implications for transgender subjects. While gender non-conforming bodies are excluded from the 'lovely sight' of the queer lover, they nevertheless (and maybe for the first time) emerge as victims who are worthy of protection. Devalued otherwise, it is in their spectacular vulnerability that they gain value and currency. I will illustrate this with the moral panic surrounding a highly mediatised incident at the Drag Festival in 2008, which launched the hate crime discourse firmly onto the German landscape. This highlights the need to take concepts such as homonationalism or homonormativity beyond their privileging of the 'homo'. As Riley Snorton and I put it:

> we must question a conception of transgender as first and foremost victimized. Rather, it is necessary to interrogate how the uneven institutionalization of women's, gay, and trans politics produces a transnormative subject, whose universalized trajectory of coming out/transition, visibility, recognition, protection, and self-actualization largely remains uninterrogated in its complicities and convergences with biomedical, neoliberal, racist, and imperialist politics. (2013: 67)

In the following, I will tackle the homonormative affect of love alongside the transnormative affect of injury. Both congeal in a structure of feeling – to reframe José Muñoz's (2000) engagement with Raymond Williams – that excludes queers of colour, or lets them participate only by turning others into 'affect aliens' (see Ahmed 2008). As the 'love that dare not speak its name' comes out in public, which acts become speakable? I begin by revisiting the burgeoning literature on queer love and gay marriage, and end with queer of colour kitchen-table conversations that recast demands to perform dominant love in a climate of systemic violence.

LOVE, THEORETICALLY

Judith Butler is in town (Butler 2007). The foyer of the London School of Economics is packed with a young giddy crowd. I arrive half an hour before the talk, too late to secure a seat in the main lecture theatre, and am herded into a side room where the talk is televised. This must be the intellectual equivalent of pop fandom, I think. Or of England playing. Even in the side room, the air is thick with exhilaration. We become spectator participants to Butler's mediated, yet larger than/live performance on screen. From the critical questions – Are women's and gay rights now instruments in the 'war on terror'? How have sexual freedom and progress become tools in the civilising mission? *Is this what we have fought for?* – we are swiftly moved to humour, as Butler ponders (and I paraphrase from memory and notes):

> Do I want to kiss in public? Yes. Do I want everyone to watch? *(Pauses, laughs.)* Do I want *everyone* to watch? *(Laughs hard.)*

The two separated halls simultaneously erupt into laughter, thickening our critical audience into community. We are progressives against the war, united by our critique of the state, which has appropriated our struggle for sexual expression and misdirected it against those to whom we have allied ourselves: the Iraqi prisoners in Abu Ghraib violated by torture methods purported to 'sexually liberate' them, the growing populations in West and Central Asia whose deaths and abandonment are legitimized by their 'backward', 'barbaric' gender regimes, the migrants tested on their views on homosexuality in the Dutch civic integration examination, which foreshadowed the proposed reform of the German nationality law. As discussed in the introduction, the 'Muslim Test', tested applicants on their women- and gay-friendliness alongside their proneness to terrorist and 'undemocratic' beliefs and practices.

Like many queers of colour at the time, who were battling the growing racism of LGBT movements in relative isolation, I welcomed the uptake of explicitly anti-racist discourse by a famous queer theorist. I nevertheless could not help but wonder what makes Butler's joke so common sense (or queerly sensible) that it instantly glued together this white-dominated audience. Indeed, just over a year later, the first home-grown critique of gay imperialism disappeared from print in Britain.[2] In my earlier discussion of Butler's talk (Haritaworn

2008b), I asked what I called the tired old positionality question: *Are all kisses the same?* I argued that kisses are embedded in, and invited or concealed from, various public spheres, not merely with regard to their subjects' gender, but also their colour.

> Thus, two same-sex kissers who are brown may not be read as transgressive outlaws, but on the contrary as secretive, repressed, closeted victims who are exceptionally brave and in *need* of liberation by their already-liberated (white) siblings, as well as by the state. Kissing, as a spectacle of sexual freedom, encapsulates the very discourses of gendered modernity which Butler critiques. Vice versa, the transgressiveness of the white queer kisser is never outside these discourses, either. In fact, collective imaginings of brown homophobic onlookers may prolong … this moment as playful, transgressive and queer. (Haritaworn 2008b)

In the following, I will follow around some of the kisses that have circulated in Berlin. I read these kisses in conversation with critiques of love, romance and gay marriage. Critics of gay marriage have delivered the most strident analyses of how value accrues to same-sex couplings in a context of ongoing homophobia and transphobia. In the place of standardised couplings, radical queer marriage critics have sometimes proposed alternative forms of queer intimacy, which are more likely to be set in dark alleys (see Berlant and Warner 1998). As chapter 4 ('Queer Nostalgia') further explores, this is sometimes accompanied by a nostalgic longing for more threatening and subversive kinds of queer desire. In contrast to this preoccupation with respectable and subversive performances of queer love in queer counter-cultural discourse, love and sex talk rarely make an appearance at queer of colour kitchen tables in Berlin, even if expressions of love continually surface in countless acts of care. Indeed, I will argue, queers of colour in Berlin are marginal to a community of feeling that is assembled around (or even in opposition to) love and marriage.

In his essay 'Feeling brown', José Muñoz (2000) engaged Raymond Williams's idea that subordinated formations (the working class in Williams, queer Latin@ performers in Muñoz) are accompanied by particular 'structures of feeling', which Williams defined as impulses that do not yet reach the status of social movements:

> a social experience which is still in process [but] which in analysis (though rarely otherwise) has its emergent, connecting, and dominant characteristics, indeed its specific hierarchies. (Williams 1978: 132)

Foregrounding the theatricalisation of 'brown feelings' in queer Latin@ plays, Muñoz interpreted these as critiques of dominant affect: 'Acting white has everything to do with the performance of a particular affect, the specific performance of which grounds the subject performing white affect in a normative life world' (Muñoz 2000: 68). This has implications for queer Latin@s' ability to belong. In a culture dominated by whiteness – 'a cultural logic which can be understood as an affective code that positions itself as the law' – Latin@s and other 'oppositional groups' are 'exiled from paradigms of communicative reason and the larger culture of consent' (2000: 68). In fact, Latin@ affect is 'often off', 'spicy', 'over the top and excessive' (2000: 69–70). This nevertheless holds promises, as Muñoz explores with regard to queer Latin@ plays.

We might argue that this emotional register fits more easily into the realm of cultural production more than that of activism. Performed on stage, 'spiciness' and 'exoticism' may translate into value and capital. The emphasis on cultural productions further lends itself to a revaluation of queer of colour formations as anti-identitarian, as also expressed by Muñoz's better-known concept of 'disidentification': 'neither an identification nor a counter-identification – it is working on, with, and against a form and a simultaneous moment' (2000: 70). Lifting the burden of proof off multiple minoritised subjects who remain squeezed between queer and other collectivities whose own identitarian logics are often uninterrogated, we might take Muñoz's work to denaturalise dominant affects further. Thus, while Muñoz targeted whiteness rather than queer whiteness, and reserved the term 'structures of feeling' for queer of colour socialities, I am interested in how the concept can be deployed to denaturalise gay imperialism and other queer ascendancies. Specifically, I suggest interrogating queer 'structures of feeling' as affective performances that can either be actualised or failed. Thus, like the national affects discussed by Muñoz, white queer affects and 'sensibilities' such as love, sex radicalism or transgression are harder to perform for queers of colour, particularly where we refuse to consent to or authenticate queer racism.

Sara Ahmed (2004a, 2008), as so often, helps us to further demystify queer love. I find two of her figures particularly useful here: first, the loveable object and likeable subject and, second, the affect alien. Drawing on Freud, she explores the relationship between love and identification as a process that distinguishes between the ideal subject and the ideal object: 'The object becomes ideal only through approval by loved others; idealisation creates both likeable subjects and loveable objects' (Ahmed 2004a: 129). In this, the 'investment' in the ideal object is not 'about' the object but for the subject, who needs it in order to approximate its ego ideal and accumulate value (2004a: 127). As illustrated by declarations of multicultural love, not all objects are equally positioned to meet this expectation.

In such a narrative, 'others', including ethnic minorities and white working-class communities, in their perceived failure to love difference, function as 'a breach' in the ideal image of the nation. Their failure to love becomes the explanation for the failure of multiculturalism to deliver the national ideal. (2004a: 139)

Interestingly, Ahmed shows that multiculturalists are not alone in embracing love, but that white hate groups, too, profess to act in the name of love. At the same time, such far right groups attack their anti-racist critics for failing to love the vulnerable nation: 'By being *against* those who are *for* the nation ... such critics can only be *against* the nation; they can only be *against* love' (2004a: 123). I wish to build on this examination of love and hate as racialised affects by asking what happens if the haters are not white, and the lovers not straight. What if the lover who needs protection is queer – an ideal object who loyally repeats rather than 'breaches' the ideal image of the nation?

Besides objects that fail to be ideal, Ahmed (2008) presents us with bodies that fail on a more substantial level. She notes that the fantasy of the happy multicultural nation requires the production of affect aliens such as the 'melancholic migrant' who, in his backward orientation towards bad experiences and lost belongings, stands in the way of multicultural happiness. We can similarly describe queers of colour as affect aliens to a queer-friendly public gathered around love. Queer love, in its 'sticky proximities' (see Ahmed 2011) with freedom, choice, visibility and equality, chimes well with the dominant affects of a neoliberal multiculturalism where anything can be freely chosen, and where all have 'equal opportunities' as long as we possess the same capital to compete (see Grewal 2005; Melamed 2011). If queer lovers are scripted 'as worthy multicultural global citizens', in Jodi Melamed's terms, this scripting nevertheless requires the simultaneous appearance of hateful Others 'doomed by their own monoculturalism, deviance, inflexibility, criminality, and other attributes' (2011: 87).

Indeed, to be a neoliberal citizen who loves well means to perform one's emotion in distinction from uncultivable poor and racialised populations who are reduced to base instincts and impulses. As theorists of neoliberal affect have argued, the self-actualised citizen who has successful relationships must constantly work on hir emotional and communication skills (see Rose 1989; Skeggs 2010). In contrast, as repetitively rehearsed in globalised tropes of crime, pathology and violence, racialised and colonised subjects always already fail at acquiring such skills. As the next chapter ('Hate') discusses in greater detail, youth of colour in Germany are frequently characterised as hateful, criminal, violent and undeserving of care on account of their failure to display love and empathy, and to manage their anger and hatred. Who is deemed capable of love and worthy of care is reformulated under finance capitalism, whose ideal citizen is the investor who self-actualises by taking good risks, in contrast to criminalised and pathologised populations who are *at risk* (Martin 2007).

In historicising love and hate, we can go back further in time to trace these affects to racial and colonial capitalism. The 'What's love got to do with it?' panel at the American Studies Association annual meeting in Los Angeles (Finley et al. 2014) applied Denise Ferreira da Silva's (2007) distinction between 'universal' and 'affectable' subjects to love. Colonial love here is described as a universal stance that only civilised, reasonable subjects are capable of. Racialised and colonised populations are incapable of learning how to love reasonably because they are incapable of escaping their 'natural' bodily instincts and impulses such as hate and anger. In the 'Family of Man', where white norms of family, nation and empire must be inculcated into affectable populations, racialised and colonised peoples remain in a child-like position where they must learn, but constantly fail, to conform to cis-heteropatriarchal bourgeois moulds of gender and sexuality. To love authentically, then, is twice unattainable for queer people of colour, who are excluded from dominant love on account of their racial as well as their gender and sexual non-conformity.

The pressure on queer subjects to uncritically embrace celebratory representations of queer love must of course be understood within a context that has recently decriminalised and depathologised same-sex intimacies. Heather Love (2007a) remarks that there is a 'premium' on happiness which, as a qualifier of good citizenship, looms large for queers. Queers invest in romance and happiness because they are haunted by unhappy endings:

> Emotional conformism, romantic fulfilment, and gay cheerfulness constitute the dominant image of gay life in the contemporary moment. Not only are gays being represented as shiny, happy people in major media outlets, but traces of the history of gay unhappiness are being expunged as well. While the unrelenting stigmatisation of homosexuality characteristic of earlier moments is hardly to be yearned for, the current appearance of homosexuality in the mass media as a happy and healthy lifestyle poses a new set of problems. (Love 2007a: 56)

She links the question of gay happiness with that of assimilation and normalisation by asking how the path laid out in front of us has come to look so much like the straight path. Coming out stories often follow a pre-given formula: 'painful and confused loneliness; exposure and awakening; acceptance and integration into the community' (2007a: 52). Love asks why gay people desire to join the very institutions (like marriage and the family) that were historically used to demonise and exclude them. The answer, she suggests, lies in their affectivity. Not only do these objects and scenes promise us normalcy; more importantly they promise us happiness. Applying a critical race and mad/disability studies lens, we can look beyond the promises made to those who invest in happiness towards the penalties for those who fail to perform it. We can understand happiness as a form of consent in a context that punishes and pathologises non-conforming emotions such as anti-racist anger or sadness, and sorts 'happy' or 'functional' populations from 'unhappy' or 'dysfunctional' ones that must be segregated from the realm of life, and the properly alive (see Haritaworn 2012).

The promise of happiness pervades the larger gay marriage movement. In her introduction to the seminal collection *Against Equality*, Yasmin Nair (2010) critiques the developmentalist progress narratives that undergird gay marriage narratives:

> The history of gay marriage supposedly goes something like this: In the beginning, gay people were horribly oppressed. Then came the 1970s, where gays – all of whom looked like the men of the Village People – were able to live openly and have a lot of sex. Then, in the 1980s, many gay people died of AIDS – because they had too much sex in the 1970s. This taught them that gay sex is bad. The gays who were left realized the importance of stable, monogamous relationships and began to agitate for marriage and the 1000+ benefits it would bring. Soon, in the very near future, with the help of supportive, married straight people – and President Obama – gays will win marriage rights in all 50 states, and they will then be as good and productive as everyone else. (Nair 2010: 1)

A further relevant framework is feminist critiques of romantic love, which emerged with patriarchy's need to consolidate itself and domesticate women in the face of evidence that heterosexual family life presents women with a raw deal. Romance, as produced and consumed through novels and later film, serves to re-attach women to patriarchy, as it locates their happiness in finding the 'right' man. Berlant (2006) points to the 'cruel optimism' that secures women's endurance in the very objects and scenes that contribute to their attrition. This is if anything compounded for the 'love that dare not speak its name', as well as for interracial intimacy, both of which are romantic precisely because they are tragic (Haritaworn 2012). Thus, queer novels such as the *Well of Loneliness* formulaically find a doomed ending (Love 2007b). Queers, especially those interpellated by the particular race and class configurations of this genre, arguably inherit a particular duty to rewrite such unhappy endings, that release queer intimacies from the clutches of death. The new-found visibility of gay marriage and same-sex kisses bears this promise. Queer romance becomes a rallying cry not only for individual happiness but for an end to collective suffering.

In contrast to straight romance, queer romance at first sight allows for optimism without cruelty. Yet, while sameness has been fetishised in queer narratives that promise a love that is equal and unmarred, queer relationships remain shot through with, and surrounded by, differences that gay marriage, if anything, further institutionalises. Thus, romantic arguments made in favour of gay marriage, such as being able to sponsor one's immigrant partner to enter or remain in the country, or being able to inherit the joint home, keep in place racist borders and a capitalist system where wealth and entitlements are inherited rather than fairly distributed (see also Chávez 2013). As Priya Kandaswamy (2008) points out, the former argument merely expands power differences in heterosexual marriages to citizen gays, while the latter ensures the reproduction of capital regardless of sexual orientation.[3] Matt Udora Richardson similarly states: 'The crux of [the gay marriage] movement is led by [people who] already have a considerable amount of upward mobility, so marriage is the icing on the cake' (in Bailey et al. 2004: 91).

The rewards for performing queer love are thus greater for some than for others. For queers of colour, who deviate from already deviant cis-genders and heterosexualities, attachment to gay marriage and other queer structures of feeling is a failed affective performance in that it rarely produces access to benefits.[4] Black queer and/or feminist critics in particular have highlighted the exclusion of even straight Blacks from the benefits associated with marriage and the family (Cohen 1997; Collins 1991; Ferguson 2004; Roberts 1997). In her seminal article 'Punks, bulldaggers, and welfare queens', Cathy Cohen (1997) highlighted the competitive, anti-intersectional stance in the Queer Nation manifesto 'I hate straights' and other radical queer texts and projects. This dichotomy between oppressed queers and powerful heterosexuals ignores how people who are poor, Black (and we might add trans and disabled) receive very limited 'entitlement and status … from obeying a heterosexual imperative' (Cohen 1997: 442). On the contrary, racist rules and figurations such as the marriage bans during slavery, anti-miscegenation rules, and the recurrent moral panic over Black and Latina 'welfare queens', have targeted poor people, people of colour, and other bodies targeted by eugenicist policies of population control, precisely in their heterosexuality. Cohen illustrates this by citing the 'culture of poverty' thesis of the influential Moynihan report, which labelled the Black family as a 'tangle of pathology' that 'retards the progress of the group as a whole' (Moynihan 1965: 29–30, cited in Cohen 1997: 455–56).

Building on Cohen and other Black feminist and queer of colour theorists, Priya Kandaswamy (2008) takes issue with the claim that gay marriage is a redistributional gain that extends ideals of welfare and civil rights to an overlooked constituency. She reads the pathologising figure of the Black welfare mother – whose poverty is blamed on her own refusal to get married – against the newly respectable figure of gay marriage. Kandaswamy questions this supposed civil rights victory in the context of the shrinking of the welfare state, especially the lower tiers that served to redistribute capital to poor people (but were long reserved for 'deserving' white working-class people). In contrast, gay marriage gives access to the welfare state's top tiers to those who may have been excluded on the grounds of their sexual orientation, but were entitled on the basis of race and class all along.

Chandan Reddy (2011) makes a similar argument by proposing that we view gay marriage as a 'hybrid' between the welfare state, whose safety net has again been largely reserved for white citizens, and the neoliberal security state, which reduces equality to 'the equal right of each to egotistic pursuit in civil society' (2011: 9). He states:

> For many U.S. citizen white gays and lesbians, the gay marriage project actually brings together these two differing visions of the state, that of the so-called *welfare state* and that of the *neo-liberal security state*. Advocates for gay marriage will often speak of marriage as a distributional right – extending access to the so-called safety-net [...] while at the same moment characterizing the so-called 'right to marriage' as about neo-liberal fairness and equality. (2011: 11)

To Reddy, queer complicities with neoliberalism are further reflected in shifts in queer organising structures, which have undergone considerable profession-alisation and institutionalisation. While proponents of gay marriage associate it with the goals and ideals of the welfare state, the legal and policy elites who form the campaign frequently work within neoliberal frameworks. Reddy comments:

> Ironically many of these lawyers and policy elites are embedded in institutions like Lambda Legal defense, NGLTF, etc. that began as institutions attached to and seeking to engage the exclusionary contradictions of the welfare state. That is, the legal, policy and electoral initiatives for 'gay marriage' have transacted and expanded the neo-liberal state within the very institutions that had their historical horizon of possibility within the contradictions elaborated by the welfare state. (2011: 9)

I will return to and expand on Reddy's view of gay marriage as a 'hybrid' between the welfare state and the neoliberal security state in the conclusion to this book. In the German context, gay marriage was instituted around the same time as the infamous law of the blood was reformed, extending citizenship benefits and privileges that had already been shrunk to a pittance. I will propose that we think of the queer lover as not merely a link, but a 'transitional object' (Winnicott 1953) between the welfare and the neoliberal regime, which ushers us into consent with death-making techniques and horizons by queerly regenerating them as progress and love of diversity.

But the question 'Is gay marriage racist?' goes further than merely expanding entitlements for people with race and class privileges (now regardless of their sexuality). In the US, gay marriage proponents have actively demonised people of colour, in particular Black people, as especially homophobic. When Proposition 8, the ban on same-sex marriage, passed in California, in the same election cycle that ushered in Obama, the gay and progressive media, and many participating in the large-scale mobilisations protesting the ban, blamed African American and Latino voters (Bassichis and Spade 2014). The competitive stance identified by Cohen once again surfaced, as many linked the loss of gay rights to the victory of the first Black president (Roberts 2009). Academic critiques of the antiblackness that enabled this queer moment are only just surfacing, ten years after Black queer activist Kenyon Farrow (2010 [2004]) posed the question 'Is gay marriage anti-Black?' Then already, the media figured gay marriage as white and opposition to it as Black, by locating homophobia in a seemingly monolithic 'Black church'. According to Farrow, this ignores the ways in which the Christian right, known for its white supremacy, has appealed to Black churches to paint opposition to gay marriage as in line with Black family values – 'this, even though Black families have consistently been painted as dysfunctional and are treated as such in the mass media and in public policy' (Farrow 2010 [2004]: 23). The circulation of the 'Black homophobia' discourse is thus a function of the wider antiblackness of the gay movement and the nationalism into which it is assimilating. This assimilation is ultimately achieved by appropriating Black experiences of segregation and Black languages of resistance and methods of civil rights. Prefiguring many of the critiques cited in this section, Farrow shows how the argument that gay marriage is the last frontier of civil rights serves the interests of the most privileged strata of the gay movement.

> The white gay civil rights groups [like the Christian Right] are also anti-Black, however they want Black people to see the struggle for same-sex unions as tantamount to separate but equal Jim Crow laws. Yet any of this examination reveals that histories of terror imposed upon generations of all Black people in this country do not in any way compare to what appears to be the very last barrier between white gays and lesbians' access to what bell hooks describes as 'Christian capitalist patriarchy'. That system is inherently anti-Black, and no amount of civil rights will ever get Black people any real liberation from it. (Farrow 2010 [2004]: 29)

Farrow's analysis chimes with developments in Europe, where gay rights 'victories' occur on a highly racialised ground that smacks of racial regress rather than sexual progress (see Haritaworn et al. 2008). This highlights the need for a transnational analysis that is able to attend to the travels of not just gay marriage but of the racialised regimes, methodologies and structures of feelings that accompany it. Reading the German drama of queer lovers and hateful Others alongside the gay marriage movement in the US suggests that the racialisation of gender violence is not parochial to north-west Europe but, rather, a globalised phenomenon. Transnationally, racism has been a method for the production of respectable and innocent genders and sexualities that are worthy of visibility, recognition and protection. Justice and liberation here become co-terminous with the pathologisation of populations who, in the newly gay-friendly societies of the West, are forced to bear the residues of gendered and sexual violence. These populations – including Muslims and Arabs in north-west Europe, African Americans in California, Palestinians in Israel/Palestine, Africans everywhere – become interchangeable in the face of rapidly travelling scripts and methods of activism on the one hand, and punishment and pathologisation on the other.

The drama of queer lovers and hateful Others is crucial in the conversion of queer intimacy from perversion into love. The queer lover requires the simultaneous emergence of a hateful Other who is already disposable to the neoliberal multicultural community (Melamed 2011). In this, straight people of colour – always already homophobic – are not the only affect aliens forced to bear the residue of gender violence in the newly gay-friendly context. Queers of colour, too, emerge as unrecognisable – and threatening – to queer structures of love and happiness.

KISSING IN PUBLIC PLACES

I remember this demonstration organized by the LSVD. It was in 2009. You probably know this story. A few white people stood in front of [Habibi, the falafel shop at the corner of Adalbert- and Oranienstraße] and put up a poster saying 'Habibi is not lovely'. The owner of the shop couldn't understand it at all and didn't know how to react. He was really shocked. I guess despite the demonstration he didn't get what was happening. I guess no one had bothered to explain it to him. *[Describes how the shop owner went to the queer business where he worked at the time to find out more about the allegations.]* He talked to us really nicely. From the start he addressed [my transgender colleague], he was very relaxed about it. It was clear to me from the start that he didn't have a problem with us. And he explained the incident to us once more. It was a total misunderstanding. There were two tourists, it was quite late, almost time to close shop. There was only one worker left in the shop and he wanted to collect the bill. He didn't speak English, so these two gay guys – they were from Israel – misunderstood him. So embarrassing. The man, since he didn't speak English, tried to use his hands to explain. He tried to show he's closing shop by rolling up the shutters *(makes a rolling gesture)*. The two of them thought he was grabbing a stick and turning violent. (Anonymous interviewee)

This interviewee captures well how queer kisses circulated through Berlin in the late 2000s – here in two overlapping layers of manufactured realism, involving a gay Israeli couple kissing in an Muslim-owned shop, and a 'kiss-in' denouncing the shop as homophobic and 'not lovely' (in a queerly racialising mimicry of its name, Habibi). Kisses thus form part of a structure of feeling that excludes most queers of colour in the city. The sociality, the 'specific dealings, specific rhythms' (Williams 1978: 133, cited in Muñoz 2000: 68 fn 2) of the kiss/in are such that to participate in it would be akin to self-hate. The kiss described in this account is a non-performative in Sara Ahmed's (2004b) sense: it does not do what it claims to do. It nostalgically conjures multiple murderous pasts – the AIDS crisis and, in the characteristically twinned figures of the Jewish victim and the queer victim (see Kuntsman 2009a), the Holocaust. Yet in the place of a 'homophobic' public that has the power to let queers die, the present kiss-in targets a small racialised business whose survival depends on the queers living in and moving through this rapidly gentrifying neighbourhood. It thus invokes a very different horizon of social death, that speaks the language of protecting queer life.

Queers of colour become affect aliens in this landscape of feeling because they do not love and desire the same bodies and objects. Like the owner of Habibi, they do not find the displayed kisses lovely, and thus forfeit their own ability to be lovely. In fact, cynicism and brutal humour are the dominant (un) emotional performances at the queer of colour kitchen table. You've got to laugh in the face of all this awfulness. This does not mean that love, sex and romance are absent from the kitchen table, whose participants (in no particular order) get crushes, get laid, or get married along with everyone else. Given their hostile environment, this is no small feat, and queer of colour acts of love, towards both self and collective, should indeed be noted and celebrated. Yet these intimate acts convert differently for racialised than white bodies. They do not warrant protection and accrue value and vitality in the same way. Furthermore, as queer love – a white structure of feeling that requires the abjection of racialised bodies – is rapidly becoming a site of disidentification, other investments become more urgent. As the interviewee just cited describes, the destruction wrought by the kiss-in necessitates acts of care – care for the neighbourhood, care for racialised people, whether queer or not – that queers of colour frequently feel called upon to do. In the case at hand, it involved dialoguing with the falafel shop owner and doing damage control for his business by introducing him to the organisers of the alternative Kreuzberg Pride who, however white-domi-nated this space also is, were in a position to accept him as a sponsor of the event, thus restoring his spoilt reputation. In contrast to dominant queer love, with its standardised, clear-cut figurations and affects, such acts of care are often spontaneous, messy and contradictory. We might say that love in the wake of the kiss-in can mean taking care of the mess left behind by white queers. This naturally involves support and solidarity for people of colour, who may or may not be queer or even especially queer-friendly. Queer of colour investments thus follow a different calculus, which enables different acts and objects to surface as worthy of investment (see also Lamble 2014). In this instance, queers of colour take care of the neighbourhood in ways that could not be further removed from the 'cleaning up' logic of urban regeneration. While frequently dismissed as 'identitarian', these intimate performances are external to the rules of queer identity politics. They are hard to document or enumerate and rarely rise to the status of a social movement (see Kuumba 2001). Their success cannot be counted through measures of publicity or visibility. On the contrary, in a context of embodiment where visibility regularly attracts further violence, these acts are often successful precisely because they occur behind the scenes.

This contrasts with the acts of queer love that are now appearing everywhere. Gay kisses are ubiquitous all of a sudden. They are invited into a public that long confined them to the 'little-trafficked, badly lit areas' (Berlant and Warner 1998: 558) of the closet, the asylum, the prison and the public toilet. While queer bodies and sexualities radically claim space and gain visibility, their circulation is not random. They cluster in specific sites: newspaper articles about an academic study commissioned by the LSVD, the Simon study which proved what by then everyone already knew: that 'migrants' are more homophobic than 'Germans' (for example Grassmann 2007). Posters of kisses and actual kiss-ins that are staged in racialised and white working-class neighbourhoods to mark these, in the terms of one organiser's website, as 'problematic hot-beds' full of homophobic 'chavs' (Maneo 2008a). One example is a kiss-in staged in front of a Hamburg mosque, by the local newspaper, in a formerly migrant area whose main gentrifiers are white gay businesses. Another is a poster campaign by the LSVD to educate the inhabitants of disadvantaged 'problem' neighbourhoods that 'love deserves respect'. What kind of worlds do these queer figurations make? Which futures do they orient us towards, which do they foreclose? If the new intimate publics congregating around the queer kiss brim with transformative affects and aesthetics, these citations are nevertheless post-political: they promise to change the world, while reinscribing hegemonic ideals of privacy, property and nation.

Let us take a closer look at one of these gay kisses, which adorned an article on the Simon study in the liberal/left-leaning paper *Süddeutsche* (Grassmann 2007).[5] The study was commissioned by the LSVD, funded by the government, and named after its principal investigator, a gay psychologist (Simon 2008). The article's name aptly invokes the drama of queer lovers and hateful Others along with its setting: 'Migrant kids against gays: Homophobic Berlin'. It loyally repeats the study's quantitative findings as evidence that homophobia is a problem 'especially with Turkish-descended youth' who, we learn, scored 2.08 on a 5-point scale of homophobia measured in school children. These findings, the article suggests, should be a cause of concern in a cosmopolitan city like Berlin, where 'a gay politican has been elected mayor twice', and where 'there

Figure 3   Screenshot of online article 'Migrant kids against gays: Homophobic Berlin'

Source: *Süddeutsche*, 26 September 2007.

should be a certain tolerance toward homosexuals' (Grassman 2007: n.p.). Yet 'homosexuals' are curiously absent from this report, whose sole focus is 'migrants' and their dysfunctional phobic aversion towards 'homosexuals'.

In other reports, too, the inclusion of queer intimacy is confined to an aesthetic level. Like the *Süddeutsche*, the left-wing *Tageszeitung* chose an image of gay male intimacy for its article on Simon's (2008) study. Interestingly, it is the hugging protagonists of *Brokeback Mountain* who warn us about the increasing 'homophobia' of Berlin youth this time. Scripted in intensely local terms, both the queer lover and its hateful Other are products of transnational travels that bring multiple scales – here of city, nation and West – into coherence in a way that whitens these spaces and brings them into familiarity and familiality while erasing racialised subjects from them.

I will here focus on the two bodies chosen to visually mediate Simon's findings in the *Süddeutsche*, as I am interested in the particular 'orientation' (Ahmed 2006) that they bear towards us. The two young men seem incidental to the text, their photo taken maybe from one of the online Pride archives that are now often circulated. They remain anonymous but nevertheless look comfortably familiar in their gender presentation as well as their whiteness. Their muscle tees hug their gym-built torsos tightly, swelling and folding in just the right places. There is no baggy excess, no angled planes hiding badly fitting binders. Their hair is short but slick, their 1970s sun shades signify camp rather than sissy: an aesthetic but virile masculinity that a straight girl might wish for in a boyfriend who could dress a little better.

The bodies of the two kissers claim space, open up towards us. Their kiss takes place in public, on a square maybe. To a queer observer the spectacle might evoke nostalgia, reminding 'us' of the kiss-in of the late 1980s (whether or not we are of its time and place), that icon of radical queer history and AIDS activism which, queer historiographers tell us, gave birth to queer theory and politics (see Seidman 1996). It is the ultimate symbol of transgression and in-your-face direct action. It claims space in a hostile public that is far from friendly towards queer and trans people and would carelessly watch 'us' die (Cvetkovich 2003). In Puar's terms, the two cis-men, formerly marked for death through AIDS, are 'folded (back) into life' (Puar 2007: 36). The kiss we are watching is not diseased, pornographic or repugnant, but is out in the open. It is drawn out and savoured; no quick fumble hidden away in a public toilet or a closet. It is uncensored; proudly displayed under a rainbow flag.

The public kiss in front of our eyes has an audience, but one that is far from hostile. 'We' appear to stand close by, with more witnesses gathered opposite in the background, gathering around the two lovers. As readers and onlookers, we become witnesses to their queer love. Not only do we approve of it, we would protect it even, from Others who lack 'our' openness, who are excluded from view. This imag/ining of sexual liberation as always already achieved belies, of course, the recentness with which full humanity was, formally, extended and which is, substantively, still sorely lacking (see Haritaworn 2008b). I would argue that the gay kiss, and the new desire to flaunt, sponsor and circulate it, fulfils a specific role in allaying and displacing continuing anxieties around queer intimacies. 'We' are able to witness this love communally because of Others who abstain from this communing, who may even need to be kept away, because their intrinsic hatred makes them want to injure this love. The stance into which the straight 'we' is interpellated, in contrast, is not necessarily a loving one. Nowhere in the accompanying article are straights asked to love queers (who remain curiously absent from it); rather, queers are tolerated as an inevitable byproduct of a free society.

This stance is a protectionist one. 'We' can come closer because others hate them. By positioning its heterosexual audience oppositionally – white bodies that open up intimately, versus brown bodies that shrink back, moved by their own backwardness – the kiss thus mediates a new membership paradigm, which enfranchises a new subject but in the same breath disenfranchises others. As we shall see, the queer intimacies which become a pleasant sight in the ideological field staked out by Simon and his funders, commissioners and disseminators differ markedly from the gender non-conforming bodies that materialised as the moral panic's first victims. In its whiteness, its coherence, its liberated desires, and its normative desirability, the innocent victim of 'Muslim homophobia' repeats hegemonic values of the neoliberal nation (privacy, respectability, beauty, freedom, choice) in ways that will be complicated for the gender non-conforming subject. Nevertheless, the drama of the queer lover and the hateful other carves out an affective territory big enough to include bodies and desires that transgress the bounds of respectability.

The gay kisses accompanying the Simon study had real-life companions. In 2006, the anti-violence hotline Maneo began to organise yearly kiss-ins that targeted Berlin's 'problem areas': on the one hand, the abandoned zones in the former East, whose *plattenbau* high-rises have become the epitome of white working-class dreariness and backwardness; on the other, Kreuzberg, Neukölln and other formerly degenerate inner-city areas. As the website states: 'We don't accept any *No-Show* [orig. in English] areas. Every kiss counts, every kiss deserves protection' (Maneo 2008b). The 'we' of this statement is an ascendant one, which works towards an expanded whiteness that coheres by performing its gay-friendliness in the role of the teacher. The racialised other, already known to be deficient and in need of education, must learn that it is not ok to attack gays (as distasteful as they may appear). Indeed, the *Protect every kiss!* campaign was sponsored by the (then left-wing) local government and covered by various newspapers and TV shows. The kiss-ins inscribe themselves into an existing local landscape, yet they also invoke other times and places. They are organised on 17 May – declared International Day Against Homophobia at the International Conference on LGBT Community Human Rights that accompanied the first World Outgames in Montréal in 2006 – thus signaling membership in what Joseph Massad (2007) calls the gay international.[6] In 2009, after targeting sites racialised as Muslim or working class, the kiss-in takes places at the Memorial to the Homosexuals Persecuted under National Socialism, which was commissioned by the LSVD and completed a year earlier by Scandinavian artists Elmgreen and Dragset. Besides metonymically placing the racialised homophobia panic beside a past which must never repeat itself, the event also references the 'recent events surrounding the Eurovision Song Contest in Moscow', which are going viral at that time (Maneo 2009). In 2010, the Maneo kiss-in takes place in front of the Ugandan Embassy. According to the English-language press release, 'Homophobia is global – but not internationally socially acceptable… We bring the kiss – a symbol for love - out in the open to demonstrate publically against homophobia, in Uganda and in all the countries of the world' (Maneo 2010b).

While referencing the history of radical AIDS activism – a nostalgic referent to times when most straight people would watch queers die – these kiss-ins perform, and claim space in, a more ambivalent public. They are expressions of what I (in chapter 4) will call queer nostalgia, which rehearse a new community whose shame, anger and radicalism belong more with a repressive past than a progressive present, and with bodies and places that refuse to catch up. Today's kissers occupy space very differently. Rather than sick perverts outside the law, they are state-sponsored envois that closely collaborate with the police. They still address a neglectful state, but one that is willing to fund them to target poor racialised neighbourhoods that are already heavily policed and socially abandoned. In contrast to the 1980s kiss-in, this performance of queer sexuality draws its spectators in without repelling the straight 'us' or repressing the queer 'them'. The gay kiss, domestic, romantic and vulnerable, performs a middle-class model of care and citizenship whose guarantor is no longer the welfare state but the militarised state. This kiss, which celebrates life in the face of death, is not only nostalgic but also melancholic: It performs diversity for a community that no longer feels safe with diversity but still desires it, and needs it for its progressive identity.

This diversity is, of course, a single-issue one. These kisses are often white, young, non-disabled, non-trans, male – 'attractive', 'normal', palatable and assimilable. The depicted bodies look innocent and deserving of protection.[7] They also look as if they could belong. The queer intimacies publicised today have little resemblance to the sick freak or pervert. Their intimacy is not in our face (it's in theirs – the white 'we' ceases to be shocked by it). In narratives of homophobic violence, we often hear that all the victim did was give his boyfriend a kiss goodbye (Maneo 2008c). He certainly did not make out with him on the train. The vulnerable gay subject is domestic and respectable. Sometimes he is directly characterised as monogamous and middle-class (Mosse 1997). The couple depicted in front of the Hamburg mosque (see Figure 4) are described as:

> Bank employee Andre H. (33) and student Christopher N. (30)… [They] are married and love each other. (Eicker 2007)

The two are an interracial, white and East-Asian, couple. Interraciality (but only where it is part-white) parallels homosexuality in German and other West European exceptionalisms. The two models of transgression are twin symbols of a free and modern society where intimacy is freely chosen and no longer governed by tradition, culture or religion (Haritaworn 2012).

In mainstream gay activism, such claims to visibility are often written in the languages of advertising and performed as consumer citizenship (see Grewal 2005). In 2008 and 2009, Maneo and the LSVD run advertising campaigns that promote gay kisses. The LSVD 'Love Deserves Respect' campaign is launched by gay mayor Klaus Wowereit, who is quoted as stating:

Figure 4   Kiss-in in front of mosque (May 2007)
Source: Photo credit *Hamburger Morgenpost.*

That a kiss between two human beings causes hate and violence is sad and impossible to understand. Unfortunately, in the past months numerous homophobic hate crimes have happened. Society's openness and tolerance must be defended with all the measures provided by the law. (LSVD 2009)

The body of the queer lover intimately translates a state of exception where the boundaries of 'all the measures provided by the law' can be continually pushed (Agamben 2005). This opens up new possibilities for performing sexual citizenship. The exceptionalist, militarised state offers queers a dual place: as icons of western freedom, but also as symbols of western vulnerability, whose protection warrants ever harsher measures.

The posters themselves focus on the queer lover. They feature three couples marked as ambiguously interracial. The 21,000 posters, sponsored by the city, target areas which, according to the website, are 'disadvantaged' (LSVD 2009). They carry the trilingual caption (in German, Turkish and Arabic): '*Love Deserves Respect*'. At their bottom is a spattering of logos by private and public sponsors.[8]

The posters are arranged as triptychs: three lesbian, straight and gay 'couples' – most white, some vaguely multiracialised – appear next to each other. Queer interracial intimacies here appear as what Susan Willis (1990), commenting on the invention of the Black Barbie and the commodification of Black femininity, has termed 'serial replicants'. This has an aesthetic function, in that it unites a

Figure 5   Lesbian part of the triptych *Love Deserves Respect* by the Lesbian and Gay Association Germany

Source: Photograph by the author.

gay and straight audience in their shared desire for an Other who is rendered palatable in hir proximity to whiteness (hooks 1992). It further depoliticises the depicted intimacies by representing them side by side, Benetton-style, as if they were on a level playing field (see Lury 2000). The transgressive, queer, inter-racialised body is elevated as the symbolic border guard of a community that derives its exceptionalism from its fantasised role as the witness and protector of transgressive love, also and especially that love which the Other fails to respect. The body marked as Muslim plays a particular educational role in this drama. On its own, in its single form (as just Muslim) it works as the constitutive outside – as a location of backwardness and deficiency that needs to be educated, assimilated or quarantined. In its multiple form, however (as Muslim and queer), this body symbolises how the border can be crossed: The racialised-appearing kissers in the posters perform their own kind of exceptionalism as 'exceptions to the rule' that all Muslims are homophobic (see Haritaworn et al. 2008).[9] As Jen Petzen (2005) argues in her analysis of an earlier LSVD poster campaign (whose caption translates as: 'Kai is gay. So is Murat. They belong to us. Always!'), they promise a belonging that nevertheless requires relinquishing ownership and agency by declaring itself as belonging *to us*.

It is important to note the long-standing hybridisation between the forms and conventions of queer arts and capitalist advertising, each of which authors aesthetic methods and forms of transgression that become valuable to the other. The *Love Deserves Respect* triptych invokes the famous bus poster by ACT-UP

artist Gran Fury *Kissing Doesn't Kill: Greed and Indifference Do* (1989), which
has also been popular among queer curators in Berlin (Kedves 2014). The poster,
designed amidst the AIDS crisis, was also a triptych featuring a straight, gay and
lesbian kiss. Its kissers differed from those of the *Love Deserves Respect* campaign
in both their race – most of Fury's kissers were people of colour – and their counter-cultural style. But the citationality of queer art and multinational advertising
goes further: while Fury mimicked Toscani's 1980s advertising photographs for
Benetton, Benetton later produced and circulated its own posters of queer and
straight 'lovers', in the 'Unhate Campaign' of November 2011 (*Spiegel* 2011).
The campaign, of which I became aware after numerous queer acquaintances
had shared it on social media, aimed for the characteristic shock effect through
which the company brands itself. Among the series of six photo-shopped posters
of unlikely kissers, five were gay and all were international or interethnic. Two
of the 'couples' most commonly remarked upon ironically restaged the 'war
on terror': besides a kiss between Pope Benedict and Egyptian imam Ahmed
al-Tajjeb, Benjamin Netanjahu and Mahmoud Abbas were also shown kissing.
Just like the kisses staged in Berlin, the ones of the Benetton campaign claimed
to give visibility to the ideal of tolerance. But while 'hate' and terror – affects
which, as the next chapter discusses, are thoroughly racialised as Muslim – were
supposed to find their happy ending in a diversified and secularized version
of Christian love, the kiss between pope and imam was quickly censored by
the Vatican.[10]

As this book goes to press, another same-sex kiss involving a kisser marked as
Muslim is going viral, as part of a series of anti-Muslim cartoons by the French
magazine *Charlie Hebdo* that became the target of an attack in early 2015 which
was quickly ascribed to Muslims (e.g. Fisher 2015). The November 2011 cover
of the magazine, which followed a previous attack, depicted a white man with
glasses and a pencil behind his ear (wearing a T-shirt with 'Charlie Hebdo' on it)
locked in a kiss with a brown man marked as Muslim by his beard, his headwear
and his exaggeratedly long nose. In the background are the smoking ruins of the
magazine's office. The caption of the cartoon reads 'L'Amour Plus Fort Que La
Haine' (love is stronger than hate). It performs a sexual freedom that is signified
by a 'love' that is painted as hard to tolerate, debatable even: the salivating kiss
between a pairing whose racial and sexual mismatch render it so grotesque that
only the freest of all would restrain from hating it. This debatable sexual freedom
is subordinated to a bigger freedom of speech that is untouchable, and signified
by the 'harmless' pencil behind the bespectacled white cis-male intellectual's
ear. The pencil is a popular motif in the revival of cartoons that accompanies the
#jesuischarlie moment. Wielded by 'fearless' artists drawing pencils alongside
the weapons of hateful terrorist it, like love, is described as the stronger weapon.

What renders the representational strategies of an advertising campaign
by a multinational company, gay NGOs and a left-wing local government so

similar? While capital has clearly appropriated queer methods and aesthetics, it is important to realise that the same holds true the other way round. If the kisses on the billboards and in the streets are designed to encode mobilisation, this is a reflection of what I call plastic activism: something that tries to look like a movement but is really the work of a few professionals and their graphic designer. Nevertheless, an analysis of neoliberalism alone cannot help us make sense of the new palatability and placeability of queer intimacies. In the following, I will describe the queer lover as a victim subject whose genealogies of control and abandonment are located in ongoing histories of racism.

QUEER INJURIES

Visual projects such as the *Love Deserves Respect* campaign index a changed political landscape where dominant identity politics is learning the language not only of capitalism but also intersectionality. By professing allegiance to love, diversity and tolerance, a single-issue agenda is thus able to masquerade as multi-issue in order to gain representational power and a competitive edge over migrant organisations in struggles over public funding and recognition.

In Germany as elsewhere, there is no shortage of queer victim subjects. Post-colonial and transnational feminists have helped us understand the rescue missions that frequently undergird neo/colonial missions of 'white men saving brown women from brown men' (Spivak, 1999: 284–311). As early as October 2001, Paola Bacchetta, Tina Campt, Inderpal Grewal, Caren Kaplan, Minoo Moallem and Jennifer Terry noted the 'co-optation of Muslim women as "victims" of violence or of "Islamic barbarism"' in the war on terror (Baccheta et al., 2002: 306). Besides war and occupation, the 'victim subject', in Ratna Kapur's (2005) terms, has been of central importance to the global violence against women movement, whose dominant issues have alternated between female circumcision, *sati*, dowry murders, trafficking, pornography, female infanticide, the veil and honour killing. Kapur argues that while the movement has posited a unitary female subject, it is the body of the 'truncated Third World woman' that has been most frequently mobilised: 'it is invariably the abject victim subject who seeks rights, primarily because she is the one who has had the worst happen to her' (Kapur 2005: 98, 115). This is amplified by the dominant genre of political grievance. Kapur highlights the centrality of personal testimonials in public tribunals, which regularly contain horrifying graphic accounts. Besides repeating patriarchal and colonial images of women in the global south as 'thoroughly disempowered, brutalised and victimised' (2005: 115), these mobilisations also reinforce female victimisation by appealing to the patriarchal state in general, and its criminal justice system in particular.

Kristin Bumiller (2008) points to a similar protectionist turn in the violence against women movement in the US, which has come a long way since its early days. She reminds us that the shelter movement was not only profoundly anti-state, but that it did not draw biopolitical distinctions between service 'users' and 'providers' on the one hand, and 'deviant' and 'normal' masculinities on the other. Rather, in a violently patriarchal society, 'any man could be a rapist', and any girl or woman could experience violence – but also support others through the same experience (Bumiller 2008: 10). This contrasts with today's dominant iconography of 'innocent, white, and/or angelic' victims who must be protected from dark-skinned strangers in dangerous areas (2008: 9, 19). Bumiller locates the institutionalisation and professionalisation of the feminist anti-violence movement in a neoliberal context that gives rise to 'expanding systems of medicalization and criminalization' as well as to a social service bureaucracy. Sexual violence in particular is turned into a social, medical and legal problem.

Like much feminist analysis, Bumiller's and Kapur's accounts foreground a heteronormative scenario of violence and anti-violence. Nevertheless, their critique of gendered investments in racialised moral panics is highly relevant for the analysis of both feminist and gay anti-violence organising in Germany. There, anti-violence activism is rarely questioned in its institutionalisation and professionalisation, and remains acutely under-researched in its relationship with the prison and medical industrial complexes. Evidence of racism in the German shelter movement, which has often figured 'perpetrators' and 'victims' as 'Turkish', has mainly come from anti-racist feminist shelter workers (Aktaş 1993; personal communication with Nivedita Prasad in 2012). Even less has been written on the racialisation of the gay anti-violence discourse in Germany, which has loyally repeated the racialised terrain carved out by earlier feminist activisms. The main anti-violence organisation in Berlin, Maneo, is alleged to have forged racialised hate crime statistics that portray men of colour as violently homophobic (Blech 2009, Ruder 2011). Its sister organisation LSVD, meanwhile, actively inscribed itself in the global feminist discourse by taking a leading role in the public scandal over the country's first mediated case of 'honour killing' (Haritaworn and Petzen 2011). The association organised a vigil for the victim, Hatun Sürücü – a (presumably heterosexual) woman of Kurdish origin raised in Germany whose positionality could not have been further removed from the LSVD's constituency. Nevertheless, by mimicking an honour crime panic that was going viral (see Schneider 2005), the association was able to create a lasting discursive link between gay rights and women's rights on the one hand, and Muslim mal-integration, religiosity, violence and crime on the other, thus converting its work into the highest currency.[11] Sürücü has become a mainstay for the association, which has periodically unearthed her case whenever the moral panic needs a repetition (e.g. LSVD 2014).

Besides these overlaps between feminist and gay languages and visualities of violence and anti-violence, there are also important differences. As Bumiller reminds us, the non-trans female victim of heterosexual rape, however innocent and respectable, is always already confirmed as passive and submissive, thus seemingly engendering her own victimisation.

> Contemporary media is replete with images of violated women. The brutalized bodies of women with blackened eyes, open wounds, and as bloodied corpses are abundantly displayed in media reports about crimes and crime trials. (Bumiller 2008: 16)

In late 2000s Berlin – the same time that gay kisses were mushrooming – there is a similar abundance of images of gay men as violated, bruised and beaten in the gay and alternative media. Yet the depicted subjects are not abjected to the same deathly realm. On the contrary, the white, male, gender-conforming body that draws attention to the newly emerging hate crime discourse is just as alive as its kissing equivalent. Spectacularly 'injured', he (sic) nevertheless remains virile, coherent, attractive and distinctly able-bodied.

An example is the November 2009 cover of the monthly gay magazine *Siegessäule*, which features a mock-injured torso clad in sportswear. The dark-haired model's pretty pout sports a colourful band-aid for children. The cover's citation of gay S/M culture and its fetishisation of physical violence and transgression of race, class and age borrow from the feminist victim subject, without however locking the gay male body into a passive, emasculated stance. It renders the hate crime discourse sexy to a gay audience. Multivalent, already queered, and multiply subverted, this performance loyally repeats the nation (see Haritaworn 2008b).

The February 2009 issue of *Zitty*, the big monthly listings magazine, also features homophobic hate crime. Addressing a mainly heterosexual audience, the issue strikes a less sexual register in order to render the gay body attractive and identifiable to its readers. After re-telling the sad story of one victim of hate crime, the lead article turns to the work of Maneo, whose head is portrayed as a lonesome hero and saviour of gay men:

> The shelves in his little office with the slightly yellowed blinds bend under the weight of the files, against the walls there are information panels that are used for public actions. The bodies of the abused are on them, alongside short protocols of the violent event. 'Pushed off the bike and called names', one of the panels says; beside you can see a man's naked upper body. His torso is coloured partly blue, partly green and yellow by the punches and kicks which rained down on him. His 'mistake': he wore a pink shirt that night. (Bombosch 2009: 16–17, my translation)

The vulnerable, injured body – which is rendered graphic through text rather than image – screams for 'us', as readers and witnesses, to take urgent action. Its spectacular vulnerability enables us to come close in the face of deep remaining ambivalence, without threatening the visual coherence of the gay male body. 'We' do not stop to wonder about the origins or trajectories of these images and texts: to question the injury would mean to trivialise it; and to appear stuck in a homophobic past long overcome.

It is tempting to theorise these images and the political strategies that they represent as 'wounded attachments' in Wendy Brown's sense. Brown has critiqued the privileging of pain in identity politics, which to her is a resentful 'formulation of justice which, ironically, reinscribes a bourgeois ideal as its measure' (Brown 1993: 394). Focusing on feminist, gay and anti-racist identities, her article claims that these activisms often demand inclusion into the privileges possessed by 'bourgeois men', without contesting the liberal capitalist regime that disentitles large parts of the population in the first place.

> [Middle-class identity] embodies the ideal to which nonclass identities refer for proof of their exclusion or injury: homosexuals who lack the protection of marriage, guarantees of child custody or job security, and freedom from harassment; single women who are strained and impoverished by trying to raise children and hold paid jobs simultaneously; people of color disproportionately affected by unemployment, punishing urban housing costs, inadequate health care programs, and disproportionately subjected to unwarranted harassment and violence, figured as criminals, ignored by cab drivers. The point is not that these privations are trivial but that without recourse to a white masculine middle class ideal, politicized identities would forfeit a good deal of their claims to injury and exclusion, their claims to the political significance of their difference. (1993: 395)

The privileged, in such politics, are objects of desire but also of a 'resentment' which 'retains the real or imagined holdings of its reviled subject – in this case, bourgeois male privileges – as objects of desire' (ibid: 394). Ironically, activists thereby also perpetually restage their own exclusion from the universal ideal. They invest in their own subjection because the survival of their identities depends on the repeated performance of their exclusion. They attach themselves to the wound because the wound is the site of their identity formation.

Brown's analysis analogises all sorts of oppressive and anti-oppressive acts and conditions, as if they were on a level playing field, and as if they did not intersect. However, to stay just with the example of race, there is a difference between being ignored by a cab driver, and being criminalised or denied health care. Prison abolitionist movements point the way beyond a 'white masculine middle class ideal', without however evading the centrality of antiblackness, class oppression and other factors that land some in prisons at much higher rates than others. Furthermore, despite its foregrounding of injury, Brown's argument lacks a disability lens: both phenomenologically and rhetorically, wounded attachments would look different from the perspective of actually injured bodies. It is no coincidence that both the gay kissers and the 'injured' bodies circulated in the racialised homophobia panics look distinctly able-bodied. Finally, and most importantly for this discussion, Brown's proposition of resentful identity formation presumes a single-issue activism whose prime interlocutor is an undifferentiated 'middle class'. This is complicated by our case of a white – and hardly nonclass – gay identity politics whose target of resentment is not 'the bourgeoisie', but working-class people of colour who are already rendered disposable by intersecting necropolitical regimes of borders, policing, gentrification and war. Hate crime activism is thus possible without attributing pain to those who have the power to punish queer resentment. On the contrary, white straight people emerge as the protectors and rescuers of injured queers from homophobic people of colour. Furthermore, investing in victim subjectivity is more than merely an identitarian pitfall. Rather, the drama of queer lovers and hateful Others is biopolitically productive in that it enables a proliferation of rescuable identity categories that, as we shall see next, far surpass the homogenous subject of homonormativity.

COLOURFUL SUBJECTS

Trans people have often been positioned as the innocent Other of homonation-alism. Recent critiques of the campaign for trans people in the military aside (see Geidner 2013), the trans subject has mostly been located on the receiving end of the 'war on terror'. For example, trans people have been described as the (unraced and mistaken) victims of counter-terrorist surveillance at airports and other sites of compulsory identification (for example Puar 2007: 252 fn 74; Thaemlitz 2007; Wilchins 2003). Exposing the exclusionary workings of a homonormative politics of respectability that has employed gender conformity as a key strategy for assimilation remains important (For example Gossett 2013; Mock 2013; Namaste 1996; Rivera 2002). In Dean Spade's (2004) terms, efforts to include the trans were long 'LGB-fake-T', and are haunted by a long tradition of sacrificing trans rights and protections for quick legislative gains. While all this is true, it is important to acknowledge that trans people are far more than the movement's embarrassing margins. As this section illustrates, white trans and genderqueer people in Berlin have actively inserted themselves, and gained substantially, from the racist panics over crime and violence, neighbourhood and nation. This complicates an account of *homo*nationalism that exclusively foregrounds a homonormative identity politics. Rather, gender non-conforming subjects have exerted agency in ways that trouble dichotomies of 'assimilated gays' v. 'transgressive trans people'.

As already flagged in the last chapter, the racialised homophobia discourse found its first bodies not in the gaybourhood where it was first scripted, but in the genderqueer scene in Kreuzberg. Ironically, the homonationalist episteme, forged in years of homonormative activism, rendered respectable by the Simon study, and popularised by journalists close to the big gay organisations, found its first real-life 'case' in a queer left-wing setting. This section follows around the production of an 'event' that was key to the birth of a respectable trans subject worthy of coalition and served to cement a view of Kreuzberg and later Schöneberg as degenerate queerphobic spaces. In questioning how the incident became an 'event', I am also interested in whose suffering becomes uneventful in its course, and confirmed as the 'ordinary, chronic, acute, and cruddy rather than catastrophic, eventful, and sublime' (Povinelli 2008: 511). Writing on forms of 'state killing' and 'letting die' in an Australian context of settler colonialism, neoliberalism and war on terror, Povinelli reads the spectacular violence circulated under the sign of 'terror' alongside the slower modes of violence against poor and Indigenous people, whose premature deaths appear natural or self-inflicted.

This contrasts with the 'eventfulness' of the scene that lent the moral panic its first bodies. The incident itself was highly contested – those involved variously described it as a drunken traffic altercation that was neither racialised nor particularly gendered, or as a 'hate crime' committed by members of a Turkish fascist organisation. Nevertheless, the story that circulated most widely and rapidly was that a group of 'lesbians' had been beaten up by a group of 'Turks'. Like the Habibi incident discussed above, it followed a particular script and featured a particular set of characters. The 'crime scene' this time was the Drag Festival, an alternative event that invited people 'from all over Europe and Israel' – a geopolitical boundary that marks the community to be celebrated and protected as western – to come together for four days (Drag Festival 2008a). The characters were a nationally mixed group of performers and visitors, including drag kings, genderqueers and trans people, who on their way home from the closing party at the famous alternative club SO36 got involved in a street altercation in the course of which several of them were injured. The backdrop was Kreuzberg, at its most dangerously diverse. In the words of a visiting performer: 'I was very surprised that such a thing happened in the most queer friendly street in Berlin' (Zoé 2008a). Both the alternative subcultural setting and its queer and genderqueer inhabitants, then, markedly differed from the assimilationism of professional gay organising. Nevertheless, and despite the alternative media spaces within which it took place – including left-wing newspapers, Indymedia, queer, trans and gender studies e-discussion lists – the debate that ensued followed the well-trodden homonationalist path mapped out in advance by white non-trans gay men working for the homonormative organisations.

I argue that these happenings converted into an event because after years of plastic activism, the raced and classed setting of Kreuzberg, and the presence of queers on this well-tilled soil (queers, moreover, participating in an internationally publicised festival), the story appeared instantly familiar. The production of the event involved putting forth a recognisable narrative of sexual and gender oppression. The first pieces of information were published by the Drag Festival organisers themselves. In a press release published the next day, which included a call for action, the organisers referred to what had happened as homophobia:

> In order to raise awareness of the attack, but also of the increasingly homophobic climate in Kreuzberg, there will be a demonstration on Mariannen Square [where the attack happened] on 9 June at 7pm, with the motto 'Smash Homophobia!' (Drag Festival 2008b)

The press release and the demonstration were taken up by several newspapers, magazines and news websites. All of these represented the event as 'homophobic' rather than transphobic. Many described those beaten up contrary to their identities, as 'women' or 'lesbians' (Antifaschistische Linke Berlin 2008; Indymedia 2008; Jungle World 2008; *Siegessäule* 2008; Luig 2008).

Besides interpellating particular bodies and intimacies, the debate produced particular ideas about the space of Kreuzberg. It is the 'good mix' Kreuzberg that emerges here, a Kreuzberg that is diverse and alternative, and needs defending. Media reports of the Drag Festival incident described the 'perpetrators' as unambiguously Turkish. The Drag Festival press release authors appeared to go out of their way to avoid this racist ascription, naming the 'perpetrators' as Grey Wolves and fascists rather than Turkish:[12] 'This is not, however, a "migrant" problem, as often described by some right-wing German populists' (Drag Festival 2008b). Instead, they highlighted that festival goers had also been harassed by drunken German football fans in the area, thus placing the spectre of white working-class homophobia beside that of racialised homphobia. While invoking the sign of (Turkish) fascism rather than Turkishness enabled the authors to identify their own speech as anti-racist, this did not prevent readers from recognising the 'fascists' as 'Turks'.[13] For example, a reporter of the left-wing daily *Tageszeitung*, who had participated in the festival, described the 'perpetrators' as 'a few Turks', whom she swiftly linked with the 'usual Oriental scene in Berlin-Kreuzberg [which] now seems sinister to me'. In the same section, she invoked a 'brutal' masculinity and an 'aggressiveness in the street which is against everything that cannot be understood through traditional norms' (Luig 2008). The invocation of fascism did not, therefore, interrupt the circulation of the sexual knowledges popularised by the Simon study, as well as in several years of homonormative activism. It served, rather, to prevent an ascription of racism to the Drag Festival organisers themselves: we did not name the homophobes as 'Turks', hence we are not racist. Furthermore, given the significance of fascism to German identities and counter-identities, it served to displace all allegations of oppressiveness onto the Other, who thereby became the origin of not only homo/transphobia but also of racism and fascism. It served, finally, to 'politically correct' the actions which followed: a day after the incident, a few thousand mainly white queers marched through not only Kreuzberg but also Neukölln, thus gluing the '*multikulti kiez*' and the 'ghetto' into one 'neighbourhood' imaginable as Muslim, and demanding similar, albeit unspecified, intervention.

How did the sign 'Turkish' and its political euphemism, 'Grey Wolf', come to stick, in Sara Ahmed's (2004a) terms, to the bodies of 'the perpetrators'? Neither their ethnic nor political identity seemed clear in the accounts of the 'victims' themselves, who again did not all position the events in the same way. One person with whom I emailed after the incident, for example, described the perpetrators as conspicuously 'blonde'. While there is of course no obvious relation between hair colour and ethnicity, his choice of describing the perpetrators in this way is nevertheless significant given the privileging of hair colour in German practices of phenotyping (with 'blonde' being an implicitly 'white' marker). Even the presence of Grey Wolves in this narrative was largely based on the account by an individual in the group of queers, who, according to my informant, had provoked the attackers in 'a "game" to see who is more macho, but this game got lots of us beaten up'. To cover up their responsibility in escalating the violence, my correspondent continued, the person then claimed to have seen a Grey Wolves sticker on the car of the attackers, and thereby began a 'conspiracy theory' which quickly became the source of new truths about 'Kreuzberg' and 'migrant homophobia'.

Even though the supposed 'Turkishness' of the attackers was thus contested, it nonetheless quickly became common knowledge. In Sara Ahmed's terms, affect sticks to certain bodies, is read as residing within them, and emanating from them: fear, or fearsomeness, is already in the bodies of men labelled 'Turkish', so that the mere mention of gender violence alongside Turkishness (the location of a club, a faint imag/ining of a sticker) is enough to 'recognise' the perpetrators as Turkish. This affective reading, it seems, has nothing to do with racist histories, representations and iconographies of violence. As Ahmed (2000) explains in her earlier work, the thing about the stranger is that they are not strange at all, 'we' already know them – which is why 'we' easily *re*-cognise them.

Unsurprisingly maybe, the wider media cited and repeated these ascriptions. The special issue in the alternative *Jungle World* carried the title 'Homophobia among Turks and other Germans' (Bozic 2008). Three years after the 'honour killing' debate and one year after the Simon study, the *Jungle World* authors can take for granted the existence of 'Turkish homophobia' as an object that can be known, defined, described and acted on. The Turkishness of homophobia is further authenticated in the subtitle: 'Bissu schwül oder was?' (You gay or what?), which is deliberately misspelt, with additional dots on the '*schwul*' (gay), in a mockery of Turkish. Not only can homophobes be known at first sight – they are, of course, Turkish, it's in their culture, they cannot even *say* gay, they lack a basic vocabulary for homosexuality. But 'we' know them intimately. 'We' speak their language, while they can only ever mimic 'ours'.

This cultural imperialism is threaded throughout the issue. The five articles repeat and build on an Orientalist archive of gender and sexuality that is by now familiar. The main article (Bozic 2008) quotes the Simon study as stating that homophobic attitudes among migrant youth are 'significantly more wide-spread', and as citing 'religiosity' and the 'acceptance of traditional norms of masculinity' as causes of homophobia. Further sources of expert knowledges are the LSVD, Maneo and Café Positiv, the same white non-trans gay organisations that have been instrumental in fomenting moral panics over 'homophobic migrants'. As in earlier media reports (see chapter 1), they are cited as experts discussing the problem of 'migrants' harassing gays. The only gender non-conforming sources in the article are the press release by the Drag Festival, and statements by Fatma Souad, an organiser of the queer Turkish night Gayhane in SO36. Souad is paraphrased as saying that 'Gay and transsexual Turks' (cited in the male form, 'Türken') who 'question ideas of masculinity' and are treated as 'fouling the nest' (Bozic 2008: 3).

While the special issue is described as a response to the Drag Festival incident, the positionalities and visualities that it invites into a sympathetic public are quite different from the injured female-assigned, gender non-conforming bodies, some of whom were migrants and visitors from abroad. The central actors of the issue are non-trans white gay men, the same gay activists who have long invested in the 'migrant homophobia' debate and will benefit from the resulting policy changes. In the lead article, 'transphobia' is mentioned only once, but 'homophobia' or '*Schwulenfeindlichkeit*' (hostility towards gay men) 22 times. On the whole first page, there is not a single reference to transphobia. On the contrary, the issue's subtitle specifically announces a Pride event that is happening in response to the incident as 'protesting against sexist [sic] incidents in Kreuzberg and Neukölln'.

Nevertheless, drag is chosen to visually mediate the topic of 'Turkish homophobia' on the cover of the special issue. In front of an urban silhouette, 'queers' are beating up 'Turks', two opposing groups whose stark contrasts are marked through their colouring and shape. While the 'queers' are wearing colourful clothes—three wear little dresses, one wears leather – the 'Turks' are grey, monochrome and covered. Several of them are labelled as 'Gräue Wölfe' ('Grey Wolves', again misspelt with an additional umlaut on 'grey'). The 'queer'

Figure 6   'You gay or what? Homophobia among Turks and other Germans'
Source: Cover of *Jungle World* 26 (26 June 2008).

diversity of features and hairstyles – long, blond, curly, red, shaved – contrasts
with the 'Turkish' uniformity of styles and expressions – moustache, short hair,
monotonous face. The 'queers' are painted in lively, moving swings and strokes
– they kick, punch, bite, threaten their adversaries with colourful sex toys. The
'Turks', on the other hand, are in straight lines – they are square and rigid, leaning
backwards, or immobile, fixed, standing still. Their 'primitive' look appears to
be racial: the big noses, bent bodies, long arms, which hang at the level of the

genitals, seem suggestive of far right iconography, rather than of a left-wing newspaper. The two groups move in different directions. While the 'queers' are moving towards the 'Turks' (albeit with force), the latter move backwards. Their homo/transphobia appears to be at the same time a refusal, in Sara Ahmed's (2006) terms, to orient themselves towards the 'right' objects. The passivity of the Oriental, who can only be shaken up by force, has a long genealogy, from Karl Marx's writings on India and China (Avineri 1968) to Raphael Patai (1973), whose early anthropological study *The Arab Mind* recommended anal sex as a torture method for Arab men. According to Patai, being forced into a passive role violated their masculinity and therefore constituted the ultimate degrading act.

In fact, the image covering the *Jungle World* uncannily reminds me of Abu Ghraib, the prison torture scandal which was allegedly inspired by Patai's 'findings'. Jasbir Puar (2007) has, of course, helped us understand Abu Ghraib as a spectacular performance of Orientalism, rather than as the scandal of cultural offensiveness that it became in the liberal media. Abu Ghraib created knowledges of Orientalised sexuality, knowledges which the debate on 'migrant homophobia' implicitly cites and repeats: the idea that Muslim men have a particular, 'traditional' masculinity, that they are especially homophobic, but also eternally sodomised according to an older fantasy of an Orient that was homoerotic rather than homophobic (Massad 2007). At the same time, this racialising performance produces 'queer' sex in particular ways. Anal sex is at once a tool of liberation and indistinguishable from rape. On the *Jungle World* cover, this double signification is extended to other queer and trans practices and identities: the use of vibrators, BDSM, leather and drag. This euphemising of sexual violence (as freeing rather than violating) is enabled by the use of the cartoon – a medium that, as also illustrated by the *Charlie Hebdo* cover analysed above, invokes a humour that is by definition excessive. As with the same-sex part-'Muslim' kiss on the French cover, the *Jungle World* cartoon stages its scene as a battle that brings the 'war on terror' home. And again, this representation is as ambivalent towards the queer bodies as it is dehumanising of the racialised ones: while the queers are clearly the victors, they are painted in decidedly unflattering ways. The drag queens especially catch your eye with their big build, their bad style, their furry bodies and faces. The drag spectacle highlights the contradictions of the LGBT participation in racism and war. It has little of the normalcy and attractiveness of the gay kiss. It is, on the contrary, a freak show, which amuses, makes us voyeuristic, draws us in, and repels us at the same time (see Ahmed 2004a). The war is here waged sexually. Its weapons are anal plugs that are still smoking, a rubber baton that is forced into an anus, high heels that aim between the legs. The most effective weapon (judging by the atypically emotional face of the Turkish 'victim') are the protruding genitals of a drag queen or trans-feminine person, which are equipped with a big piercing. This transphobic representation characteristically aims at the disgust that modified genitals evoke in many non-trans people, and still blends seamlessly with the claim of 'German' progressiveness and 'Turkish' regressiveness.

The ambivalence with which trans and genderqueer narratives of spatialised and racialised violence are incorporated by this issue of the *Jungle World* is reflective of the contradictory context of trans citizenship. The prior emergence of a moral panic around 'migrant homophobia' has created space for a certain trans and genderqueer voice to enter into the public discourse. However, this narrative foregrounds experiences of injury and violence rather than expressions of gender non-conforming agency that might threaten a gender system that constructs trans bodies as worthless. Normalised subjects emerge in this narrative as benevolent saviours of injured bodies and identities, whose innocence and deservingness derives from their need for protection from Others who hate them. The injured narrative that is circulated between gender non-conforming people and their audience leaves intact a system of compulsory heterosexuality and forcible gender assignment, which instead becomes imaginable as 'tolerant' and 'protective' against Others who are converted into the real origins of violence and thus become the constitutive outside to an expanded, inclusive community. Ironically, the limited space generated by this victimology is quickly ceded to the same homonormative subjects who have traditionally excluded gender non-conforming voices and experiences from their spaces.

This was also the case one summer later, in 2009, when the moral panic returned to the gaybourhood in Schöneberg. The last chapter discussed the 'Smash transphobia!' demonstration in Frobenstraße in greater detail. Here, it is noteworthy that the demonstration, organised by NGOs that variously support trans people, migrant gays and sex workers, served to briefly foreground migrant trans sex workers but ultimately evaded sex work and racism by putting an undifferentiated transgender victim subject on the map. Due to the proximity of Frobenstraße, one of the poorest postcodes in Berlin, to the gaybourhood, the homonormative organisations were able, after a decade of trying, to paint Schöneberg as a dangerous area in need of attention and policing.

The representations of queer lovers and injured trans people examined here point to continuing contradictions, but also increasing proximities between transgressive and assimilationist, and between radical queer, trans, gay and LGBT forms of organising. It is important to highlight these convergences alongside the ways in which homonormative organisations continually incorporate and profit from victimologies involving more vulnerable bodies. At the same time, there have been many powerful initiatives by queers of colour to scandalise the large gay organisations' treatment of people of colour communities. The LSVD in particular has responded to this by making efforts to shed its reputation as a white, non-trans, male organisation. Besides increasing representation and services for women and trans people, it has on several occasions attempted to pass as a gay migrant self-organisation, by employing individual people of colour who are willing to authenticate its politics in exchange for jobs, salaries and media influence. Such attempts are nevertheless not always successful. Queer of colour groups have repeatedly refused the LSVD's patronage and publicly critiqued its racism and imperialism (Bernhardt 2006; Petzen 2005). For example, when the LSVD in 2003 attempted to use the self-organised group GLADT (Gays and Lesbians aus der Türkei) in order to provoke migrant associations to 'clarify their relationship to homophobia' (in the title of a press release that painted migrants as backward, mal-integrated and violent), queers of colour organising under the banner of QEKON (Queer and Ethnicity Conference) countered by publicly demanding that the LSVD clarify its relationship to racism (citations from Petzen 2008). On 17 May 2014, the Migrationsrat (migration council), an umbrella organisation of over 70 migrant self-organisations, followed this kind of trans and queer of colour leadership by publishing a statement, aptly timed, on the same International Day Against Homophobia that has been the occasion for the kiss-ins in racialised communities discussed above, 'Migrant self-organisations take responsibility in the fight against homophobia and transphobia'. While ostensibly complying with the temporal and biopolitical scripts of the moral panic, the statement subverts these scripts by reclaiming people of colour leadership over the problems of homophobia and transphobia. It not only cites a study that it conducted with its membership that confirmed an overwhelmingly positive attitude towards LGBT issues, but also holds white society accountable for trying to make sexual and gendered progress 'at the expense of people with migrant histories, people of colour and Black people' (Migrationsrat 2014b, my translation).

This is but one illustration of the amazing successes in building new anti-racist alliances that cross hetero/homo divides and promise to begin with, rather than cannibalise, a multi-issue agenda; these alliances have resulted from the LSVD's transparent attempts to divide straight and queer people of colour, and, most importantly, from the hard work of queers of colour. But there are setbacks as well. While homonormative organisers, at the time of writing, seem increasingly discredited, problematic coalitions such as the one leading up to the demonstration at Frobenstraße have not so far resulted in any demands for accountability. As the trans and queer of colour critiques explored in the following suggest, this has resulted in a violent erasure of trans of colour positionalities in particular.

AFFECT ALIENS

I chose silence on [Transgender Day of Remembrance] because on this one day the world spoke names of fallen siblings they did not know, share space with and care after in life. My body and being craved silence and solitude as well-meaning folks turned their lens for one day on fallen trans women of color while living trans women of color continue to be exiled from such spaces daily. (Mock 2013: n.p.)

Writing in New York City, a context with a sizeable trans of colour community, Janet Mock, in a blog post entitled 'Not all memories are created equal', explains her decision to stay alone on Transgender Day of Remembrance rather than join one of the busy commemoration events that have proliferated since the 2000s. More cynically, Riley Snorton and I have argued that one of the most urgent tasks at present is 'explaining the simultaneous devaluation of trans of color lives and the nominal circulation in death of trans people of color; this circulation vitalises trans theory and politics, we claim, through the value extracted from trans of color death' (Snorton and Haritaworn 2013: 67). This is echoed by critics from the kitchen table who, in this city with a much smaller queer of colour let alone trans of colour community, openly critique a mode of coalition that trades 'my race for your gender'. In this organisational climate, 'the one who has had the worst happen to her' (Kapur 2005: 98) does not matter, save as a number to be added up, or a thing to be accumulated, on annual reviews and funding proposals.

The queer of colour kitchen table emerges as a site where affect aliens, whose ways of being emotional (or unemotional) lack currency and are unintelligible or even dangerous to 'queer' structures of feeling, can congregate. There, other kinds of love and resentment are permissible, which elsewhere would be considered pathological and punishable rather than valuable, and most certainly perceived as 'fouling the nest'. This does not necessarily make the kitchen table a 'safe space' – indeed, many in this group have rejected practices of teaching or organising that make such unrealistic and unhelpful promises, or that all feelings are equally permissible. Conflict did occur – for example around the degree of self-organising that participants wished to enforce, the degree of criticism of white gay or queer scenes that folks thought was possible or desirable in public, and the differing sides participants took over rifts in the wider migrant, gay migrant and women of colour scenes, for example around anti-Black racism or transphobia. Nevertheless, I have been struck by the loyalty and willingness among participants to work things out, and the time people have for each other's survival choices, in the face of impossible conundrums such as having to hold down jobs in the local gentrifier bar, or the NGO known for its racism or transphobia. The kitchen table has been a space of prefigurative activism and radical becoming, whose primary concerns have shifted and changed over the years – from speaking up against and educating about anti-Muslim racism and criminalisation through racialised hate crime discourses, to supporting participants through health crises and trans or disabled coming outs, to making direct interventions to tackle trans misogyny in women of colour communities, to participating in wider struggles against policing, gentrification and borders. In contrast to other spaces of radical becoming, the complicating of identities that has occurred at the queer of colour kitchen table never struck me as leading to a loss of radicality and other ideals of power cognisance and transformation.

Part of this radicalism has been a willingness to critique, in the face of repeated experiences of being punished, labelled and disowned. While far from anti-intellectual – reading and writing are part of the queer of colour kitchen table and the interlocking social movements that have given rise to it (see SUSPECT 2010b) – participants have used their organic intellectual skills to critique formal academic structures and the gendered, racialised and classed formations that they foster.

Q: You once said something interesting about genderqueers in Neukölln... That Neukölln is white, young and genderqueer.

A: Well, they're not just white, young and genderqueer, they're all gender studies students. This is a really elitist group, they don't do this out of any inner motivation but they have clear political conceptions to turn their lives and themselves into uber-queer projects. And they're all the same! They wear same asymmetrical hair cuts and the same clothes. [*Talks about how Queer used to have so much potential and so much to do with queer of colour lives.*] Now it's all white washed, H&M'ed, in comes your Neukölln crowd. And I'm really asking myself what they're doing in Neukölln. What's their relation to people there. If it's pure victim tourism.... They feel so marginalised that they think they're on an allied level with people of colour. [*Argues that this often occurs through cultural appropriation*: 'Decoration – it's so cool, all those Arabic letters that you can't read, let me stick that on my cloth bag.'] Even if they choose to live in coal oven flats with holes and mould on the ceiling they're basically doing it for fun.

I am struck by this analysis, whose critique of traumatised citizenship does not stop at homonormativity or even transnormativity. Rather, queer left styles, which are often heralded as alternatives in debates over gay marriage, homonormativity and homonationalism, become perceivable as themselves contingent on racism and classism. Again, this renders problematic the kinds of coalition that have arisen in the changed environment shaped by queer regeneration.

This point was also brought home by Meivi, a trans ally who has diasporic links to Latin America and Spain. In the following passage, she remarks that the trans scene that has formed in Berlin is much younger than the one in the places where she grew up. She also highlights that this new scene does not make any noticeable efforts to reach out to people of colour. In particular, she is scandalised by the unapologetic absence of trans women of colour:

I'm very surprised about this new trans scene in Berlin. I'm really surprised by the absence of women mostly, and I'm really surprised by the total absence of women of colour. That for me is a totally different position from where I used to live.

She contrasts this with the everyday conviviality with trans women that she experienced in the places she had lived before.

I used to live in a neighbourhood where I had contact with trans women because they were my neighbours or shop in the same store. Not because we agree politically … but this is a class thing as well. How do you work, where do you work, there are like trans women working as a hairdresser.… I mean, there are a lot of people out there, since thousands of years and they are still there, and they are still fighting every day, not just against transphobia but against racism and class oppression, and have to survive every day. And changing the societies, it's necessary, but not every society has to change the same way. And western models, I *wish*, will not be copied everywhere. Even though they try to push it in every way. And actually it's the same with western feminism. It's white middle-class feminism, but it's not the only feminism that exists. And there are a lot of agendas that have left many of us out.

What is the implication of exporting transnormative movements to places where the gender binary has been less successfully enforced – whose gender non-conformities were first treated as a failure to be civilised, then as a failure to be properly modern lesbians and gays, and are now, with the rise of the T within the LGBT, once again confirmed as pre-modern? Dispensable to white trans movements in their life, trans-feminine people of colour are nevertheless becoming valuable in their death. Meivi illustrates this with regard to the relatively recent arrival of Trans Day of Remembrance in Berlin – another globalising anti-violence methodology that, even more spectacularly than hate crime activism, vitalises some trans subjects by fetishising others in their death (see Bhanji 2013; Lamble 2008; Snorton and Haritaworn 2013). Meivi describes the event as 'totally unpleasant, often very apolitical as well … and racist, openly or closed':

A: It was very funny, it was one of the first times that I attended an event in Germany where I hear so many names that are familiar to me, like Pérez, Rodríguez, whatever, and hearing that I have a very weird feeling. I have the feeling that people are not contextualising the thing.… So apparently how many people are killed in Brazil, and how many people are killed in Monaco. … Brazil is, I don't know, maybe twenty times the size of Monaco. There are a lot of people, and class issues, who are working in many spaces where they may be more vulnerable. But one of the reasons [they are vulnerable] is because people are poor. Not only because they are trans but also because they are poor. And they are exposed to a lot of violence that comes from poverty. So I don't want to minimise at all the violence against trans people, but I think it's necessary to contextualise and also, like, it's very disrespectful, fucked up and makes me very angry, this white construction again, and this denial of anything else.

J: Why do you think TDOR are interested in women from Latin America?
A: I don't think they are so interested in trans women from Latin America.
J: Only when they're dead maybe?
A: Maybe.

What does it mean if the only representation of queer and trans people of your diasporic collectivity are the butchered names of dead people? Another witness told me the mispronunciations were followed by laughter, and a statement along the following lines: 'These people did not die in vain: they brought "us" together today.' While there have been many attempts to reclaim TDOR in the service of the lives and survival of trans women of colour, the event described by Meivi appeared untouched by them.

There is now a growing body of writings on how neoliberalism and the prison industrial complex affect trans people without race and class privileges. What is still rare, however, beyond isolated voices such as Janet Mock's, whose incisive and moving words I have cited above, is an interrogation of trans complicities. Abjected from the innocent romance of the gay kiss, I have argued, the trans subject has nevertheless gained significant currency as a result of its utility to the hate industry: the trans body's spectacular vulnerability to violence renders it the exemplary victim subject. Nevertheless, these biopolitical and necropolitical conversions do not accrue value equally to all trans people. Like queer love, trans vulnerability, too, becomes visible as a structure of feeling that produces affect aliens who may be mourned but are rarely missed.

CONCLUSION

I was at a friend's living room, all white people, there was a guy I had known for a while, he had just finished taking hormones: He is a cis-male now who was trans in the past. He had some spare medication at home which he didn't need any more. I said I'm having trouble finding a doctor who would give me health insurance. I'll buy them off you. And very kindly he gave them to me for free later on. The other white people in the room asked him to share some of his experiences as a white trans person in Berlin, he was living in Kreuzberg. So within maybe 4–5 minutes he started talking about how the

Turks in Kreuzberg and Neukölln were looking at him when he was walking on the street, make derogatory comments and so on. And I said 'Turks, what do you mean by Turks?' And then he said 'Oh yeah, and also the Arabs.' I went silent. There were three other people in the room … they all looked at me because they knew that what he said was disgusting, and they knew that I would have a problem with him. And I mean I'm not stupid, I saw their eyes, and they were saying 'Let it go,' that his pain is more valuable, needs to be more visible than mine. So I let it go, but it built. So a week later I said to the other three, 'Do you know how fucked up that was? When he was narrating that transphobic experience in the street, how does that construct my own experience as a trans Arab? It means I'm transphobic. And if you're giving out medals, he has a right to talk about transphobic experiences in the street, then honey give me some medal.' … So they were talking about white injury at the expense of perpetrating another injury in the same room, and rendering that completely unspeakable. (Charlie Abdullah Haddad)

I end with this statement by Charlie Haddad as it helps me make sense of the processes that have enabled some queer narratives to find a public while others get trapped in queer living rooms (or under queer tongues). The 'experiences' that are described here do not give us unmediated access to violence against 'trans people', 'queers of colour' or other newly desirable subject positions that have become recognisable under conditions of gay imperialism and homonationalism (see SUSPECT 2010a). Rather, Charlie's re-telling of different scenes of violence – the street, the queer living room – invites us to question the very economies and relations of production, circulation and exchange through which truths about violence are manufactured and attachments to scenes and states of injury occur.

This re-telling enables us to understand violence narratives as materially impactful forces that generate and distribute bio-value. Formerly degenerate subjects find speakability, visibility, publicity and vitality in front of publics and counter-publics that come together for the first time on a racialised terrain populated by violent, criminal and *criminally homophobic* bodies, whose degenerate properties are much harder to contest. 'Gay-friendly Berlin' takes shape in affective landscapes and biopolitical narratives of 'Kreuzberg and Neukölln' as the 'dangerous' inner city that belongs to 'Turks…. Oh yeah, and also Arabs.' Yet the circulation of queer bodies and intimacies is uneven. While some bodies become visible in this built environment, others disappear from view. And while some stories roll off tongues easily, others are best let go. The ones that body forth are current and become currency, in Adi Kuntsman's (2009b) terms. They are rewarded, gain 'medals' as Charlie puts it. They accumulate bio-value by converting the suffering queer body into a resource whose energies (increasing along with the severity of injury) can be extracted to accumulate capital.

Nevertheless, if the promise of inclusion is made to many, the returns yielded from these 'intimate investments', as Agathangelou et al. (2008) might say, are not the same from all queer starting points. Charlie's statement brings to the fore how the transgender body, whose ascent from the prison and the asylum is painfully recent and incomplete, becomes interesting within a changing landscape shaped by gentrification, 'war on terror', and moral panics over crime and integration. Long excessive to 'LGB-fake-T' politics, its spectacular proximity to death (as the always already injured or dying target of hate) makes it the ideal victim subject. This complicates earlier theorisations of wounded attachments and traumatised citizenship.

Wendy Brown's (1993) argument, introduced earlier, that claims to recognition are often made in the cadence of the wound is helpful, especially in understanding the global purchase of hate crime activism as the latest single-issue politics.[14] Nevertheless, wounded performances do different work for different bodies. In the place of a universally injured subject, it may be more helpful to examine the conditions under which some 'injuries' become spectacular while others appear self-inflicted or banal. This is well-illustrated by the changing landscape of transgender recognition which, as Charlie demonstrates, does not open equally to all trans people. While it invites some as experts, consultants and coalition partners, often those who happen to be least vulnerable to violence as a result of their race and class privileges and professional qualifications, trans people of colour become even less able to tell stories that attain the status of the political. They are capacitated mainly in their (social or actual) deaths. According to Charlie, a trans Arab who refuses to authenticate a racist aetiology of violence has no value in this exchange system. In the absence of a queer community that is willing to consider racialised trans (especially trans-feminine) lives as vulnerable and trans women of colour as coalition partners, to describe oneself in the terms of queer injury would constitute a failed performance. In the structure of feeling that is the queer living room, to raise one's voice and participate in violence talk would only mean to risk losing fragile ground. There, violence and anti-violence talk follow a racialised binary of perpetrators (non-trans people of colour) versus victims (white trans people), where to be a trans Arab means to be 'transphobic'.[15]

Indeed, as we shall explore next, the case of the U.S., where hate crime laws already exist, shows that gender non-conforming people of colour who experience violence rarely receive protection from the criminal 'justice' system but are more likely to be criminalised themselves.[16] The policing of multiple forms of violence extends to the queer living room. Sharing one's experiences of them not only fails to elicit empathy but makes one sound mean, incoherent and undeserving of community. For queer and trans people of colour, anti-racist, anti-violence talk can land us in a corner where we are forced to watch the space around us contract, at multiple scales: from the gender non-conforming body to the queer living room to the gentrifying neighbourhood. In this economy of anti-/violence, value and pathology are not distributed randomly but follow the powerful lines where populations are carved out, resources (from hormones to housing) distributed, and chances of life and death extended or withheld.

3

HATE[1]

In her lecture 'Death and rebirth of a movement: Queering critical ethnic studies', Cathy Cohen (2010) tentatively opens up the possibility that from the ashes of white conservative LGBT movement another queer politics and theory might arise. This movement would be accountable to young people of colour who, in a neoliberal context of neglect, militarisation and institutional and interpersonal violence, are prepared for premature death (see Gilmore 2007), regardless of their sexual and gender identity. In calling for such a 'politics that springs from the lives of folks of color' (2010: 131), Cohen once again challenges both the identitarian assumptions of an institutionalised and professionalised movement that requires lives worthy of survival to look queer, and the post-identity claims of a queer canon whose default stance towards racialised subjects is one of indifference or competition.

Given this lack of accountability, it may be unsurprising that the setting for Cohen's intervention is a critical ethnic studies conference rather than a queer or gender studies setting. This reminds me of the stakes involved in doing radical queer of colour scholarship in variously disciplined spaces.[2] While gender studies is expanding in ways that often repeat rather than interrupt the harnessing of dominant women's and LGBT movements to the projects of nation and empire, ethnic studies is facing a brutal backlash, despite some of its gatekeepers' attempts to perform themselves as respectable multicultural citizens. As critical ethnic studies is reinvented as an insurgent knowledge formation that resists rather than diversifies capitalism, colonialism and imperial war, it enters into possibility as a site for anti-racist queer and trans scholarship.[3]

One of the dominant political methods that Cohen singles out, besides marriage and gays in the military, is hate crime activism. She thus echoes Yasmin Nair's (2008) humorous characterisation of gay equality campaigns as the 'usual Holy Trinity of Hate Crimes Legislation, Marriage, and Don't Ask Don't Tell'. Both join a steadily swelling chorus of voices that critique the hate crime paradigm, now one of the top issues for LGBT movements globally, for strengthening a criminal 'justice' system that disproportionately targets people who are poor, of colour, or unable or unwilling to conform to norms and standards around gender, sexuality, health and consumption. These critical voices have so far been limited to the US, currently the leading exporter of punitive methods and technologies (e.g. Conrad 2012; Spade 2011; Spade and Willse 2000). The experience there suggests that those categorised as needing protection from violence often end up criminalised themselves for supposed hate crimes against whites, heterosexuals and other structurally more powerful people (Bassichis and Spade 2014; Smith 2007b, 2011). As trans and queer of colour organisations like the Audre Lorde Project, FIERCE, Gender Just and the Sylvia Rivera Law Project have shown, this is compounded for sexually and gender non-conforming people who are poor and of colour (e.g. Sylvia Rivera Law Project et al. 2009). For many, this was amply demonstrated by the fate of CeCe MacDonald, an African-American transgender woman who was first violently attacked and then sentenced to prison after her attacker died in the ensuing fight. Similar criminal *in*justice was done to the New Jersey 7, a group of Black lesbians who likewise defended themselves and were subsequently, all but one, sentenced to prison (see Incite! 2008; Support CeCe n.d.).

Nevertheless, what I call the hate/crime paradigm – the 'sticking', in Sara Ahmed's (2004a) terms, of criminality and pathology to bodies and populations that are always already seen as hateful, where *hate* functions as a racialised psy discourse – must be further unpacked. The German context, where terms like *Hasskriminalität* (hate crime) and *Hassgewalt* (hate violence) arrived very recently and are far from naturalised, may be instructive here. Until the late 2000s, violent homophobia was not primarily understood as the deed of hateful individuals or as something that is necessarily a cause for incarceration. Foregrounding a transnational race, gender and disability studies lens and placing it in critical dialogue with affect studies and scholarship on biopolitics and necropolitics, I argue that the hate/crime paradigm travels within a context where capital, identity moulds and carceral and biomedical methods cross borders instantly, while critiques and alternatives often do not.

This chapter examines how the hateful homophobe, who, in a north-west European context of war on terror and crime is immediately recognised as Muslim, arrived in close proximity with another figure of hate, the *Intensivtäter* – the multiple, chronic or 'intensive offender' – that is in turn forged in close hybridity with anti-Black methodologies that target poor, racialised communities in the US. In the late 1990s, he (sic) became the latest folk devil whose basic incapacity for empathy and integration (often figured as mental and physical deficiency) has produced consent not only for faster, harsher prison sentences for young people but also for the cultural exiling of barely nationalised populations from the realm of human intelligibility and entitlement.

By starting with the proximities and overlaps between sexual and criminal 'justice', carceral and biomedical discourses on hate, violence and crime, and racialised, perverse and mad figurations, we may approach the ascendancy of queer, multicultural and disabled subjects in a different way, one that abolishes rather than diversifies systems of murderous inclusion and frees us to perceive, formulate and strengthen radical alternatives.

HATE AS A PSY DISCOURSE

Many are now aware that the label 'criminal', including in its 'hateful' variation, is more likely to stick to racially and sexually oppressed people than on racists, homophobes and transphobes. Few, on the other hand, have asked how the label 'hate' may function in a similar way. This may be to do with the sense that 'people have fought for this', as a senior colleague from the US stated to a group of queers of colour and allies in Berlin, who asked what the recent arrival of the 'homophobic hate crime' discourse in Berlin might mean for racialised people. Even those who reject hate crime as a model of organising often partly remain within its logics. Thus while the *crime* part of 'hate crime' is sometimes debunked, its *hate* counterpart is rarely interrogated. While learning immensely from the compelling anti-violence methodologies formulated in radical women of colour and queer and trans of colour activisms in North America, including community accountability, prison abolition and transformative justice, I am struck by how 'hate' (now as 'hate *violence*' rather than 'crime') has survived as a rationale for much of this work.

My intention is not to dismiss these important responses that have taught me so much about community building against multiple forms of violence, including those carried out by the state as the most powerful bully of poor, racialised and gender non-conforming people. Rather, I wish to propose that we further expand our abolitionist imagination by asking how hate is ascribed in tandem with not only crime but also pathology, in ways that defend and expand not only the prison but also psychiatry and other institutions of 'care' and reform. In particular, I argue that hate always already emanates from racialised bodies and 'minds' in ways that call for their assimilation and segregation in the form of treatment, education, policing, confinement and deportation. In taking this further step and interrogating 'hate' alongside 'crime' and 'pathology' as twin pedagogies that educate us about the need for murderous systems of inclusion, we may draw on affect studies as a useful methodology to examine how meaning is ascribed to racialised bodies and populations. Particularly helpful to me is Sara Ahmed's argument that affect sticks to bodies differentially, producing affect aliens such as the 'melancholic migrant', who, in his backward orientation towards lost belongings and bad experiences, stands in the way of multicultural happiness (Ahmed 2004b, 2010). In considering the hateful Other as an affect alien who threatens a nostalgic vision of a violence-free community, I am further struck by the call for action that this figure demands from its onlookers. It appeals to authoritative intervention and thus demands a distinctly institutional critique. In particular, it is noteworthy that figures like the melancholic migrant, the Black rioter and the hateful homophobe invoke psychiatric authority – the diagnosing, profiling and 'treatment' of 'depressed,' 'schizophrenic' or otherwise 'maladjusted' populations, who are unable to control their impulses or function in a civilised society. Following insights by anti-racist disability and mad studies scholars, we can trace how the trope of the mental and physical inferiority of racialised populations has informed successive projects of colonialism, slavery, genocide and immigration, and continues to underwrite carceral, biomedical, military and other regimes of control and reform (Gorman 2013; Kanani 2011; Tam 2012).

In paying closer attention to the sites where bodies are sorted into populations according to evaluations of their 'stock', I am inspired by current engagements in critical race and ethnic studies, which interrogate how subjects and populations are carved out for life and death, often along older lines of degeneracy that must be understood within ongoing histories of racism, eugenics, colonialism and genocide, and the spatial practices of segregation, confinement and deportation that have arisen from them. Some of these engage with biopolitics and necropolitics in asking how racialised bodies become recognisable as those against whom, in Foucault's (2004 [1978]) words 'society must be defended'.

If this is more apparent with regard to death-making processes, it has equal purchase on the question of how subjects become viable for life, public visibility and citizenship. In our introduction to *Queer Necropolitics* (Haritaworn et al. 2014), Adi Kuntsman, Silvia Posocco and I note that the vitalisation of (white) queer subjects often stays close to the sites where queer and trans people were (and often continue to be, post-homo/transphobic claims to the contrary) sentenced to social or actual death. Gay assimilation requires an ascent from madness and criminality that is best performed as expertise over those who properly belong segregated. What might an abolitionist project look like that attends to 'caring' alongside more obviously punishing institutions and examines processes of exclusion alongside processes of 'murderous inclusion'?

Narratives of hate are instructive here. In the crime reports, activist writings and media texts on violent crime and homophobic hate crime that I review here, the two forms of crime regularly appear alongside each other as related labels invoked to profile working-class, racialised youth. They work at each other's service, making those marked as hateful – who fail at emotional management – appear destined to become violent, criminal and in need of punishment or reform. The hateful personality resembles the 'dangerous individual' described by Foucault (1978). In his reflection on the growing presence of psychiatric experts in court, Foucault noted a shift from the crime to the criminal, where what is punished is no longer something that has already happened but something that might happen in the future, a potential for harm that can be forecast by dissecting its carrier's inner workings. As Nikolas Rose and Dorothy Roberts have each observed, this is currently rehearsed with the rise of biopsychiatry and biocriminology, and the renewed attempt to identify future criminals by their genes or forebrains (Roberts 1993; Rose 2010; see also Breggin 1995). But while Roberts, from her Black feminist perspective, highlights the survival of scientific racism in discourses on crime in experiments on Black inner-city school children in the US, Rose, commenting on the same 'material' but from a purely Foucauldian perspective that misses race, comes to a different, somewhat optimistic conclusion. Unlike the older criminological figure of the 'born criminal', he argues, the new scholarship, about whose uses and abuses he remains partly open, is distinctly post-eugenics in that it only assumes a *potential* for violence which must first be triggered (see also Singh and Rose 2009).

I propose that this binary view of biology versus social construction, natural versus social science, nature versus nurture misses the point of how publics are seduced into viewing some as less than human and come to consent to their banishment from this category and its benefits. In fact, the personality profiles that I will review next are all designed to appear post-race and post-eugenics and distance themselves from purely biological explanations. In media case studies as in statistical reports, perpetrators are described as young men of colour who have suffered family violence, school exclusion, failed social mobility and discrimination. Moreover, marking the end of eugenics as the beginning of social constructionism becomes problematic when we revisit accounts by early twentieth-century eugenicists that already fused social and biological explanations and were less purely biologistic than we imagine today (see Halmi 2008). A more useful approach might therefore be to examine how seemingly opposite frameworks of nature versus nurture, punishment versus care (and we might add gays versus Muslims) combine to script racialised bodies as degenerate in ways that usher into consent highly diverse constituencies, including those that position themselves on the right side of power. Narratives of hate, which, as I will illustrate, is often described as an emotion that is both caused by harm and harm*ful*, are productive in this. Hate is similar to anger, whose oppressive ascriptions have been more widely explored and contested, including in anti-racist and feminist discussions of oppression and resistance to pathologisation (e.g. hooks 1996). Both are often described as responses to bad experiences and belittled as excessive, irrational and misplaced. Yet, unlike hate, anger has also been described as a righteous reaction against oppression, as in this frequently cited Malcolm X statement: 'Usually when people are sad, they don't do anything. They just cry over their condition. But when they get angry, they bring about a change' (see Breitman 1994).[4] A prime gender studies example is the figure of the angry Black feminist, whose anger is celebrated and glorified even as those who are interpellated this way are also regularly demonised and pathologised. Hate, in contrast, lacks positive connotations and reclamations. It is seemingly irredeemable and, though constantly explained in proliferating aetiologies, it characterises the humanly inexplicable.

I will explore how case studies of violent perpetrators nevertheless often take the generic form of empathy narratives, honing in on evidence of child abuse, poverty, discrimination and other 'bad experiences' that at first sight look like understandable reasons to feel bad. Nevertheless, if the causes of hate are understandable, the hateful reaction and subsequent action are not, rendering them immediately atrocious. This serves to rewrite the old chain of race, class and crime as one of present or absent empathy with suffering. To hate is to reveal one's impulsiveness and irrationality as well as one's failure to perform oneself as a civilised subject who has the capacity to master hir destructive impulses, empathise with others' pain, and prove hir potential for change.

In the personality profiles that follow, the hateful perpetrator appears as the constitutive outside to the neoliberal citizen, who manages and is able to talk about hir feelings, and expresses and takes responsibility for hirself, thus constantly striving towards emotional intelligence, communication and self-actualisation (see Rose 1989). If this is a strategy of classification through which, as Beverley Skeggs (2010) argues, the white middle class distinguishes itself from the reformable white working class, the racialised perpetrator remains uncultivable. Hir hate is a failure to love and forgive, to perform hirself according to the Christian values of an avowedly secular community and as a peaceful subject in times of war. Indeed, in the personality profiles and unassailable statistical regression analyses that I will examine, one's propensity to crime rises with one's degree of religiosity for Muslims but not for Christians, as the love of thy neighbour renders the latter more peaceful and tolerant.

Is it a coincidence that hate has become a Muslim property, that it is gaining currency as the bulk of the racialised in north-west Europe are re-cast as Muslim, as one globally interchangeable population (see Yıldız 2009)? What bodies appear as hateful in different times and places? In the German texts that I examine below, English-speaking studies of crime that have been formulated in the anti-Black context of the US are effortlessly assimilated into an anti-Muslim framework that is itself highly transnational.[5] How do the hateful criminal and the hateful homophobe each bring home globalised spectres of Muslim terror and Muslim rage, re-posing the seemingly unanswerable question 'Why do they hate us so much?' for diverse constituencies and at various scales? As I shall explore next, the figure of the hateful Other has also been key to the dual emergence of a respectable queer subject who is innocent and worthy of inclusion and recognition, and of a gay-friendly community that is willing to protect it.

THE HATEFUL HOMOPHOBE AND THE INTENSIVE OFFENDER

I sometimes show my students two YouTube videos, next to each other, in the same projection.[6] One is from the year 2007 and is a TV news clip based on closed-circuit camera shots. It is on the 'Serkan A. and Spyridon L. case' which, true to its status as a 'case', served to familiarise German TV audiences with a new figure of moral panic: the *Intensivtäter* (intensive or repeat offender), a thus far administrative category whose punitive application and criminalising impact on young people of colour has been compared to the 'three strikes' policy in the US.[7] As Lauren Berlant (2007) notes 'the case' is pedagogical and exemplary in that it offers 'an account of the event and of the world', and is the primary communicative action through which biopower, in the name of experts, sorts individuals into populations. The case is also crucial to moral panics over crime, which, according to Julia Oparah (formerly Sudbury 2005), need offending bodies primarily in order to demonstrate the need for tough action regardless of actual crime numbers. This is also the case with Serkan A. and Spyridon L., who beat up an old white man on the Munich subway just before Christmas. The media describe the victim as a frail pensioner who tells the judge: 'I have been a teacher my whole life and then ...' (Arnsperger 2008). For months, the act is replayed on TV with an intensity and brutality that has its own performative force (see Ahmed 2004a). It is central in manufacturing consent for faster, harsher sentences for young people and leads to debates about whether 'criminal children' who bring us to the 'end of our patience' (in the words of Judge Kirsten Heisig [2010], whom the moral panic made a media star) should be put in closed homes or education camps. This is the second famous *Intensivtäter* case after the 'Mehmet case', which, in November 2001, produced consent for the deportation of children born and raised in Germany who, until then, had secure status. Both are spectacular cases in Ruthie Gilmore's (1999) sense: their dramatic mediatisation creates consent for new instruments of criminalisation even as crime statistics are falling.[8] But while fewer youth offend, the criminal energy of these 'terrible few' is so intense that 'we' have to act quickly. Both hate and intensity produce an affective urgency that justifies quick and ruthless intervention.

The other video is called *CCTV* (*Überwachungskamera*). It also shows a terrible attack by young people marked as poor and racialised, this time against two white men who are kissing in a night-time parking lot. Unlike the first, *CCTV* is no documentary but an advertising film for a local gay anti-violence NGO called Maneo (also author of some of the posters and kiss-ins discussed in chapter two). It is shown at the Berlinale, on public television and in the advertising programme at Berlin cinemas. It precedes 'Serkan A. und Spyridon L.' by a year – yet its plot, visualities and technologies bear uncanny resemblances to this 'case'. The hateful Other exists even before the figure finds its bodies and materialises into the very action it has been fore/cast to perpetrate.

In the videos, the homophobic migrant and the intensive offender look identical. They are recognised through the same forensic media and the same affective scripts. The frail pensioner and the bashed gay men slide into one sentimentalised, white, victim subject. Their interchangeability is confirmed by a growing army of experts who loyally repeat each other. For example, the report *Violence Phenomena among Male, Muslim Youth with Migration Background* (Toprak and Nowacki 2010) cites the Simon study (2008), which is in turn commissioned by the biggest gay organisation LSVD (the Lesbian and Gay Association Germany) which designed and distributed the kissing posters discussed above. And when Judge Heisig, long the most prominent expert on the *Intensivtäter*, dies (first we hear by suicide, then at the hands of Arab family clans), both the LSVD and Maneo publish obituaries to a 'valuable partner and supporter' (Maneo 2010a).

In the Simon study, the LSVD press releases, the articles and special issues on the Drag Festival and the many reports on violent Muslim youth, the profile is near identical. To stylistically retrace the formulaic manner in which the hate/ intensive offender is profiled: He (sic) is *badly integrated* and *religious* but only where he can be construed as Muslim. The most influential of the violence reports, the Pfeiffer study (Baier et al. 2010), whose findings are disseminated through headlines such as 'Young, Muslim, brutal' (*Spiegel Online* 2010), goes to particular lengths to highlight, in typical post-Christian/secular and divide-and-rule manner, the positive effects of a Christian socialisation (including for Christians who are not white Germans) in *reducing* rather than *increasing* delinquent behaviour. Moreover, and synonymously, the hate/ intensive offender *is non-German*. For Pfeiffer and colleagues (Baier et al. 2010), school children who 'do not themselves have German nationality or were not born in Germany, or to whose biological parents the same applies' cannot call themselves German (2010: 12). But when they tick 'No' in answer to the question of whether they perceive themselves as German, they are classified as badly integrated. These studies are thus performative (Ahmed 2004a): they remind both participants and readers that Germanness equals whiteness. In a citizenship context that has only just let go of its blood principle and is, for the first time, softening the biological borders of its nationality law, this is crucial. The figure of the criminal (and the criminally homophobic) migrant is a central technique by which the border is forcefully redrawn.

The border runs not only through blood but also through space. The hateful/ intensive offender is described as coming from a 'rural-patriarchal family' (LSVD 2003). He is not from here, no matter how many generations have been here before him (see El-Tayeb 2011). He is described as investing in 'honour' and thus placed in fertile kinship with 'honour killers'. He is from 'problem neighbourhoods' or 'places of self-segregation', where 'immigrants form big proportions of the population' (Haug 2010; Ohder and Huck 2006: 60). These are the same areas that urban planners now praise for their 'good social mix' (TOPOS 2008; see Lees 2008 for a critique). To live there means something other to the immobile, racialised subject than to the mobile, white – including white queer – subject, whose arrival and displacement of dangerous bodies and intimacies is a symptom of the area's recovery and 'regeneration'.

The hate/intensive offender is further characterised by his pathological attachments. He has few 'German' (or, in Simon, 'homosexual') friends, his whole 'gang' is delinquent, which is further correlated to the fact that their language of communication is Turkish or Arabic (Baier et al. 2010: 64; Haug 2010: 69). If bilingualism was briefly celebrated as intercultural competence, it has now lapsed back into its older, deficient status. It signifies backwardness: it is a 'bad orientation' (in Sara Ahmed's terms) to bad objects, bodies, communities and places (Ahmed 2006).[9]

Another feature of the hate/intensive offender is his adherence to 'violence-legitimating masculinity norms' (*Gewalt-legitimierende Männlichkeitsnormen*, GLMN for short), which in the qualitative studies is generically scripted as the signifying chain of Oriental despotism: violent dad, submissive mom, no communication skills, no impulse control (Baier et al. 2010: 64; Toprak and Nowacki 2010: 61). How does this clunky new label, mystifyingly abbreviated as 'GLMN' serve to reformulate larger debates about the correlation between masculinity and violence? We might compare this account to feminist accounts of the family as a site where violence is normalised and gender difference is enforced and reproduced. While criminologists have long assumed a higher tendency to violence in 'boys' (that is, male-assigned children), this is rarely accompanied by a critique of male socialisation. On the contrary, formulae such as GLMN work to insulate violence in 'chronically delinquent' boys who can be profiled and segregated from 'regular' boys (Roth and Seiffge-Krenke 2011). Nevertheless, this distinction is not stable or secure, as shown by the ongoing attempt to find objective criteria to distinguish boys whose violence must be acted upon from those who are merely acting out and for whom violence is a 'normal' step on their 'normal' path to masculinity.[10] GLMN also offers new solutions to the old eugenicist problem of how to identify families that pass on violence. In particular, it is a variation on the old classist theme of the 'bad child from the bad family' (Rose 1989). But while, in the generalised trope, delinquent children spring from excessive gender *symmetry* (working mother and weak or missing father in the white or Black working-class family), in its Orientalised variant, the intensive offender results from excessive gender *difference* (weak mother, authoritarian father) (Toprak and Nowacki 2010: 61). As Black feminists and queer of colour critics have argued with regard to the 'cultures of poverty' thesis, which blamed Black and Latino families for producing dysfunctional children, racialised families are treated as sexually and gender non-conforming regardless of their apparent heterosexuality (e.g. Cohen 1997). And, as anti-racist disability theorists have shown, this 'disablist' view of racialised communities as deficient and as reproducing problematically rarely becomes legible through a lens of disablism (see Gorman 2013). The conceptualisation of violence as 'GLMN' thus serves both to repeat white middle-class, heteronormative, non-disabled reproduction as the uncontested norm and to normalise the everyday, banal violence through which categories of race, age, gender, disability and class are upheld.

Racism is also normalised and Orientalised in other ways. While both the hateful homophobe and the *Intensivtäter* are often discussed in terms of under-privileged, underachieving and failed masculinities, the *Intensivtäter*, as the older and better-researched figure, reflects this in greater detail. He (sic) lacks in 'structural integration' also measured as 'educational aspirations'. The high rate of children racialised as Muslim who leave school without qualifications is not the responsibility of one of the world's most class-differentiated educational systems but of deficient, uneducated parents who fail to 'integrate' their children.[11]

These failures are measured ever more imaginatively. Besides the tried and tested pathologisation of bilingualism, experts bemoan the fact that racialised parents doom their children to limited horizons, limited verbal and emotional skills, and limited social capital, by failing to play parlour games with them or to send them to *Schützenvereine* and *Trachtenvereine* (rifle and traditional costumes clubs) (Baier et al. 2010: 64; Toprak and Nowacki 2010: 61). Integration here becomes the nostalgic performance of a petty-bourgeois Germanness that exists mainly as a *Heimatfilm* fantasy.[12] If this parochial landscape seems an odd site for the reproduction of the globalised affects of neoliberal citizenship (imagine learning conflict resolution skills at the local rifle club!), this is in part enabled by the *Intensivtäter*'s spectacular performance as an affect alien, who is unable to talk about hir feelings and to express hirself other than through violence. He is the constitutive outside of a neoliberal citizen whose autonomy, self-responsibility and emotional intelligence are evidenced by hir capacity to constantly work on hirself (see Rose 1989; Skeggs 2010; Toprak and Nowacki 2010). This narrative is at least as much about the integration of the national into the transnational as about the integration of the migrant into the nation. The dis-integrating migrant, who is redundant to both the national and the global, becomes the container into which these trans/national anxieties are displaced, enabling the nation to globalise without losing its identity.

Besides his bad attachments to bad places and intimacies, the hate/intensive offender suffers from '*perceptions of discrimination*' (Haug 2010: 19). This 'trait' again brings home the workings of bio- and necropower in the invention of this population. Violence is always already in those thus labelled, as well as in anyone who could be caught in this extensive profile. It cannot happen to you; to mention or even perceive it in its most toned-down version (as 'discrimination' rather than racism) increases your risk of being criminalised as well as pathologised as paranoid. We can contextualise this with the punishable status of anti-racist discourse more generally. In Germany, use of the term 'racism' is largely confined to the 1933–45 era (see Barskanmaz 2011; Melter and Mecheril 2009). *Ausländerfeindlichkeit* (hostility against foreigners) has been a common euphemism which, nevertheless, psychologises and de-politicises racism as a somewhat natural reaction to 'foreign' bodies that are, by definition, outside of and antithetical to Germanness. Even this limited frame is turned on its head in the figure of the *Intensivtäter* and the wider debates about migration and integration that it has mediated. In these debates, the real problem, from which the 'politically correct' obsession with hostility against foreigners has apparently distracted us, is revealed to be 'hostility against Germans' (*Deutschenfeindlichkeit*) (Shooman 2011).[13] Set in the schoolyards of Kreuzberg and Neukölln, this drama lets the taboo word 'racism' finally enter the German language, but only to turn the victims into perpetrators and anti-oppression discourse into both completely unspeakable and punishable language. We must understand this drama in its institutional logics whose murderous orientation Angela Davis aptly sums up as the 'school-to-prison pipeline' (Davis 2003). In Germany, too, schools prepare many children for social death rather than enhancing their life chances and thus participate in what Liat Ben-Moshe (2010) calls the trans-institutionalisation of surplus populations between institutions of care, punishment and reform. This again intersects with the pathologisation of the political as *Deutschenfeindlichkeit* or homophobia, a term that queer scholars have often contested and yet continually repeat (see Bryant and Vidal-Ortiz 2008).

In the Simon study of 'migrant' versus 'German' school children, homophobia finally *becomes* a phobia – 'a psychological tendency to react to homosexuals with a negative evaluation', which includes 'negative affects or feelings, negative cognition and negative behavioural tendencies'.[14] The conversion of sexual oppression into a psychological problem of dysfunctional youth radically disappears from view the everyday and institutional stuff that makes the world, in so many ways, hard to survive for sexually and gender non-conforming people. Instead, it turns it into a property of deficient bodies who are precluded from life chances on the basis of their mental and physical 'traits'. The metonymy between the 'German' and the 'homosexual' victim is highly productive in sexually expanding and racially contracting a German identity that no longer needs to feel guilty for the Holocaust but, as chapter four explores in greater detail, itself becomes its victim. For gays, too, were persecuted, and the hatred of homosexuals carries the same names as the hatred of Germans: 'German pig', 'German whore', 'gay pig', 'pig eater' (Heyl et al. 2008; Schütz 2010; Schwab 2009).

In contrast to the hate crime debate, which loudly claims its historic heritage, the noisy hauntings of the wider violence debate remain unspeakable to the point of punishment. The intensive offender appears as a new phenomenon that requires new methodologies. The spatial and cultural typology of the patriarchal family in the ghetto is joined by a multitude of statistics that correlate an 'integration index', 'religiosity scale' and other 'factors of influence' (such as 'violence in the family', 'family in proximity to poverty' and 'life in disadvantaged housing areas') in countless regression analyses.[15] The numbers thus produced must be understood in a historical context that simultaneously birthed racism, eugenics and statistics as kindred 'white logic[s] and white methods'. As Zuberi and Bonilla-Silva's (2008) collection of the same name demonstrates, these indeed have the same fathers in scientists such as Francis Galton.

The memory of this history enables us to understand violence narratives and their numerologies in their racist, classist and eugenicist echoes, as well as in their transnational travels. This is why seemingly disparate and parochial 'debates' such as the (currently revived) 'culture of poverty' thesis in the US and the crime and integration panics in north-west Europe produce easily transposable explanations that nevertheless appear intrinsically local and authentic.[16] How might we turn around the gaze and begin to travel, too, borrowing analytics that help us come to grips with these highly mobile racist scripts of bodies, minds and spaces? For example, Sherene Razack's analysis of race, space and Canadian settler colonialism has purchase for the European inner city. In Razack's analysis, the racialised inner city and the reservation are cast as degenerate spaces producing degenerate bodies: the Indigenous and racialised people who live there are always already cause and origin of violence (both in the figure of the racialised perpetrator and in that of the non-rapeable woman of colour) (see Razack 2002a, 2002b). Race, class, gender and colonial violence thus disappear and become utterly unremarkable, self-inflicted phenomena which naturally inhabit racialised bodies and their surroundings.

PROFILING THE *INTENSIVTÄTER*

The search for the *Intensivtäter* does not stop at constructionist explanations. Besides being a focus of criminological, sociological and pedagogical expertise, he is also the subject of psychologists and psychiatrists.[17] In the descriptions of the psy experts, he becomes a type, a personality profile, a genus. No longer at stake is the punishment of deeds that have already been done. In risk profiles, 'at-risk' children aged 5 or younger are prepared for 'early detection'. This is Foucault's shift from the crime to the criminal. In the collection *Intensive Adolescent Offenders: Interdisciplinary Perspectives*, a youth psychiatrist (Huck 2011) complains that the *Diagnostic and Statistical Manual* of the American Psychiatric Association (*DSM*, which long included homosexuality and 'gender identity disorder', and still lists many queer and trans practices and identities as mental disorders) has no diagnosis specifically for intensive offenders. At the same time, the existing *DSM*, whose menu of diagnoses has grown exponentially since its first edition (from 60 to soon over 400), is invoked continually. Among the existing labels, Attention Deficit Hyperactivity Disorder (ADHD) and Anti-Social Personality Disorder (ASPD) are cited repeatedly.

While a genealogy of these diagnoses is beyond the scope of this chapter, both resound heavily with eugenicist spectres of degeneracy and are deeply raced and classed in their application. Rachel Gorman describes hyperactivity as the successor of 'moral imbecility', which was frequently diagnosed in children of colour considered 'turbulent, vicious, rebellious to all discipline; they lack sequence of ideas and probably power of attention' (2013: 275).[18] More harmlessly, it seems, the *Intensivtäter* debate invokes ADHD as a prognostic tool to spot future chronic delinquents as 'difficult babies' (Roth and Seiffge-Krenke 2011: 256). In North America, the widespread diagnosing of ADHD and commonplace medicating of children has been linked with the aggressive marketing of pharmaceutical companies (Breggin 2007). The expansion of this diagnosis into unsaturated European markets must be observed against the background of a medical industrial complex which capacitates bodies anew (Puar 2011). We must ask how the medical industrial complex, as many working on the intersection of race and disability have shown, 'treats' bodies differentially (Hutson 2009; Roberts 1997: 97). We must further interrogate how it renders surplus populations productive beyond their labour power. In the context of neoliberal racism, bodies labelled chronically delinquent are – not incidentally – those affected disproportionately by the exodus of manufacturing and the resulting mass unemployment.[19]

This is also apparent in the second diagnosis cited in the *Intensivtäter* debate: Anti-Social (or Asocial or Dissocial) Personality Disorder. On the checklist of this diagnosis are 'traits' such as 'failure to conform to social norms', 'lack of the capacity for empathy', 'irresponsibility and disregard for social norms', 'impulsiveness', 'low threshold for discharge of aggression, including violence' and 'incapacity to experience guilt'.[20] Here the carceral and the biomedical are intertwined in a manner that recalls older eugenicist notions of the innate criminal – and personality disorders are generally considered 'incurable'. In the words of two psychologists in the same collection, who support the view that chronically delinquent youth represent their own 'type' (the 'LCP' or 'life course persistent' type), it can 'hardly be assumed that individuals of the LCP type will learn pro-social behaviours as adults' (Roth and Seiffge-Krenke 2011: 255–56). Both chapters cite the increasingly popular brain and gene theories which treat violence as hereditary. This may occur either biologically or socially – aggressiveness can also be caused by violent damage to the head!

Recalling the debate over the born versus socialised criminal, this logic fuses not only nature and nurture but also science and Christian morality: the frontal brain is the seat of both impulse control and conscience. It also brings to mind the scandals over proposals to experiment on children in Black and Latino neighbourhoods in the US in the name of preventing violence and rioting, and the recurrent calls for brain scans and gene tests to 'screen and intervene' (Rose 2010).[21] In the UK, researchers have begun to assemble risk profiles that include 'bio-markers' alongside social factors such as alcoholism, poverty, experiences of violence and ethnicity, and may soon become available to judges, teachers and doctors for diverse purposes.[22]

Again, a transnational perspective is important here. While the German experts rely heavily on the English-speaking literature on ASPD, which interchangeably describes an 'anti-social', 'dissocial' or 'asocial' type, I have not so far spotted the term *asozial* in the German literature, possibly because this was the exact term that the Nazis used to mark poor people, sexual deviants and Rroma and Sinti for sterilisation or internment. Nevertheless, we can take Sherene Razack's thoughts on the degeneracy of racialised bodies and spaces – which are only ever perceptible as origins and never as targets of violence – further by attending to the return of explicit eugenics to Germany: from the racist theory of German politician Thilo Sarrazin (2010) that people of Turkish origin have lower and Jewish people higher IQs, which hit the headlines around the same time as the *Intensivtäter* panic and is cited in the debate on the panic over the 'cultural practice' of cousin marriage and violence reports that open with demographic prognoses about the disproportionate growth of migrant populations (Haug 2010).

These are narratives of decline which locate the social and biological downfall of the nation in the reproduction of racialised populations. Following queer of colour theorists such as Rod Ferguson and Cathy Cohen, we may juxtapose these improper heterosexualities with queer investments in reproduction and regeneration through figures such as gay marriage, rainbow families and the queer lover who comes to life in the shadow of the degenerate bodies and the regenerating buildings of the gentrifying ghetto. The vitalisation of the queer subject is necropolitical in that it occurs in or close to the very death worlds from which Others are ghosted (Haritawornet al. 2013, 2014; Mbembe 2003).

The queer subject's new vitality contrasts with the inescapably asocial heritage of the *Intensivtäter*. So far, this appears to occur in a random rather than a systematic manner. A study by Ohder and Huck (2006), a criminologist and a psychologist who reviewed files kept of youth with this label at the prosecution service in Berlin, highlights constructionist explanations but suddenly begins to list the 'physical', 'mental' and 'social conspicuities' of the surveyed individuals. These include: 'speaking impairment (stammering, mute)', 'motoric conspicuity (hyperactivity, coordination problems)', 'chronic visible physical conspicuity (stunted growth, limping)', 'brain organic conspicuity (early-childhood brain damage, Down syndrome, epilepsy)', 'conspicuities with harm of others ("extraversion") [or] of self ("introversion")', '(delusional) distortion of perception', 'running away from home', 'prostitution' and 'suicide attempts' (Ohder and Huck 2006: 60).[23]

While the figure of the *Intensivtäter* has disability, class and race written all over it, his innate deficiency – physical and mental inferiority, poverty, social and sexual deviance, a criminal, mad or alcoholic genealogy – distinguishes him from the recognisably disabled subject, the homonormative subject, the reformable working-class subject and the good multicultural subject. The hate/ intensive offender remains ungrievable in this landscape of commemoration and the futures that open up from it. While his prognosis seems bleak he is at first sight also an object of care and reform. In media representations of hate/ violence, offenders' own experiences of abuse are described with apparently sensitive detail. Toprak, thus far cited as an expert of the *Intensivtäter*, is in the aftermath of the Drag Festival debate invited to apply his tried and tested diagnostics to hateful homophobes, who indeed stem from the identical suspect group. In an interview in the Berlin queer magazine *Siegessäule*, he states:

> Similarities consist in offenders' difficulties to talk about their emotions. They never learned to talk about their inside and to resolve conflicts, since this isn't considered masculine. (Toprak 2011: 15)

Serkan A. and Spyridon L., the well-mediatised *Intensivtäter* case discussed above, have likewise suffered. Serkan A.'s father is violent, his mother mentally ill. Serkan A. was in a children's home, Spyridon L. in a youth psychiatric institution. Yet 'our' empathy contrasts with their emotional coldness, as in the following profile of Serkan A. in *Stern* magazine:

> The Munich crime policemen were speechless faced with such coldness. Psychologists speak of a shallowing of affect. [A violence researcher is cited:] 'These youth have difficulty talking about their feelings. We don't know if it's a deficit in language or a deficit in experience.' (Doinet et al. 2008)

This empathy narrative nevertheless orients us away from Serkan A. 'Our' empathy with him contrasts with his lack of empathy, his utter lack of emotion, which is firmly rooted in him. His dismissal from the realm of humanity and the humanly intelligible nevertheless occurs in the name of reform. The pedagogues and masculinity researchers, in particular, occupy themselves with the question of how we may teach the intensive offender, in spite of everything, to manage his anger and his hatred and develop empathy for his victims (see Ohder and Huck 2006). 'Our' speechlessness nevertheless already points towards the futility of such attempts.[24] As 'we' are left to join the dots, the question that comes to the fore is, indeed, whether well-meaning efforts may not be completely wasted on young minds so deeply steeped in hate.

CONCLUSION: TOWARDS AN ABOLITIONIST IMAGINATION

What lessons are there in thinking through the queer metonymies of sexual and criminal justice, carceral and biomedical knowledges, and racialised, perverse and mad figurations that I have traced in this article? Beginning with a queer of colour critique of queer whiteness, I have ended up with an institutional critique that is inspired by an abolitionist imagination of (in Angela Davis's words) 'a world without prisons – or at least a social landscape that is no longer dominated by the prison' (Davis and Rodriguez 2000: 218). This abolitionist imagination must extend to psychiatric and other institutions of 'care' in ways that resist nostalgic longings for a welfare state that, for racialised people, was always ambivalent.[25] In the place of any wishful thinking that young people labelled violently hateful are simply in the 'wrong institution', we should attend to the symbiotic relationship between punitive, biomedical and other 'helping' apparatuses, each of which serves to administer surplus populations that, profiled by one, become recognisable to the other. This is especially relevant for racialised and colonised populations, whose conformity to white norms (especially of gender and sexuality) and identities has always been the remit of experts of punishment as well as of psychiatrists and other experts of 'care' (see Chan et al. 2005; Vergès 1999).

Besides understanding the close relationship between criminalisation and pathologisation across multiple formal and institutional sites,[26] an abolitionist imagination might also involve attending to the way punitive and pathologising logics undergird informal sites, including those that identify as alternative, radical or progressive. I have suggested anti-violence organising against *hate* as one such site, which, given the global spread of hate crime activism and the twin carceral and biomedical paradigms that undergird it, demands a transnational critique.

I propose that hate is a problematic sign to organise under for several reasons. First, describing violence as hatefully motivated partly misses the point. What of the many acts of violence accompanied by glee or solidarity with others rather than by hate and lack of empathy? The most powerful face of violence may indeed not be hateful at all but indifferent and neglectful towards those who must have inflicted it upon themselves or appear unworthy in a meritocratic system that will give you equal opportunities if only you try hard enough. Hate thus has the same individualising, depoliticising tendencies as neoliberal discourse overall. Most worryingly, its usefulness as an anti-violence method is limited by its tendency to stick to racialised bodies that are unable to perform a global multicultural citizenship fit for neoliberal subjectivity, to borrow from Jodi Melamed (2011). It serves as the latest descriptor of disposable populations marked as monocultural, irrational, backward, criminal, patriarchal *and homophobic*. Besides producing consent for ever more dehumanising measures and representations, the figure of the hateful Other also becomes the ground against which all racialised people must perform conformity to our oppression. I have described it here as a psy discourse that disciplines, but it is also a productive ingredient of governmentality in that it incites us to become docile subjects who labour hard to not appear hateful when confronted with dehumanisation.

While critiquing victim/subjectivity as a political paradigm, my analysis complicates an account of injury as universally experienced and mobilised. For example, Wendy Brown's (1993) discussion of the 'wounded attachments' of dominant identity politics is helpful in explaining the global purchase of hate/crime.[27] Nevertheless, the drama of queer lovers and hateful Others brings to the fore the differential status and effects of these figures of violence and anti-violence. How do narratives of injury perform different work depending on their authors? Why do trauma narratives attached to homornormative victim/subjects circulate at such volume and speed while experiences of racism, poverty or police violence remain unspeakable and unremarkable? To return to Charlie Haddad's sobering analysis, how do white transgender injuries become grounds for citizenship claims while trans of colour injuries must be managed in private, buried under the tongue, because to voice them would be to lose one's small claim to queer community and the meagre resources that come with it? The examined personality profiles bring home the immense pressures on the survivors of race and class oppression to present themselves as unscathed by it, and to bear it as its containers and recipients.

In formulations of queer necropolitics that go beyond a happy inclusion framework of sexual citizenship, the paradox of who must die so that 'we' can live (or rather, who must live so that 'they' can be killed with impunity) is clearly brought to the fore. While focusing on the forces that are death-making, we must simultaneously ask what a queer and trans politics would look like that genuinely fosters survival, a task that may well begin with race and class oppression rather than with hetero- or even homonormativity. Such a politics would create spaces where safety is not won by bolstering regimes of exploitation and neglect, and where the violence of the most powerful becomes a bigger scandal than the acts of those subjugated, who need not be innocent in order to deserve solidarity and for whom healing and transformation would take much more than the diversification of the unbearable status quo.

4

QUEER NOSTALGIA

The drama of queer lovers and hateful Others is simultaneously a narrative of time. In 2008, the Memorial to the Homosexuals Persecuted under National Socialism was inaugurated in Tiergarten park in Berlin Mitte, a stone's throw from the Holocaust Memorial, which pre-dates it by three years. A staple landmark on the queer visitor's sightseeing tour, the 'Homo Memorial', as it is endearingly anthropomorphised, has assumed a privileged place in the commemoration of the Nazi past as both ultimate evil of racial and sexual oppression and mythical origin of a global LGBT community.

This chapter examines the campaign for, and the aesthetic and affective qualities of, the memorial as performances of a presentism that restages the drama of queer lovers and hateful Others as a repetition of an atrocious past that is finding new incarnations in racialised populations that terrorise queers in the present. Drawing on writings on queer temporality alongside intersectional historiographies of National Socialism, which question the privileging of the concentration camp as the most important site of queer oppression, I argue that these commemorations of past terror ironically work to bolster murderous logics in the present.

As so often in dominant historiographies, this is reflected both in who is remembered and in who gets to do the remembering. As many have pointed out, scripts of the Nazi past rehearse a narrow range of permissible memories, acts and affects. The correct memory goes along with a correct affect: a white non-Jewish German guilt that is unattainable to those facing racism in the present. Not incidentally, the bodies that are made to bear the residue of anti-Semitism are the same that contain the residue of homophobia. The disposability of racialised youth is thus confirmed in yet another register.

The chapter argues that these acts of remembrance do more than merely grieve or work through traumatic pasts, as debates on temporality often assume. Rather, their desire for the past has become a dominant political orientation. I term this orientation queer nostalgia: an active investment in murderous times and places that the nostalgic subject ostensibly seeks to overcome.

PEDAGOGIES OF THE PAST

How do contemporary agendas of LGBT inclusion, visibility and recognition invoke the past? Much scope remains to harness queer temporality as a methodology to grapple with this moment of murderous inclusion, and to further think about the distinction between valuable subjects and pathological populations. Writers have given us various tools, including critiques of progress, anachronism, teleological time, and homonormative time telling; debates about futurity and non-consequential time; relationships between presentism and whiteness, and between affect and memorialisation; and a radical re-thinking of what forms of violence even reach the status of an event (Dinshaw et al. 2007; Edelman 2004; Freccero 2007; Freeman 2007, 2010; Muñoz 2007; Povinelli 2008; Puar 2007). For example, queer remembrance practices are thoroughly inscribed with a presentist identity politics that interprets the past according to contemporary conceptions of sexuality (see Freccero 2007). Furthermore, critiques of teleological time have helped us debunk the narrative of linear time that locates LGBT and other social movements on a march of progress from a terrible past to a just future (Puar 2007). How can we use these tools to render scandalous a view of Black, Indigenous, Muslim, Arab, Asian, Rroma, African, Caribbean and Eastern European genders and sexualities (depending on who the significant Other is) as backward, overpopulated, underdeveloped; deficient, criminal, pathological; patriarchal, homophobic, transphobic; failed masculine, feminine, heterosexual; undeserving and in need of control? How can we tell the time of LGBT inclusion in a way that renders imaginable futures that are more than extensions of the murderous present? What is at stake in identifying 'this moment'? As critiques of the homonationalism debate have shown (see Puar 2013), it is necessary to revisit 'the event' – from the war on terror to neoliberalism – in a way that acknowledges colonialism and slavery as the architectures, as Sunera Thobani (2014) might say, that give rise to globalised frameworks of LGBT inclusion.

The past orientation of queer regeneration, however, goes beyond a mere sorting of bodies along a backward/progressive continuum. The following pages trace the past – and the bodies and spaces that appear stuck in it – as a terrain of *queer nostalgia* that white subjects, far from trying to get away from it, have actively sought out and invested in. In contemporary mobilisations, the past figures multiply, ambivalently and contradictorily: it takes us back to an imagined community before assimilation, when 'we' had more meaningful things to do than shop and party. It promises, maybe, the resurgence of times that were more radical and 'real'. Progress, ironically, involves a continual return to the past. This repeated move across time expands the horizon of liberation (and liberalism) to places and communities that must need it and want it in the face of the rights gained here and wrongs done there. 'Our' past is like 'their' present, and thus predestines 'us' to act on 'their' behalf. This is illustrated in the description of the Hirschfeld-Eddy Foundation, a subsidiary of the Lesbian and Gay Association (LSVD) that is currently expanding to do development work in the 'South' and the 'East'. The foundation's name fuses the names of homosexual Jewish German sexologist Magnus Hirschfeld, who died in 1935 in exile, and Fannyann Eddy, a lesbian activist who was killed in 2004 in her home country Sierra Leone (Hirschfeld-Eddy-Stiftung n.d.). When, in 2008, a part of the Spree river bank is named after Hirschfeld, a speaker of the foundation states that 'Germany has a special responsibility to advocate for the rights of homosexuals and transgenders' (Queer.de 2008). Notably, the exceptional past that is invoked in order to justify German involvement in Africa in the present is not that of past German involvement in Africa.

The past is thus a fertile site for queer investment and indeed regeneration. The drama of queer lovers and hateful Others is a narrative of time that maps its subject and object onto present/future and past respectively. While the queer lover heralds a progressive love that knows no gender or colour, the homophobic 'foreigner'/'Turk'/'Muslim' figures as a racialised surplus that drags us back into a past that s/he (archaic, patriarchal, rural) never left. If the past enters into the hateful Other, the reverse is also true: in texts about the past, the hateful Other makes a foreboding (or afterboding) appearance that warns of atrocities that will repeat themselves if action is not taken now. If, as we saw in the last chapter, hate crime has been fast assimilated into local history, globalising LGBT hate crimes protections are 'invented' as local 'traditions' – to borrow from Hobsbawm (1983) – of women-and-gay-friendliness, even where local languages literally still lack words for them. 'Our' past and 'their' racialised presents (and presences) thus slide into each other.

This is compellingly demonstrated by Gloria Wekker's (2009) discussion of homonostalgia. Writing on the Netherlands, whose dominant identity as a 'free' and 'tolerant' forerunner with regard to gay rights is confirmed by its status as the first country to fully legalise gay marriage, Wekker observes that nostalgia for a better past has become a dominant structure of feeling in white Dutch gay communities. She illustrates this with a 2002 public statement by Pim Fortuyn, the infamous far-right gay politician, that 'Islam is a backward culture' and that he 'doesn't feel like re-doing the emancipation of women and gays'. The happy past of Dutch liberalism is periodised as the time before immigration: 'the good old days when there were no Muslims yet' (Wekker 2009: 1). This account of Dutch homonostalgia ironically throws into question the dominant narrative of the Netherlands as a long-standing forerunner in terms of LGBT inclusion. Thus, the LGBT-friendliness of Dutch nationalism requires relativisation: if things could be better, it's because they *were* better in the mythical past. Just as the idealised past has its constitutive cut-off point in immigration, the gay-friendly community has its constitutive outside in Muslims who are always already not-from-here.

Wekker's observation of nostalgia as a positive account of the past interestingly departs from a more common focus on melancholia, mourning, grieving, trauma and loss in queer and other scholarships (see Freeman 2007). In the introduction to their collection *Loss: The Politics of Mourning*, Eng and Kazanjian (2003) call for a politics of loss and mourning that engages a range of 'twentieth century losses', including genocide, slavery, lynching, AIDS and apartheid, from the 'perspective of what remains' (Eng and Kazanjian 2003: 2, 5). Drawing on Benjamin and Freud, particularly the latter's distinction between mourning and melancholia, they foreground a depathologised concept of melancholia as creative, productive and political. The past here remains an ultimately harmful experience that must be psychically resolved. In contrast, Wendy Brown's (1999) discussion of 'left melancholia' describes the past as an object of desire. Building on Stuart Hall's critique of the left during Thatcherism and Benjamin's earlier critique of left melancholia, Brown argues that the left in the post-socialist era clings to dated and fetishised objects, visions, methods and ideals. This ultimately renders it a conservative force that refuses to understand the relevant contradictions of the present and to grasp the possibilities for radical change that it offers up.

Against a view of melancholia as problematic, Heather Love (2007b) calls for an embrace of 'backward' feelings such as shame, depression and self-hatred. Working with yet another archive – early twentieth-century lesbian novels – she links the continued appeal and resonance of these writings with the ongoing effects of an oppressed past that, according to queer progress narratives, should have long been overcome. Love stresses that the affirmative turn from shame to pride, rights and visibility, and from negative past to positive present and future, leaves behind those who are unable to perform happiness and optimism. In the place of positive representations, and inspired by the Chicago-based feeltank's motto 'Depressed? It might be political', she revalues 'bad' feelings as a means of acknowledging the persistence of the past in the present and the continuing effects of homophobia (2007b: 26).

The queer texts that are the subject of this chapter are similarly 'backward' in that they actively seek out the past and frequently warn of its return. However, the register that they strike is not antithetical to queer progress. They combine an affirmative orientation that celebrates rights and visibility – especially in relation to *their* backwardness – with one that actively dwells on past damages. Furthermore, these texts differ from Wekker's homonostalgia for a happy past of gay friendliness. Indeed, the queer nostalgia explored in the following is for an unhappy past of homophobic persecution.

REMEMBERING HATE

The Nazi era is more than an exceptional or parochial era that properly belongs to Berlin. It is a fertile terrain for diverse transnational artists, audiences and visitors, whose various investments in the city – from capital to affect – bring home the need to treat ostensibly local histories as irretrievably global. In Germany and elsewhere, the Nazi past has figured as a key myth of origin for LGBT identity politics. This view is complicated by Koray Yılmaz-Günay and Salih Wolter (2013), who highlight the coexistence of complicity and persecution during this era. Examples include anti-Semitism in homosexual scenes, the relatively open homosexuality of high-ranking Nazis such as Ernst Röhm, and the continued existence of many homosexual bars through the war (Yılmaz-Günay and Wolter 2013; see also Haag 2008).

These authors problematise a view of homophobia as synchronous with the Nazi past. Most male-assigned 'homosexuals' were persecuted under Article 175, a penal law that was introduced in 1872. The law was in force throughout the Weimar Republic, the 'sexually free' inter-war era that is often imagined as the real predecessor to today's 'queer-friendly' Germany. It persisted until 1994, long into the democratic regime. In 1957, the Federal Constitution Court explicitly upheld it as conforming with the morality of the German people (Yılmaz-Günay and Wolter 2013).

This challenges the privileged place of the Nazi era, and of the concentration camp, in LGBT identity politics. Even during the National Socialist period, a minority of those criminalised – estimates range between 6,000 (Yılmaz-Günay and Wolter 2013) and 10,000 (LSVD 2009) – were sent to concentration camps. Those targeted for killing, according to both Yılmaz-Günay and Wolter (2013), tended to be Jewish or otherwise racialised and were not exclusively targeted for their sexuality. In fact, sexually persecuted people were not targeted for extermination on the grounds of deficient 'stock', but for reform of problematic behaviours (see also Haag 2008).

In both German and global LGBT discourses, the focus on the Nazi era as the site of ultimate sexual oppression rests on an analogy of homophobia and anti-Semitism that exceptionalises the Holocaust as the site of ultimate racial oppression. This analogy works competitively and anti-intersectionally. Yılmaz-Günay and Wolter argue that much of gay organising in Germany has mobilised a discourse on the 'only forgotten victims' that assumes a competitive Other in the 'recognised' Jewish victim (2013 [2011]: 67, my translation).

This tendency to remember analogically, competitively and anti-intersectionally was intensified in the campaign for the Memorial to the Homosexuals Persecuted under National Socialism, which closely repeats the older and bigger 'Holocaust Memorial' (Memorial to the Murdered Jews of Europe) in colour, material, form, location, and in the volume of controversy that surrounds both.

Scripted as a local story, the Homo Memorial has become a marker of queer history and identity globally. Commenting on its circulation through US gay media, Jennifer Evans argues that its international reception confirms 'Berlin's unique place as a living memorial not only to victims of one of the most heinous regimes of the twentieth century but also to ongoing human rights struggles in the so-called liberal West' (2014: 76). Its production must be contextualised with the proliferation and centralisation of 'Holocaust remembrance sites' in the reunified Berlin. Zablotsky (2012) cynically revisits the birth of a 'national memory district' after reunification, when urban planners embarked on filling the *leere Mitte* (empty centre) of the border region, to cite the title of Hito Steyerl's well-known documentary, as part of Berlin's re-development as an entrepreneurial city and tourist destination (Zablotsky 2012: 55, citing Rosenfeld and Jaskot 2008: 11; see also Ha 2013).

While Jews are apparently privileged in these memory objects, Zablotsky argues that they codify Jewish difference and repeat its alienation from the nation. Rather than being 'for' Jews, memorials consolidate a post/genocidal Germanness by aestheticising, ritualising and spectacularising the violent past. They are a transcendental site where Germanness can be performed as innocent through the display of 'correct' memories, affects – including guilt and *Betroffenheit* ('affectedness', an untranslatable emotion reserved for white non-Jewish German identities) – and conducts – including *Kranzniederlegungen* (throwing wreaths and kneeling in front of memorials) (see also Shapira 2014).

This resonates with Allen Feldman's (2004) proposal that memories of violence are objects whose mode of circulation and consumption demands inquiry. Describing human rights violations as biographical artifacts and commodities, Feldman traces their circulation through various 'theatres' and 'marketplaces', including truth commissions and consumer media. Thus, plots of violence inherit scripts and characters from older medical settings that are 'inflected with a post-mortem aesthetic akin to the public dissection theatres of the seventeenth and eighteenth centuries', including a desire to witness the violated body through stages of diagnosis, treatment and catharsis (Feldman 2004: 167). Such trauma narratives reinscribe linear, teleological time in order to establish a clean break with the past. Institutional violence, in particular, must be archaicised and periodised so that 'post-violence reason' can be re-established, ironically by the same institutions that perpetrated the violence in the first place (2004: 168).

In Germany, too, violence plots serve to absolve white subjects and institutions from accountability. Drawing on Turkish German author Zafer Şenocak and Black German author May Ayim, Zablotsky (2012) shows how dominant forms of memory insulate the extermination of European Jews from past and future continuities of racism. In particular, they cut it off from the comparatively short but bloody history of German colonialism, which culminated in the attempted genocide against the Herero and Nama in what is now Namibia. Another little-known fact are the experiments on African and mixed-race individuals carried out by Eugen Fischer, who – not incidentally – was the teacher of Auschwitz physician Mengele (see El-Tayeb 1999). Fischer himself practised unimpeded after 1945 and even continued his experiments on Rroma and Sinti children (Zablotsky 2012: 5, fn 9).

As so often, the past is invoked in ways that recuperate the post-racial present. But, more than elsewhere, the post-racial state in Germany is de-linked from movements of resistance by racialised peoples. It is telling, for example, that the founding call of the Federal Republic, *Never Again!*, contains a missing verb. The post/genocidal identity of the nation gestures towards an unspeakable that, while generating volumes, remains productively empty. I call this identity post/genocidal as it seeks to insulate the genocide firmly in the past, while rendering death-making processes in the present unspectacular, self-inflicted, and mentionable only at great risk.

The achievement of the post-racial status quo thus results from the work of benevolent unmarked German subjects who remember 'correctly', rather than from the labour of oppressed subjects, for whom performing anti-racism remains undesirable. This is compounded by how anti-Semitism is reinvented as a Muslim problem. There now exist a host of publicly funded programmes to teach racialised youth the 'correct' relationship to the Nazi past (but not, say, the colonial past or the present of racist labour, carceral and border regimes). These programmes occur within the same segregated memory spaces. Damian Partridge (2010), following participant observation with youth groups and school classes visiting the Holocaust Memorial and Auschwitz, notes that white teachers and youth workers label youth of colour as problematic when they fail to exhibit guilt. Similarly, Esra Özyürek (2013) argues that programmes targeting youth of Turkish origin construct anti-Semitism as a 'Turkish' problem whose apparent cause lies with Turkey's failure to atone for 'its' anti-Semitism – in contrast to Germany. According to Özyürek, the spectre guiding these programmes is racialised youth who identify too much – rather than too little – with the persecuted Jews. Such identification threatens a post-genocidal view of the nation by drawing connections between past and present forms of racism.

Interestingly, Özyürek places the racialisation of anti-Semitism in a 2000s context where German citizenship has become easier to attain. As argued above, the early 2000s is also the time that homophobia becomes converted into a Muslim phenomenon. Made to bear the residues of anti-Semitism and homophobia in the post/genocidal society, the generations born and raised in Germany, belatedly 'granted' citizenship privileges, are firmly repeated as non-citizens. The pedagogical attempt to 'historically sensitize' youth of colour thus joins ranks smoothly with the arsenal of anti-homophobia and anti-violence programmes that we discussed earlier. The effort to teach racialised youth the correct emotion (there empathy, here guilt and *Betroffenheit*) distracts from how poor people of colour become disposable in the present, rendering the mention of racism-here-and-now punishable. Given the twin refusals to consider anti-Semitism a form of racism, and to consider resistance by people of colour anti-racism, these programmes ironically paint a landscape where 'racists' can be ascertained not by their failure to be less oppressive but their *failure to be white*. In this philo-Semitic script, anti-Semitism is firmly located in racialised bodies.

The performance of guilty memory (as correct memory) thus ironically reserves non-racist speech for those who can flaunt their unalloyed descent from perpetrators whose racist dispositions are firmly in the past. People of colour become guilty because they are unable to exhibit inherited guilt, more so if they disidentify with this economy of memory and affect. It is into this racialised landscape of remembrance that queer stakes to the past are inserted. As I shall explore next, the past, far from being a terrain that we must get away from, emerges as a desirable object and a fertile setting for presentist scripts of queer lovers and hateful Others.

THE HOMO MEMORIAL

While teachers and youth workers are diagnosing inner-city kids' false memories at the Holocaust Memorial, the Homo Memorial across the street in Tiergarten park is the setting for a different but related drama. Scripted in intensely local terms, the memorial has been produced and circulated in ways that complicate a parochial reading of Berlin and its pasts. It is visited by queers from all over the world, who become victim subjects as soon as they set foot in Berlin. Commissioned by the LSVD, it was produced by two white gay Scandinavians, Ingar Dragset and Michael Elmgreen, who are known for their sex-radical interventions in public space.

The memorial, inaugurated in 2008, contains several direct references to the older Holocaust Memorial. Erected within viewing distance of the latter, it echoes the older and bigger monument precisely in form, colour and material. But in the place of the 2,711 concrete slabs of the Holocaust Memorial, there is a single one, which nevertheless repeats the others queerly. The lone slab is angled, not straight so to speak. It contains one further deviation from its predecessors: inside the memorial, through a glass window, a film plays with queers kissing: first two men, then, following protests by lesbian feminists, a range of couplings including lesbian ones (see Evans 2014; Haakenson 2009).

The resemblance between the two sites of remembrance is not incidental. In 2000s gay media activism, the 'homosexual victim' is placed in the shadow of the

'Jewish victim'. In an early press release protesting the omission of homosexuals from the commemoration of the Holocaust, the LSVD states:

> So far, the homosexual victims of National Socialism have mostly been ignored in the culture of commemoration. It is time for this to change. The symbolic placement of a construction sign [as part of the protest] is simultaneously meant to mark the ideal location for the memorial: close to the Reichstag, opposite the emerging Memorial for the Murdered Jews of Europe, and neighbouring the planned memorial for the Sinti and Roma. (LSVD 2001)[1]

The quote echoes the discourse on gays as the 'only forgotten victims' who are disadvantaged in relation to Jews as the 'privileged victims' highlighted by Yılmaz-Günay and Wolter (2013). This fantasy is as post/genocidal as it is assimilationist: Excluded from the nation and its 'culture of commemoration' (which becomes the culture of the nation, so that to be commemorated is to be part of the nation), the 'gay community' nevertheless demands entry into it. Again, this recognition requires analogy and competition. In order to be recognised as victim subjects who have suffered in their own right, homosexual suffering needs to first resemble (and replace) Jewish suffering. In the narrativisation of the 'Homo Memorial', gays appear to be worse off: Not only do they still lack visibility and recognition (to the point where they must kiss in hidden spaces), they also appear more likely to experience violence in the present. When the window inside the Homo Memorial is scratched and cracked, an article in the local gay paper claims that this would not happen to the Holocaust Memorial:

> In comparison: the Memorial to the Murdered Jews in Europe on the other side of the street has more target surface, since it is bigger. There, no comparable attacks were made, only a few scrawlings. 'The attacks on the Homo Memorial have a different quality.' (Göbel 2009, citing the LSVD historian Andreas Pretzel)

This competitive post-racial fantasy is belied by the fact that both the Holocaust Memorial and other Holocaust remembrance architectures are frequently vandalised, and have become targets of repeated neo-Nazi marches and attacks (Cortbus 2014; Whitlock 2005). Peter Eisenman, the memorial's architect, even planned for this possibility by coating the memorial with anti-graffiti chemicals. The contradictions of post/genocidal memorialisation are further brought home by the scandal that erupted after the company commissioned to do the coating was revealed to be the same one that supplied Zyklon B gas to Auschwitz.

Zablotsky points out that the company was nevertheless allowed to continue to operate because it had successfully 'come to terms with its past' (2013: 69).

The competitive stance towards the old racial/religious Other characterises the Homo Memorial lobby, in which the LSVD is a dominant actor, from its incipience in the early 2000s. Yılmaz-Günay and Wolter (2013) go so far as to call the memorial 'a piece of "appropriation art"': 'The lonely slab is consciously made to appear as if exiled from the arrangement of the 2711 stelae that diagonally opposite are a reminder of the victims of the Shoah' (2013: 70). The early 2000s are also when the new racial/religious Other appears on the horizon as a competitor for funding and resources. As queer of colour observers noted then, the LSVD assumed its place on the public stage by competing with migrant associations over public resources and recognition, ultimately redefining the problem of migrant integration as a sexual one, and itself as expert on this issue (see Petzen 2005).

The politics of commemoration and of hate crime thus share an organisational and political space that is deeply racialised. They draw on overlapping aesthetic and affective languages: The white gender conforming kissers inside the memorial resemble the ones we have seen in chapter 2 ('Love'), and yet the film, shot in Tiergarten itself – a well-known cruising area – contains multiple hidden references to public sex (see Haakenson 2009). The kiss, multivalent in its homonormativity, its romance and domesticity, and its sex radicalism, brings into spectating community multiple white positionalities: a straight-but-not-narrow audience willing to protect vulnerable intimacies so long as they are recognisable through a heteronormative lens, a gay identity that demands public representation, a queer one that is nostalgic for in-your-face activism, and a self-consciously perverse one that enjoys anonymous sex.

The kiss in the Homo Memorial easily attaches itself to other intimacies, past and present. In January 2009, on the Day of Remembering the Victims of National Socialism, the LSVD organises a remembrance ceremony at the memorial. In the speech, historian Andreas Pretzel interprets the repeated vandalism as a backlash against the kiss inside, and places it in a direct genealogy with the recent cases of hate violence:

> It seems to me that the attacks on the memorial are associated with the assaults on homosexuals, as they are motivated by similar homophobic aggression against publicity and visibility. (LSVD 2009)[2]

Pretzel goes on to cite the litany of kissing victims and inner-city crime scenes that is familiar to consumers of hate crime activism. Having compared the memorial to the victims of racialised hate crime, he then goes on to establish a close identity between homosexual persecution during the Nazi past and hate violence in the present:

> We recall the state terror to which homosexuals were exposed during the Nazi period and after, and are referring at once to the here and now, are appealing to the present. (LSVD 2009)

This presentist equation of past and present struggles and identities is also conveyed in the choice of the victim subjects whom we are asked to remember. To 'keep awake in our collective memory the remembrance of the persecuted', Pretzel tells us the story of a gay couple who chose a 'love-death 70 years ago':

> Soon they would have had to go to prison, would have lost their bourgeois existence, their social reputation and not least the life happiness of a 14-year relationship. (LSVD 2009)

The intimacy we are encouraged to grieve is not any intimacy: it is performed not only as long-term and monogamous but also as very explicitly middle-class. One of the lovers, we learn, was a judge, the other owned a costume business. As so often in acts of commemoration (Kuntsman 2009a), some lives appear more grievable than others. In remembering the couple as 'what they wanted but were not allowed to be: a loving couple just like any other', the commemoration follows a lens that is as presentist as it is homonormative.

Kisses past and present thus become victims past and present, which in turn become agendas past and present. In this, the body of the victim of National Socialism, the body of the queer lover wanting partnership rights, the body of the victim of hate crime, the body of the actor in film, and the body of the anthropomorphic memorial turn into one injured body that needs our protection. This metonymy is repeated again and again. It appears in the many press releases and actions that lobby for the punishment of hateful Others, as well as in political responses such as the Green Party Action Plan against Homophobia (Bündnis 90/Die Grünen 2008). Not surprisingly maybe, in 2009 the annual kiss-in by Maneo, which, as we saw in chapter 2, previously targeted migrant and working-class areas, takes place in front of the memorial.

This placing side by side of past and present, object and bodies, racism and homophobia, is highly productive. It weds together the new discourse on 'Muslim homophobia' with the universally deplorable evils of National Socialism. To criminalise hate crime thus becomes to prevent genocide from ever happening again. The irony, that the memory of a past where oppressed people were incarcerated should lead us to a future of more incarceration, and that the policing and deportation of racial/religious Others should be an appropriate redress to the Holocaust, is lost.

CONCLUSION

In this chapter, I have highlighted the queer nostalgia that informs memories of the Nazi past. In the practices of memorialisation examined here, fascist terror is mobilised as a transtemporal affect that characterises the homophobia of a present that forebodes a return of past terror. This (retro-)actively foreshadows the racialised hate crime panic, thus refiguring the struggle against hate crime as a direct heir to the struggle against National Socialism. Importantly, these acts of commemoration turn fascist violence into a property of racialised bodies: as racist/homophobic hate in the past becomes *racialised* homophobic hate in the present, agents of terror past and present are urgently conflated.

CONCLUSION: KISS GOOD MORNING, KISS GOOD NIGHT

This book has renarrated the emergence of a queer lover who becomes a lovely sight in the shadow of racialised Others. I have described this drama as a cultural script that accompanies queer regenerations – of identities, acts, times and places – through which formerly degenerate objects and environments are converted into ones that signify value and vitality. This cultural analysis differs from a citizenship framework that measures the extent to which LGBT subjects are 'in' or 'out'. In its place, it asks 'Inclusion into what?' As Adi Kuntsman, Silvia Posocco and I put it in our joint editorial: 'Instead of taking for granted the incorporation of sexual minorities as a certain pathway to progressive politics, this Special Issue asks how inclusions can be murderous by shifting the focus from their promise to their violences' (Haritaworn et al. 2013: 445–46).

I have traced the appearance of the queer lover and its hateful Other alongside several shifts: between a perverse and a respectable queer subjectivity, between a queerphobic and a gay-friendly community, between the 'ghetto' and the colourful neighbourhood, between a difference regime defaulting to multiculturalism and one defaulting to sexual diversity, and between a welfare and a neoliberal regime. The queer lover plays a crucial role in these conversions, as it makes them appear familiar within older structures of feeling. In this conclusion, I propose that we think of the queer lover as a transitional object that mediates several important transitions. Besides further inquiring into the temporality of this narrative – what worlds does queer love make? – I am curious to trace what happens to gender and sexually non-conforming subjects in the process. For while the phrase 'We have fought for this' is often repeated in defence of rights and citizenship, what will become of this 'we' (however inclusively defined) is far from certain.

In thinking through this, I have indulged myself with a close reading of Winnicott (1953), the English psychoanalyst who introduced the concept of transitional objects and phenomena. Having carefully dismantled psy discourse in chapter 3 on 'Hate', it is not my intention to reify it here. Rather, I will attempt to explore how psy discourses have informed neoliberal imaginaries – from the 'responsible' citizen who counts and must account for hir own health, to the welfare recipient who must learn how to look after herself and her children – that appear more caring as they appear to care for queers (e.g. Roberts 2011; Rose 1989).[1]

Taking a queer leaf out of Winnicott, I propose that the queer lover is a transitional object that fulfils a wider purpose for those who surround themselves with it. Writing about early childhood development, Winnicott argues that transitional objects (first soft objects such as teddy bears, then harder objects such as dolls) and transitional phenomena (songs, tunes, lullabies) play an important role in helping children transition to a more mature and independent stage, where they are able to tolerate the frustrations and disillusionments of reality. As is often the case in psychoanalysis, Winnicott employs a highly gendered, abled and Euro-centric framework grounded in the nuclear bourgeois family, which normalises individualistic assumptions of coherent, discrete and self-sufficient bodies, minds and identities. Thus, the successful scenario for individuation is the child who is successfully weaned off 'the breast'. In contrast, 'distorted' use of the transitional object – reflective of not 'good enough' mothering – results in 'psychopathic' and otherwise abnormal identities, illustrated by the (queer?) man who 'has not married' (Winnicott 1953: 91).[2]

Much can be (and has been) said about the colonial, cis-heteropatriarchal, and disablist logics of this liberal identity ideal, which has if anything become more hegemonic under neoliberalism (see Love 2007b; Thobani 2007b). Indeed, attempts to dismantle the welfare state are often accompanied by calls to grow up, to no longer be dependent on the state's paternalism, and to become responsible for one's own health and welfare (see Roberts 2011; Rose 1989; Skeggs 2010). As Ann McClintock (1993) shows, this familial view of the social has older roots in the evolutionary trope of the 'Family of Man', which treats the white bourgeois family as the natural model for both nation and empire, each headed by the white patriarch. The continued need in formally post-colonial and post-racial contexts to relegate racialised populations to a child-like status is brought home by the figure of the mal-integrated, criminal and homophobic youth described in chapter 3 ('Hate'). There, I discussed how the shift from a welfare to a neoliberal regime is announced as a pedagogical call that reserves good neoliberal citizenship to those who are capable of becoming fully self-actualised and self-sufficient individuals. It is telling that the welfare state is feminised as being 'too soft' on crime, immigration and 'risky' (and 'at risk') populations who remain locked in poverty, dysfunction and dependency (see also Ahmed 2004a). While focusing on the exemplary failures of non-citizens, the pedagogical call to grow up interpellates rights-bearing citizens, too, who are increasingly feeling the pull of precarity. The neoliberal state, stepping in as the welfare state 'fails' – an action that is ironically an inaction, a gradual withdrawal of care – thus succeeds in weaning the child and helping it transition into the stressful and disillusioning, but ultimately necessary reality of becoming a self-reliant individual. The ego ideal of the neoliberal state indeed resembles that of Winnicott's 'good enough' mother.

In the remaining pages of this book, I propose that we think of the drama of queer lovers and hateful Others as a transitional phenomenon, not dissimilar to the soft teddy, the hard doll or the lullaby. Indeed, the narrative of protecting vulnerable queers from the failed heterosexualities and masculinities of poor people of colour helps to reassure a range of subjectivities that currently face challenges to their sense of self and community in a rapidly changing environment. These include ascendant queer and neoliberal multicultural subjects, progressives who wish to stay on the right side of racism in the face of increasingly unabashed dehumanisation, and the growing constituencies of subjects with race and class privileges who are themselves beginning to feel the effects of neoliberal restructuring.

Besides describing (or prescribing) individuation, thinking about transitions in this way further provides insight into how new collectivities are formed, and old ones morph and shift. Winnicott locates transitional phenomena mainly in the mother–child relationship and predicts they will lose their importance over time: the child eventually lets go of hir toys and lullabies. However, they do not disappear entirely. In a rare leap beyond the individualistic realm of the nuclear family, Winnicott argues that transitional phenomena 'become diffused … over the whole intermediate territory … that is to say, over the whole cultural field' (1953: 90). For the adult, the realms of art, religion and philosophy emerge as an 'intermediate area of experience' that powerfully gives rise to shared realities and solidarities. This diffusion interestingly recalls the proliferation of queer kisses, long considered immature (per)versions of proper object relations, in collective accounts of nation, Europe and West. Their transition from counter-publics to publics, as this book has argued, nevertheless remains contradictory and unstable. This is also the case for the transitional phenomena described by Winnicott. Thus, intermediate areas of experience both provide a basis for shared solidarities and remain precarious sites. Those who invest in them become vulnerable to being labelled illusory or mad, unless their intermediate areas can be brought into coherence with those of others (Winnicott 1953: 95).

The mode of inclusion that this gestures towards thus keeps the included on the border of the pathological. It chimes with the continuing ambivalence towards queer and trans embodiments and intimacies that, as I have shown, characterises the shift from a queerphobic to an LGBT-friendly society. While the ascent of homosexuality from crime and disorder remains incomplete, the pathologisation of transgender, that illusory identity *par excellence*, is hardly interrupted. Nevertheless, it is precisely the willingness to share illusory experiences that gives rise to the only kind of solidarity that Winnicott's indi-vidualistic model has space for:

> We can share a respect for illusory experience, and if we wish we may collect together and form a group on the basis of the similarity of our illusory

experiences. This is a natural root of grouping among human beings. (1953: 89)

Besides being a source of solidarity, the intermediate zone is further important in that it provides relief from the considerable 'strain of relating inner and outer reality' (1953: 95). Such strain is arguably increasing under neoliberalism, especially for the growing number of white middle-class people who now also experience precarity but lack alternative models of support (see Berlant 2011). Indeed, we might argue that the queer kiss – an object and phenomenon that increasingly circulates through intimate publics – provides comfort in uncertain times. It reassures us that the post-racial community still cares, in spite of growing evidence that poor people and people of colour are abandoned with impunity, and that a similar fate may await those in traditionally more secure locations. At this unstable intersection, the queer lover remains as a symbol of certainty, who reminds 'us' of 'our' benevolence, tolerance and love of diversity, even while the concrete acts of care that would reflect such values are rapidly withdrawn.

This does not mean that the queer lover is an unambivalent object. In addition to its connotations of illusion and madness, the transitional object is never an equal member of the family. The following list entitled 'Characteristics of relationship with transitional object' could easily describe our favourite gay or transgender TV sidekick characters:

1. The infant assumes rights over the object …
2. The object is affectionately cuddled as well as excitedly loved and mutilated.
3. It must never change, unless changed by the infant.
4. It must survive instinctual love, and also hating, and, if it be a feature, pure aggression.
5. Yet it must seem to the infant to give warmth, or to move, or to have texture, or to do something that seems to show it has vitality or reality of its own. (Winnicott 1953: 90)

My tongue-in-cheek revisiting of the queer lover as a transitional object allows us to approach this figure, not as a stable identity that is in or out, but as one whose uneven arrival in the eclectic toy box of the white heteronormative national and global family romance requires further inquiry. An excitedly cuddled object, it is nevertheless regularly mishandled. Its future is uncertain: it may well be discarded depending on its imminent uses. Furthermore, if all sexually and gender non-conforming subjects are encouraged to project our complex and uneven realities into happy queer kisses and other transitional phenomena, it has been important to me in this book to highlight that some performances are more likely to succeed than others. In chapter 2 ('Love'), I have illustrated this with the injured trans person, who has tenuously arrived among the ever-expanding repertoire of toys and tunes, but remains on the hard end of the soft-to-hard hierarchy. Similarly, as many have shown, queer migrants and queer people of colour who wish to become desirable to this new economy must be prepared to do immense amounts of identity labour that often involves cutting others off from its benefits (see Chávez 2013; Haritaworn et al. 2008; Kuntsman 2009a; Lubhéid 2008; Shakhsari 2014). In contrast, this book has focused on the organic intellectual labour of anti-racist queers of colour. How can we fail to be cuddly for white supremacy? What energies become available if we refuse to give warmth or enact vitality for a familial, national and global community that is predicated on such murderous inclusions? If the kitchen table is a small place to practise doing the work it will take to home gender and sexually non-conforming subjects back into anti-racist and anti-colonial projects, it nevertheless bears important lessons.

EPILOGUE: BEYOND THE 'MOST HOMOPHOBIC'

This book is on a small place and an even smaller community. You could say it was conceived with a small picture in mind. While foregrounding specific racial and sexual formations in Berlin, *Queer Lovers and Hateful Others* has employed a relational lens that pays attention to the ways in which identity moulds, political methods, carceral techniques, capital and ideologies travel. Such a relational approach is also proposed by Nadine Naber (2013), who builds on earlier transnational feminisms (Bacchetta et al. 2002; Grewal and Kaplan 1994, 2000, 2001) in order to formulate an anti-imperial transnational feminism that is able to investigate the effects of the 'war on terror' on women and queers in the Middle East in conjunction with Black feminist, Indigenous feminist and feminist of colour analyses of the wars on poor racialised and colonised populations in the US. Similarly, writers on the racialisation of queerphobia have attended to the travels of the 'most homophobic' figure and its globalising effects (Bacchetta and Haritaworn 2011; Haritaworn et al. 2013, 2014). As formerly homophobic societies officially become 'LGBT-friendly', the residue of gender and sexual oppression is contained elsewhere, in populations and geographies whose identifiability as backward, violent, patriarchal and irrational is grounded in longer histories of dispossession and exploitation. This is dramatically crystallised in the queering of the 'war on terror', and the ways in which gender and sexuality oppression have globally become markers of Islam in particular. Much work on homonationalism and gay imperialism has explored this with regard to the Middle East, the US and Europe (Bacchetta 2014; Bracke 2012; El-Tayeb 2012; Grosfoguel et al. 2014; Haritaworn 2008a; Jivraj and de Jong 2011; Kuntsman 2009a; Massad 2007; Petzen 2008; Puar 2007; Shakhsari 2014). Anti-Muslim and anti-Arab formations of sexuality are particularly salient in West Europe, where they interpellate the majority of the racialised, who have been transfigured from nationally distinct to globally inter-changeable populations (see Yıldız 2009).

Queer of colour kitchen tables in Berlin, the key entry point employed in this book, have often come together on the understanding that bodies racialised as Muslim bear the brunt of the racialised queerphobia panics in Germany, and that those of us, myself included, who do not bear this brunt need to step up as allies. In the 2000s, moral panics around Muslim homophobia erupted in several north-west European cities, including Berlin, London and Oslo. Set in gentrifying inner-city areas such as Kreuzberg and Neukölln, East London and Grønland, the drama of queer lovers and hateful Others evokes intensely local landscapes (personal communication with Arnika Rodriguez in 2010; see also Decolonize Queer 2011; Lamble 2014; Safra Project 2011). At the same time, its existential struggle is endlessly transposable and calls for identical forms of, increasingly punitive, intervention across vastly different national contexts. In this, the 'Turkish migrant' in Berlin Kreuzberg, the 'Pakistani' in Bradford, UK, and the provincial 'Iranian fundamentalist' all appear to be carrying the same cultural baggage, globalised as 'their religion': an inherent hatred of anything queer. Gendered knowledges of the 'Orient' have undergone considerable changes since white Europeans first began to describe West Asian, South Asian and North African genders and sexualities in paintings and travel writings (Said 1979). If Said's 'Orientals' brimmed with a rampant sexual and gender non-conformity that clearly needed restraining, today's 'Muslims' are imagined as repressed and *not free enough* (Massad 2007; Puar and Rai 2002). Similarly, gay rights were absent from public discussions of migration and multiculturalism in Germany until the 2000s. *Queer Lovers and Hateful Others* has traced some of the moments, often instantly forgotten, when categories around race, gender and sexuality shift and acquire new meanings, and become converted into common-sense truths whose production is instantly occluded from sight (see Ahmed 2004a). I have proposed that the category 'Muslim' is itself productive of a globalised Otherness against which expanded publics and counter-publics (a gay-friendly Germany, a unified Europe, a 'West') can cohere (see Yıldız 2009). In this refiguration of borders, populations and entitlements, activations of gender and sexuality and other 'invented traditions' (Hobsbawm 1983) do considerable work.

Who are the significant Others that enable the birth of the homonormative subject? Asking this question is important given that the 'most homophobic' figure differs according to geographical context. In the US, Black people and Latin@s were targets of the gay marriage mobilisations following Proposition 8, thus intensifying longer-standing practices of analogising gay and Black oppression that often fixate on essentialist tropes such as 'the Black church' (see Bassichis and Spade 2014; Farrow 2010 [2004]). In Toronto, Jamaica and Uganda have magnetised LGBT human rights activists, with campaigns focusing on 'stopping murder music' and denying visas to and freezing bank accounts of 'homophobic' individuals (Global LGBT Human Rights 2014; Gosine 2009). On the Canadian west coast, meanwhile, the prime suspects of hate crime have been South Asians. This includes Sikhs, the very group that bore the brunt of anti-immigration and anti-sodomy discourses when colonial norms of queerphobia were consolidated. Having been criminalised as too queer, Sikhs are now criminalised as not queer(-friendly) enough (Ingram 2003; Jaffer 2012). Worldwide, Russia drew the attention of the international LGBT movement during the Sochi Winter Olympics in 2014, thus projecting a longer-standing concern with East European sexualities among West European activists onto a bigger public stage, now including North America (Long n.d.).

My intention in writing *Queer Lovers and Hateful Others* has not been to cover all sites that have become interpellated through gay imperialism and homonationalism, nor to explain the various histories of sexual, racial and imperial oppression that are obfuscated by these representations. Each of these deserves a book in its own right. More work, further, needs to be done to understand racisms and colonialisms relationally. For example, this book has suggested that the anti-Muslim racism that informs the queer regenerations examined here intersects with colonial discourses that pervade imaginaries of racialised bodies, communities and inner-city spaces in Germany (but see El-Tayeb 1999; Steyerl and Gutiérrez Rodríguez 2003). The obfuscation of colonialism in public debates in Germany is in part a reflection of the peculiarity of the German labour migration regime, which did not recruit from the former colonies in Southwest Africa and the Pacific but from southern Europe, Turkey, Morocco and Tunisia. In contrast, labour migration in other West European contexts followed colonial lines, as commented upon in the name of the anti-racist party in France, Les Indigènes de la République, and the activist motto in Britain, 'We are here because you were there'. Following a European integration project that dovetailed with the Huntingtonian 'clash of civilisations', it is bodies assigned to Turkish and Arab 'origins' that have been reinscribed as unassimilable in Germany. The contract workers who migrated to the German Democratic Republic from Vietnam, Mozambique and other countries in Africa, Asia and Latin America, meanwhile, frequently lost their status when the Federal Republic expanded to 'reunify' with its socialist neighbour. While Islamophobia has become the most public mode of German racism, antiblackness has remained a constant thread – from the moral panics over Black French, British and American soldiers stationed in Germany after both world wars, whose figuration as sexual predators needs to be read in a genealogy with the hateful homophobe; to the Black German suspects who were immediately caught in a 'Muslim homophobia' net that was not spun with them in mind (see Haritaworn and Petzen 2011); to the automatic and taken-for-granted ways in which Africa and the Caribbean are becoming new targets of western LGBT rescue missions. It is no coincidence that the Lesbian and Gay Association Germany (LSVD), which has focused on 'Middle Eastern' populations since the early 2000s, now has an 'international human rights' subsidiary, the Hirschfeld-Eddy Foundation, that is partly named after a Sierra Leonian, Fannyann Eddy. Ironically, more attention has been paid to Hillary Clinton's 2011 speech to the UN and the recent discovery of Africa by the Human Rights Council (a latecomer to gay imperialism) than to the longer-standing LGBT aid regimes of the old empire, ranging from David Cameron's announcement that aid will be tied to LGBT-friendliness to the much older international LGBT funding structures that emerged in Scandinavia and the Netherlands in earlier decades (Agathangelou 2013; Ekine 2013). Ultimately, the profitable regenerability of victim and perpetrator populations renders crises transposable and targets malleable. At the same time, it is important to acknowledge that the *longue durée* of racism, slavery and colonialism magnetises some bodies for queer regeneration more than others.

As work on homonationalism, gay imperialism and queer necropolitics magnetises attention and finds a readership, we must stay attuned to the racialisation of gender and sexuality beyond the figure of the 'most queerphobic'. If Black, Arab and Muslim populations are now treated as hypersexist, homophobic and in need of civilisation, this is happening in the aftermath of colonial interventions that treated Indigenous peoples as not patriarchal and gender binaried enough, and therefore in need of civilisation. As Sunera Thobani (2014) reminds us in her prologue to *Queer Necropolitics* (Haritaworn et al. 2014), sexual and gendered racism and imperialism occur in the architecture of settler colonialism, and at the intersection of old and new empire. Making sense of this is rendered urgent for those of us writing on land that was never decolonised. I completed *Queer Lovers and Hateful Others*, a project begun in Europe, in Canada. As a settler of colour who arrived on Turtle Island at a time of Indigenous resurgence, I am challenged to rethink and revise the frameworks that inform this book. In Indigenous feminist, queer, transgender and Two Spirit discussions, there is a keen awareness of how colonial attempts at dispossession, displacement and genocide have targeted Indigenous peoples as lacking proper distinctions between genders and sexualities, as well as between human beings and non-human beings (Smith 2005). Leanne Simpson puts it thus:

> You use gender violence to remove Indigenous peoples and their descendants from the land, you remove agency from the plant and animal worlds and you reposition aki (the land) as 'natural resources' for the use and betterment of white people. (Simpson 2014)

Refusing a view of colonialism as in the past, Indigenous writers have traced the shifting manifestations of gender violence, from earlier reservation and residential school systems to contemporary regimes of adoption, foster care, policing, land theft, and the epidemic rape and murder of Indigenous women, Two Spirit, and LGBT people (Cruz 2014; Finley 2014a; Native Youth Sexual Health Network/Families of Sisters in Spirit/No More Silence 2014; Simpson 2014). Not only have they highlighted the significance of cis-heteropatriarchy and anthropocentrism to settler colonialism. The rejection of settler identities (including queer and LGBT) and the active engagement with traditional gender relations have been central strategies of decolonisation and land defence. Important attempts have been made to draw attention to the ongoing hegemony of non-Indigenous genders and sexualities in the Americas through frameworks such as colonial love, queer settler colonialism and settler homonationalism (Finley 2014b; McNeill 2014; Morgensen 2011). These intervene in a homonationalism debate that has at times evaded responsibility towards those who remain the biggest targets of gendered racism and colonialism in the contexts where we live, write and mobilise.

In describing the new queer-friendly discourse as a transitional phenomenon that occurs on the border between a welfare and a neoliberal regime, I do not wish to suggest that the neoliberal turn is the only, or even the most important timeline that we should attend to. Rather, we must locate this shift within a *longue durée* of racial and colonial capitalism. In this bigger picture, the figure of the 'most homophobic' country or community is but the latest arrival. Indeed, older colonial expansions were justified by the excessive queerness of Indigenous peoples who failed to conform to strictly binaried European hierarchies of gender and sexuality. This forces us to put the currently emerging 'especially queerphobic' figures in touch with older failed genders and sexualities that have long occupied the plane of immorality and disposability, and indeed often appear 'too queer'. In this bigger picture, the figure of the 'most homophobic' country or community is but the newest kid on a block where colonised and racialised genders and sexualities have been enmeshed and relational all along.

The racial formations emerging at this conjuncture of economic restructuring, carceral expansion and imperial war, such as the repressed Muslim woman/ queer and the chronic delinquent/terrorist, thus appear alongside other gendered figures of pathology, such as the drunken Indian (Razack 2012), the welfare queen (Cohen 1997) and the Black mugger/rioter (Breggin 1995; Hall et al. 1978). What would it mean to approach these figures within a shared horizon of transformation? What would it take to enter into kinship with the failed masculinities, femininities and heterosexualities that have become the raw material of queer and transgender ascendancies? How do we explore our genders and sexualities beyond these colonial castings, and in ways that refuse murderous invitations? If modern gender identities have been formed against a range of constitutive Others, whose primitive nature was long signified as a failure to perform proper gender identities, how do we home gender and sexually non-conforming subjects back into anti-racist and anti-colonial projects?

Given that gender violence has been central 'not simply [as] a tool of patriarchal control, but also ... as a tool of racism and colonialism' (Smith 2005: 1), such a horizon must necessarily include those who have borne the brunt of gender and sexual oppression. Exiled from both the gentrified spaces of queer regeneration and liberal multicultural moulds of respectability, the kitchen tables introduced in this book are crucial sites that wider social movements would be wise to become accountable to. Attending to them with care may well allow altogether different transitions to emerge.

NOTES

INTRODUCTION: QUEER REGENERATIONS

1. The incident that triggered the anonymous protest – the organisationally sanctioned use of the N-word by a performer at a fundraiser for the TCSD – is far from exceptional in queer spaces, in Berlin and beyond (e.g. see Farrow 2010 [2004]). That the protest was nevertheless able to reach a critical mass and a public ready to receive it (in however hostile a manner) is itself symptomatic of the densely racialised material and symbolic space within which queer politics now occurs. For examples of reports in both the mainstream and the gay press see Göbel (2013) and Zimmermann (2013). It is important to acknowledge that queers of colour were, especially in the early days, active in the TCSD and continue to make vital contributions to the organisation of the very spaces from which they subsequently often go missing as a result of racism and gentrification.

2. Identity markers such as 'racialised', 'queer', 'trans(gender)' and 'of colour' are contingent, contested, unfinished, never outside the biopolitical and necropolitical processes that this book describes, and at once crucially important for those invested in talking back at racism and gender violence. While white people, too, are racialised, and whiteness must be marked, 'racialised' is here invoked as a short-cut to describe subjects, populations and spaces that are constructed through racism (see Gilmore 2007).

3. Similarly, while earlier scholarship critiqued heteronormative constructions of the category 'migrant', it is now necessary to trace the work that new figurations such as the 'queer migrant' do. For example, Luibhéid (2008: 169) insightfully argued that most 'scholarship, policymaking, service provision, activism, and cultural work remain organised around the premise that migrants are heterosexuals (or on their way to becoming so) and queers are citizens (even though second-class ones)'.

4. As Petzen and I (Haritaworn and Petzen 2011) argue, the term 'migrant' has likewise undergone a considerable career, which cannot be understood outside histories of racism, resistance and assimilation. The term originated in anti-racist movements, where it was forged to replace the paradigm of the eternal 'foreigner', which interpellated both the contracted labourers who came in the post-war period from Turkey, southern Europe and North Africa, but also their German-raised children, Black and Asian Germans, and indeed anyone whose white German parentage is qualified or questionable (Mecheril and Teo 1994; Optiz et al. 1992 [1986]). Against this biologistic concept of national belonging and spatial entitlement, the term 'migrant' was born out of coalitions comprising people of multiple diasporic origins and generations of migration. Since entering mainstream media and political discourse, however, the term has generally been mobilised as a euphemism for the eternal foreigner. With the differential incorporation of migrants of European Union (EU) v. non-EU origin, and the new circulation of globalised ideologies of Otherness, which in the early 2000s culminated in the declaration of the 'war on terror', the category 'migrant' has undergone further shifts, making it increasingly co-terminous with 'Muslim' (Petzen 2008). In the present context, religion (especially the dichotomy

of Islam v. post-Christian secularism) has replaced nationality as the key biopolitical trope for organising difference (Yıldız 2009: 466). It is this latter synonymic usage that characterises many of the texts examined in this book.

5. See the special issue of *Feminist Legal Studies* on *Liabilities of Queer Anti-racist Critique* (Douglas et al., 2011) for an analysis of the ensuing debate.

6. For example: artactivistnia.com, blacklooks.org, blackgirldangerous.org, brownstargirl. org, darkmatterrage.com, espace-locs.fr, fabianromero.com, janetmock.com, kaybarrett. net, masculinefemininities.wordpress.com, reinagossett.com, theblackqueeradventures. wordpress.com

7. For an English version of the call for papers, see: http://femoco2013.jimdo.com/ home-1/english/ (accessed 1 August 2014).

8. 'Cis' is used in many trans and gender non-conforming communities to denaturalise non-trans positionalities and the socially ascribed gender binary. It thus bears similarities to other markers of dominant identities that often remain unmarked, such as 'white' or 'heterosexual'.

1 SETTING THE SCENE

1. A part of this chapter has appeared in Snorton and Haritaworn (2013) 'Trans necropolitics', in A. Aizura and S. Stryker (eds) *Transgender Studies Reader*, vol. II (New York: Routledge). I am grateful to the publisher for permission to use this material here.

2. Some of these questions have been insightfully taken up in the literature on queer migration (Luibhéid 2008), which invites us to think queer movements alongside race and space. In taking up this invitation, I am particularly interested in what happens if we examine variously racialised queer mobilities through the scale of the city.

3. For queer of colour critiques of Florida see Tongson (2007) and El-Tayeb (2012).

4. Schulman does mention race and class more systematically in one passage where she describes the 'racism' and 'colonial attitude' of wealthy white gay men 'coming into poor ethnic neighborhoods and serving as economic "shock troops"'. She gives the example of the 'antagonistic relationship' of gay home owners and business owners in the West Village in New York towards queer youth of colour using the Christopher Street piers. At the same time, she urges us to recognise that the 'desire to live in or to create a gay enclave was a consequence of oppression experiences', and correctly states that gentrification 'would not have been possible without tax incentives to luxury developers and the lack of city-sponsored low-income housing' (Schulman 2012: 39). Taking this further, our understanding of gentrification might begin with, rather than tack on, those queer and non-queer bodies that are displaced in the course of queer neighbourhood formation, in order to search for spatial models of safety, empowerment and belonging that are not predicated on displacement and dispossession.

5. For a critique of dominant strands of cosmopolitanism in urban studies literatures, see Goonewardena and Kipfer (2005).

6. Castells' writings on social movements and the city have also been influential in Germany (see Holm, 2012).

7. Both Castells (1993) and Knopp (1990, below) dedicate sections on non-trans women, but focus on non-trans men who are subsequently referred to as 'gays'.

8. An earlier and more race-evasive use of the 'ghetto' analogy is Levine's (1979). I problematise the notion of the 'ghetto' in the German context below.

9. Thobani does not equate the oppression of Indigenous peoples with that of non-Indigenous people of colour who have often been privileged in regimes of multiculturalism. She argues, rather, that later racisms arose in the architecture of settler colonialism, and that an anti-colonial rather than merely anti-racist framework is needed to make sense of and contest racial and other forms of oppression.

10. Milk's role in discovering and developing the Castro as a gay territory has become the subject of a 2008 biopic, whose spatial and historical landscaping could serve as a textbook example for both homo- and metronormativity.

11. While beyond the scope of this chapter, the comparative mapping of countries and cities that 'have' pride parades with those that do not is biopolitical and geopolitical in itself.

12. For critical discussions of Jenny Livingston's *Paris is Burning*, itself heavily imbued by the gentrifying moment, see hooks (1992), Prosser (1998), Muñoz (1999) and Haritaworn (2008a).

13. For an important archive of Sylvia Rivera's work, see Reina Gossett (2012).

14. The same language of 'move along' is also used in Washington DC, where police can declare 'Prostitution Free Zones' in public areas. This is frequently accompanied by the harassment and criminalisation of anyone suspected to be a sex worker, which disproportionately targets Black trans-feminine people (Saunders and Kirby 2010).

15. Razack (2002b) comments on the murder of Pamela George, an Indigenous woman who worked as a sex worker and was raped and killed by two rich white teenagers, who were acquitted as a result of the court's alliance with their colonial masculinities.

16. In Meyda Yeğenoğlu's (1998) historical analysis, too, white women became sovereign by embarking on rescue missions for Orientalised women.

17. Katherine McKittrick (2006) highlights the need to forge an urban theory that analyses cities with regard to multiple forms of racism and coloniality, including slavery and the attempted genocide against Indigenous peoples.

18. One example for the use of such colonial 'anti-gentrification' language is the No CCTV! walk that took place in Neukölln on 8 June 2012 (Genderliste 2012). According to the email announcement, gentrification is 'not only about a "beautiful" shopping world but also about the "wrong" humans sitting on park benches, the too high share of migrants and unemployed ... and the fear that those pushed to the margins could defend themselves'. The walk was organised by white left-wing activists concerned with gentrification and surveillance, whose attempt to draw attention to displacement unfortunately reified the original inhabitants who were now being displaced as less emplaced than the organisers themselves. A more creative example, which invokes rather than directly cites the pioneer discourse is the film *Offending the Clientele* (2010), which was made by the owners of a left-wing bar in Neukölln who bemoaned the subsequent take-over of the area by students and tourists from all over Germany and Europe. Its description on vimeo reads: 'Gentrification in Berlin's former borrough [sic]. The Creative Class marches in and the founders of the first szene-pub in this corner feel unwell, guilty and overrunned [sic].'

19. These statistics later came under attack as allegedly forged (Blech 2009; Petzen 2008; Ruder 2011).

20. At the time, the 'dialogue' was a common technology of the racialised homophobia panic (see Haritaworn and Petzen 2011). Staged between gay activists and the central mosque, this did not, however, allow for any real possibility to speak and be heard by the heterosexualised Other. As Anthias (2003: 282) puts it, 'dialogue becomes monologue in the colonial or hegemonic/hierarchised encounter'.

21. Eick argues that 'the anti-communist based security propaganda of the police was replaced by the increased assignment of offences to the perpetrator groups *foreigners* and *asylum seekers* as well as so-called *organised crime*' (2003: 71, my translation).

22. Eick (2003) highlights the existence of a general domain 'Targeted Foreigner Surveillance', and a spatial instrumentarium whose labels ('strained' or 'troubled areas', or 'areas suspected of becoming a ghetto') closely mirror the languages and targets of urban planners.

23. While migrants and people of colour are doubtlessly over-represented in German prisons, public statistics are scarce, and only take German versus non-German nationality into consideration. Among Berlin prisons, the male penitentiary Tegel is the only one that publishes such statistics online: in February 2009, 32 per cent of 1571 prisoners were 'foreigners', that is, people without German nationality. The remaining two-thirds may still include a disproportionate number of Black Germans and other German nationals of non-white parentage (JVA Tegel n.d.). These numbers do not include those on remand and in detention centres.

24. Besides the many, often obscure, policing instruments by the state, new forms of policing are proliferating below the state: private security firms, employed by supermarkets or housing associations, but also non-profit organisations that employ the 'poor to police the poor' (Eick 2003) in a new 'security, order and cleanliness' regime that is modeled around US-style workfare and quality-of-life discourses.

25. The role of neighbourhood watch-style associations like 'Unser Görli' ('Our Görli[tzer Park]') has been well documented (for example Indymedia 2012). Less investigation has been done into how queer and trans discourses on safety and protection, too, may be contributing to securitising public spaces.

26. Already, the report by former social landlord GSW (2010) reads more like a guide for potential investors. It was written in collaboration with Los Angeles-based multinational CB Richard Ellis, 'the world's biggest service provision company on the commercial real estate sector' (GSW 2010: 2), as well as GfK GeoMarketing, which prides itself on its expertise in providing region-specific market data (GfK GeoMarketing n.d.).

27. The same urban experts and consultants have lauded the improved 'social mix' of the area (Häußermann et al. 2007).

28. The district has commissioned several evaluation studies (Häußermann et al. 2007; TOPOS 2008) of social and rent changes in SO 36, the northern, more working-class part of Kreuzberg, which was declared a protected area in 1995. As a result, major modernisation measures can only be carried out with the permission of the district, and entail rent caps for a period of three years. The last survey took place in 2008 and, while its overall prognosis is optimistic, the authors warn that there is still considerable potential for upgrading the majority of flats, and that increased displacement pressure will result from this (TOPOS 2008: 61–62). Already, in 2008, the number of tenants who lived in their current flat before modernisation was carried out had shrunk from 35 per cent in 2005 to 24 per cent. At the same time, the difference in rents between those who moved in before and after modernisation is continuing to grow, from €0.67 per square metre in 2005 to €1.46 in 2008 (TOPOS 2008: 55). While optimistic that Kreuzberg will keep its social mix, the authors nevertheless remark: 'With these obviously considerably improved opportunities to increase the rent, the incentive naturally rises to replace an old tenant with [a new one]' (TOPOS 2008: 56).

29. According to TOPOS, there is a decrease in the average household size from 2.4 to 2.15, and of households with children from 34 per cent to 25 per cent (TOPOS 2008: 57).

30. This percentage rose from 20.3 per cent in 1993 to 30.5 per cent in 2008 (TOPOS 2008: 36).

31. For a commentary on the arrival of the gentrification concept into the German debate, as well as a documentation of both gentrification and anti-gentrification struggles, see the Gentrification Blog (gentrificationblog.wordpress.com) by German sociologist Andrej Holm, who was criminalised for his early work on gentrification.

32. Danía similarly expresses support and contrasts the new movement with the wider anti-gentrification scene:

> What's really annoying is all those slogans sprayed on houses: 'Devalue your neighbourhood' or 'Yuppies get lost'. Precisely those white queers who are the main attraction, they're the ones who're opening all the galleries and parties, and you can't distinguish them from the tourists, as both are white and middle class. They dare to say 'This is our neighbourhood', to claim legitimate speaking positions on who should be here and who shouldn't. Which is a double appropriation.

33. In 2009, the district government attempted to organise a 'task force' in Schillerkiez, a promising Neukölln location. The task force was supposed to 'cleanse' the area of drinkers, Rroma, youth of colour, and psychiatric consumers (Indymedia 2009).

34. At the time of writing, a classic example for this is the banning of the kaffiyeh in :// about blank (http://aboutparty.net/), a formerly squatted party venue in neighbouring Friedrichshain. As explained by 'some Berlin activists from the Middle East' in the anonymous open letter 'Stop Racist Door Policies in ://about blank!', the kaffiyeh is a piece of clothing worn in many Middle Eastern cultures but is in Germany associated with Palestine and hence considered 'anti-semitic'.

35. As discussed in the introduction, my use of the term 'degeneracy' draws on Razack (2002a). It is further developed in chapter 3 through an anti-racist disability studies lens.

36. In Europe critiques of queer claims to inclusions into neighbourhood, nation, Europe and West were first made by queers of colour. Since then, the concept of homonationalism has itself undergone rapid gentrification as the latest import from the US (see SUSPECT 2010a; introduction to this book).

2   LOVE

1. Parts of this chapter have appeared as Haritaworn, J. (2008b) 'Loyal Repetitions of the Nation: Gay Assimilation and the "War on Terror"', *DarkMatter* 3, Haritaworn, J. (2010a) 'Queer Injuries: The Racial Politics of Homophobic Hate Crime in Germany', *Social Justice* 37(1), Haritaworn, J. (2010b), 'Wounded subjects: Sexual exceptionalism and the moral panic on "migrant homophobia" in Germany', in M. Boatca, S. Costa and E. Gutierrez Rodriguez (eds.) *Decolonising European Sociology* (Aldershot: Ashgate), and Haritaworn, J. (2011) 'Colorful Bodies in the *Multikulti* Metropolis: Vitality, Victimology and Transgressive Citizenship in Berlin', in T. Cotton (ed.), *Trans-Migrations: Bodies, Borders, and the (Geo)politics of Gender Trans-ing* (New York: Routledge). I am grateful to the publishers for permission to use this material here.

2. See the *Feminist Legal Studies* special issue, *Liabilities of Queer Anti-Racist Critique*, on the censorship of *Out of Place* (Douglas et al. 2011).

3. The trope of the hard-working citizen who pays taxes and defends his country from perverse terrorists was also used as a strategy of gay respectabilization in the 'war on terror' (Agathangelou et al. 2008; Shakhsari 2014).

4. But see Chris Finley's work on the legalisation of gay marriage in the Colville nation, which argues that, given the centrality of heteropatriarchy in colonialism, gay marriage can be an important expression of Native sovereignty.

5. This image can be viewed on the following website: www.sueddeutsche.de/ panorama/migrantenkinder-gegen-schwulehomophobes-berlin-1.335341 (accessed 1 November 2010).

6. See the website of the International Day Against Homophobia: www.homophobiaday. org/default.aspx?scheme=3293 (accessed 27 December 2013).

7. See Lamble (2008) for a discussion of victim figurations in anti-violence campaigns.

8. The same posters have since travelled to Vienna, where they target the migrant area Simmering. In the place of the Arabic, the Viennese version bears Serbian subtitles (www.courage-beratung.at/start_index.htm). I thank Ana Hoffner for pointing this out to me.

9. This membership is of course situational, as outside this fantasy of interraciality, the queer migrant body is configured very differently, and vulnerable to intensities of violence that hate crime activists have so far rarely begun to imagine.

10. The other kissing 'couples' – including Angela Merkel and Nicolas Sarkozy, Obama and Chávez, and Obama and former General Secretary of China Hu Jintao – interestingly reference different world orders, both past and emerging.

11. In the press statement on the vigil, the LSVD states that 'archaic family understanding of honour' prevent not only heterosexual women, but also gays and lesbians, from having emancipated sexual lives (see: www.berlin.lsvd.de/cms/index.php?option=com_ content&task=view&id=20&Itemid=193 (accessed 21 November 2009). The vigil was attended by politicians and mediators working on women's and migrant women's issues, including Seyran Ateş, a lawyer of Turkish origin who has played a similar role in authenticating Orientalist gender discourses to the better known Ayaan Hirsi Ali (see Erdem 2009; Ghorashi 2003).

12. The special issue which the left-wing weekly the *Jungle World* dedicated to the incident was far less ambivalent. The author of the lead article actively critiqued the Drag Festival organisers for awkwardly evading the 'perpetrators'' ethnicity. The title of the article: 'Homophobic Turkish youth and the fear of racism allegations' (Bozic 2008).

13. We can explore the Orientalisation of fascism in German debates alongside the Orientalisation of sexism, homophobia and transphobia (Cengiz Barskanmaz 2009, personal communication).

14. For an earlier critique, see Glen Coulthard's keynote at the *Critical Ethnic Studies* conference 2012. Future critiques could focus on how the figure as a wound reifies illness and disability as undesirable and reduces them to a metaphor.

15. Of course, trans Arabs, too, have been discovered as victim subjects who authenticate racist and imperialist discourses in a way that has enabled white trans people to enter into sovereignty as their rescuers and representatives. Nevertheless, this renders an anti-racist, trans Arab positionality even more completely inauthentic and impossible.

16. See Stanley and Smith (2011). This occurs at all levels of police, courts and prisons, which have themselves been described as a site of massive and systematic gender segregation and gender violence.

3 HATE

1. Parts of this chapter have appeared as Haritaworn, J. (2013) 'Beyond hate: Queer metonymies of crime, pathology and anti-violence', special issue *Rethinking Queer Sexualities, Law and Cultural Economies of Desire* in *Jindal Global Law Review* 4(2), also forthcoming in Oishik Sircar and Dipika Jain (eds) *New Intimacies/ Old Desires: Law, Culture and Queer Politics in Neoliberal Times* (New Delhi: Zubaan, forthcoming, 2015). I am grateful to the publishers for permission to use this material here.

2. While this describes inter/disciplinary formations in the US, we also need accounts of other parts of the world, including outside the global North. In Germany, where social movements have remained very white, gender studies has had some success in finding institutional homes (see Haritaworn and Weheliye forthcoming).

3. See the CESA call for papers 2011: www.ethnicstudies.ucr.edu/CES_call4papers.pdf. Theorists and activists on these intersections have made interventions where they could, but it is interesting that while gender and sexuality studies have in some ways become more reluctant homes for women/queer/trans of colour scholarship, critical ethnic, race and legal studies are at least promising to become more open. This might reflect their lesser investment in narratives of progress, rights and protections, and their longer history of questioning how the criminal 'justice' system, even in its nicer faces, acts against oppressed people in a way that is neither accidental nor aberrant. It remains to be seen whether critical ethnic studies will expand to include queer and trans of colour scholarship in particular, whose unique contribution to wider race and ethnic studies lies precisely in its potential for dismantling the white gender and sexuality norms that are at the heart of coloniality.

4. Interestingly, googling this quote first pointed me to this self-help website: http://www.change-management-coach.com/change-quotes.html. My point is that anti-racist states labelled as depression are often pathologised even in anti-racist communities.

5. Given the pervasiveness of antiblackness in Germany, too, criminalising measures that find consent through anti-Muslim racism nevertheless regularly have anti-Black effects.

6. *Brutale Münchner U-Bahn-Schläger gefasst.* Available at: http://www.youtube.com/watch?v=zh5PW61S9Cw&playnext=1&list=PL3F633C86147B7C4E (accessed 1 June 2013) and *Überwachungskamera/Security Camera* (Social Spot Berlinale). Available at: http://www.youtube.com/watch?v=yvxR-OAGB-I (accessed 1 June 2013).

7. So far, the *Intensivtäter* is mainly an administrative category applied to youth who have been convicted of a given number of crimes (in Berlin, 10 per year) – *or who are on their way to becoming Intensivtäter*. Its main purpose, besides marking a young person out for harsher, faster sentences in court, seems to be surveillance: Thus, every *Intensivtäter* is assigned a personal police officer to watch over hir *and hir surroundings* (that is, his friends, his family, his neighbourhood). In addition to youth penal law, people labelled *Intensivtäter* are governed through a (proliferating) arsenal of pedagogical, social/youth work and psychiatric instruments, including forensic and youth psychiatry, secure children's homes and boot camps, anti-violence training, and *Sicherungsverwahrung* (safe custody), a mixed penal/psychiatric form of confinement that has repeatedly been found in violation of human rights by the European Court for Human Rights. Thank you Nadija Samour for explaining these legal facts to me.

8. The experts on intensive offenders admit to this. See Ohder and Huck (2006).

9. The category of the gang, which is often determined in highly arbitrary ways, is another globalising instrument that allows lawmakers and enforcers to criminalise

young people of colour through their proximity to other low-income youth of colour (see Critical Resistance Oakland Report 2011).

10. I thank Nina Mackert for our conversations about this.

11. For a typically muddled response to Germany's bad results in international comparisons of educational achievement such as the PISA study, see Himmelrath (2012).

12. This genre became popular after the Second World War and typically depicts a sentimental world set in the mountains, where white gender-conforming boy romances girl, that is nostalgic for an innocent Germany unspoilt by racial or sexual Others.

13. Pfeiffer and colleagues also mention *Deutscheinfeindlichkeit* as a common trait among their subjects (Baier et al. 2010: 64). The theme of 'reverse racism' (as a criminal trait) is a globalising phenomenon, as the prosecution of anti-racist activist Houria Bouteldja for 'anti-white racism' in France also illustrates.

14. 'Unter einer homosexuellenfeindlichen Einstellung ist die psychologische Tendenz, auf Homosexuelle mit einer negativen Bewertung zu reagieren, gemeint. Diese Bewertung beinhaltet negative Affekte oder Gefühle, negative Kognition und negative Verhaltenstendenz' (Simon 2007).

15. These are the 'factors' cited by the Pfeiffer study (Baier et al. 2010). For other reports, both quantitative and qualitative, that have repeated similar themes of integration, religiosity, inner-city background and inherited violence and poverty, see Haug (2010) and Toprak and Nowacki (2010).

16. The culture of poverty theory was popularised in the 1960s and attributed poverty among Black and Latino people to the dysfunctional structure of their communities and families. See Moynihan (1965); for critiques see Roberts (1997) and Cohen (1997).

17. On the dispersal of psy discourse to other disciplinary and professional formations and throughout neoliberal therapeutic culture, see Rose (2010).

18. Gorman (2013) also highlights the bifurcation of ADHD into '"hyperactive" children of colour [who] are segregated in special education, while "attention deficit" middle class youth are provided with specialised computers and tutors'.

19. There is anecdotal evidence in activist communities that children labelled difficult or disruptive, often those racialised and gendered as Turkish or Arab boys, are now given this diagnosis at school ('Racism and Mental Health' workshop at the Decolonize the City conference in Berlin, 23 September 2012). I am also grateful to Cengiz Barskanmaz and Meral El for sharing preliminary findings from research done in Berlin schools which confirms this trend (summer 2012).

20. See the following list assembled from the *DSM* and from the checklist of the World Health Organization: http://en.wikipedia.org/wiki/Antisocial_personality_disorder (accessed 1 August 2014).

21. For a genealogy of biopsychiatric attempts to reinscribe the link between race and violence, see Breggin (1995).

22. For a somewhat uncritical account, see Singh and Rose (2009).

23. Many of these terms, such as '*Auffälligkeit*' (conspicuity) sound odd in German. I argue that the choice of a more random, less medically precise vocabulary serves to obfuscate the eugenicist hauntings of this list.

24. Besides analysing how the disposability of youth of colour is euphemised through emotional narratives like these, we must attend to the institutional practices which govern the intensive offender. Liat Ben-Moshe's (2010) concept of 'trans-institution-alization' is helpful here: how are surplus populations funnelled through a cycle of

incarceration and reform? While the intensive offender is amply studied, no research has been done on what actually becomes of young people with this label (see Ohder and Huck 2006: 23).

25. Efforts to resist prison abuse by highlighting the high incidence of 'mentally ill' prisoners who should *really* be in a mental institution, often heard in the US, where many psychiatric institutions were closed as a result of neoliberal austerity measures, reify sanist notions of 'mental illness' and ignore how psychiatric institutions, too, have often given rise to scandals as violent sites of confinement. Psychiatric system survivors have long argued that similar circumstances can lead to spending longer in psychiatric care than in prison, and that, instead of a clearly defined sentence, the psychiatric patient is dependent on the whim of doctors, who have full discretion to confine hir until they declare hir 'cured' (e.g. *Dissidentenfunk* 2005).

26. On the overlaps between US prisons and military, see Avery Gordon (2006); on the transformation of the big psychiatric institution into mental health services in the community, see Voronka (2010).

27. See also Glenn Coulthard's (2011) critique, who argues, against Brown, that for Indigenous people in Canada, it is too early to let go of resentment, and concludes: 'Let's wallow in it.'

4   QUEER NOSTALGIA

1. This and the following translations are mine.

2. In an interview for a more recent article in the local gay paper, Pretzel establishes a similar metonymic link between physical violence, vandalism and migrant homophobia by suggesting that 'there are still parts of the population who feel provoked by such a kiss', and that: 'This aggression is always directed against the window, through which you can look at the inside of the stele – in other words, against the film with the gay kiss' (Göbel 2009).

5   CONCLUSION: KISS GOOD MORNING, KISS GOOD NIGHT

1. For another critical race take on Winnicott, see Eng and Han's (2006) discussion of the role of the Asian American therapist for the transracial adoptee.

2. More surprising maybe are the queer acts that Winnicott simultaneously invokes, including fist and thumb sucking and other stimulation of the 'oral erotogenic zone' (1953: 89, 96).

BIBLIOGRAPHY

Agamben, G. (2005) *State of Exception*, trans. Kevin Attell (Chicago: University of Chicago Press).

Agathangelou, A. (2013) 'Neoliberal geopolitical order and value: Queerness as a speculative economy and anti-blackness as terror', *International Feminist Journal of Politics* 15(4).

Agathangelou, A., Bassichis, M. and Spira, T. (2008) 'Intimate investments: Homonormativity, global lockdown, and seductions of empire', *Radical History Review* 100.

Ahmed, S. (2000) *Strange Encounters: Embodied Others in Post-coloniality* (London: Routledge).

Ahmed, S. (2004a) *The Cultural Politics of Emotion* (Edinburgh: Edinburgh University Press).

Ahmed, S. (2004b) 'Declarations of whiteness: The non-performativity of anti-racism', *borderlands* 3(2).

Ahmed, S. (2006) *Queer Phenomenology: Orientations, Objects, Others* (Durham, NC: Duke University Press).

Ahmed, S. (2008) 'Multiculturalism and the promise of happiness', *New Formations* 63.

Ahmed, S. (2010) *The Promise of Happiness* (Durham, NC: Duke University Press).

Ahmed, S. (2011) 'Problematic proximities: Or why critiques of gay imperialism matter', *Feminist Legal Studies* 19(2).

Ahmed, S. (2012) *On Being Included: Racism and Diversity in Institutional Life* (Durham, NC: Duke University Press).

Aktaş, G. (1993) 'Türkische Frauen sind wie Schatten – Leben und Arbeiten im Frauenhaus', in I. Hügel, C. Lange and M. Ayim (eds) *Entfernte Verbindungen: Rassismus, Antisemitismus, Klassenunterdrückung* (Berlin: Orlanda).

Anthias, F. (2003) 'Beyond feminism and multiculturalism: Locating difference and the politics of location', *Women's Studies International Forum* 25(3).

Antifaschistische Linke Berlin (2008) 'Demo nach homophobem Überfall', 8 June. Available at: http://www.antifa.de/cms/content/view/831/32/ (accessed 30 March 2015).

Arnsperger, M. (2008) 'U-Bahn-Schläger-Prozess: Die schlagen mich tot', 24 June. Available at: http://mobil.stern.de/panorama/u-bahn-schlaeger-prozess-die-schlagen-mich-tot-624986.html (accessed 1 August 2014).

Arondekar, A. (2004) 'Geopolitics alert!', *GLQ: A Journal of Lesbian and Gay Studies* 10(2).

Avineri, S. (1968) *Karl Marx on Colonialism and Modernization* (Garden City, NJ: Doubleday).

Bacchetta, P. (2014) 'Queerphilic xenophobia as an axis in Islamophobia', Islamophobia Conference, University of California Berkeley, 17–19 April.

Bacchetta, P. and Haritaworn, J. (2011) 'There are many trans-Atlantics', in K. Davis and M. Evans (eds) *Transatlantic Conversations: Feminism as Travelling Theory* (Aldershot: Ashgate).

Bacchetta, P., Campt, T., Grewal, I., Kaplan, C., Moallam, M. and Terry, J. (2002) 'Transnational feminist practices against war', *Meridians* 2(2).

Baier, D., Pfeiffer, C., Rabold, S., Simonson, J. and Kappes, C. (2010) *Kinder und Jugendliche in Deutschland: Gewalterfahrungen, Integration, Medienkonsum. Zweiter Bericht zum gemeinsamen Forschungsprojekt des Bundesministeriums des Inneren und des KFN* (Hanover: Criminological Research Institute Niedersachen).

Bailey, M., Kandaswamy, P. and Richardson, M. (2004) 'Is gay marriage racist?', in M. Sycamore (ed.) *That's Revolting! Queer Strategies for Resisting Assimilation* (New York: Soft Skull Press).

Barskanmaz, C. (2011) 'Rasse – Unwort des Antidiskriminierungsrechts?', *Kritische Justiz* 4.

Bassichis, M. and Spade, D. (2014) 'Queer politics and antiblackness', in J. Haritaworn, A. Kuntsman and S. Posocco (eds) *Queer Necropolitics* (London: Routledge).

Bell, D. and Binnie, J. (2004) 'Authenticating queer space: Citizenship, urbanism and governance', *Urban Studies* 41(9).

Ben-Moshe, L. (2010) 'Resistance to incarceration: The intersections of prison abolition, anti-psychiatry and deinstitutionalization', PsychOut Conference, University of Toronto, 7–8 May.

Berlant, L. (2006) 'Cruel optimism', *differences: A Journal of Feminist Cultural Studies* 17(93).

Berlant, L. (2007) 'On the case', *Critical Inquiry* 33(4).

Berlant, L. (2011) *Cruel Optimism* (Durham, NC: Duke University Press).

Berlant, L. and Warner, M. (1998) 'Sex in public', *Critical Inquiry* 24(2).

Bernhardt, M. (2006) '"LSVD bestätigt das schlichte Selbstbild der Gesellschaft". Der Lesben-und Schwulenverband fördert offenbar weiter die Ausgrenzung Nichtdeutscher. Ein Gespräch mit Koray Yılmaz-Günay', *Junge Welt* 79(5 April).

Bhanji, N. (2013) 'Trans/scriptions: Homing desires, (trans)sexual citizenship and racialized bodies', in A. Aizura and S. Stryker (eds) *Transgender Studies Reader*, vol. II (New York: Routledge).

Bhavnani, K. and Coulson, M. (1986) 'Transforming socialist-feminism: The challenge of racism', *Feminist Review* 23.

Bilge, S. (2013) 'Intersectionality undone', *Du Bois Review: Social Science Research on Race* 10(2).

Binnie, J. (1995) 'Trading places: Consumption, sexuality and the production of queer space', in D. Bell and G. Valentine (eds) *Mapping Desire: Geographies of Sexualities* (London: Routledge).

Binnie, J. and Skeggs, B. (2004) 'Cosmopolitan knowledge and the production and consumption of sexualized space: Manchester's gay village', *Sociological Review* 52(1).

Blech, N. (2009) 'Maneo-Umfrage gezielt manipuliert?' (Maneo Survey Purposely Manipulated?), *Queer.de*, 15 August. Available at: www.queer.de/detail.php?article_id=10906 (accessed 6 January 2014).

Bombosch, F. (2009) 'Sei anders. Sei Opfer?', *Zitty* 10 (December).

Bourdieu, B. (1987) 'What makes a social class? On the theoretical and practical existence of groups', *Berkeley Journal of Sociology* 22.

Bozic, I. (2008) 'Das große Schweigen: Homophobe türkische Jugendliche und die Angst vor Rassismusvorwürfen', *Jungle World* 26(3). Available at: http://jungle-world.com/artikel/2008/26/22074.html (accessed 6 January 2014).

Bracke, S. (2012) 'From "saving women" to "saving gays": Rescue narratives and their dis/continuities', *European Journal of Women's Studies* 19(2).

Braz, R., Brown, B., Gilmore, C., Gilmore, R., Hunter, D., Parenti, C. et al. (2000) 'Overview: Critical resistance to the prison-industrial complex', *Social Justice* 27(3).

Breggin, P. (1995), 'Campaigns against racist federal programs by the Center for the Study of Psychiatry and Psychology', *Journal of African American Studies* 1(3).

Breggin, P. (2007) *Talking Back to Ritalin: What Doctors Aren't Telling You about Stimulants and ADHD* (New York: Da Capo Press).

Breitman, G. (ed.) (1994) *Malcolm X Speaks: Selected Speeches and Statements* (New York: Grove Press).

Brenner, N. and Keil, R. (eds) (2006) *The Global Cities Reader* (London: Routledge).

Brown, W. (1993) 'Wounded attachments', *Political Theory* 21(3).

Brown, W. (1999) 'Resisting left melancholy', *boundary 2* 26(3).

Bryant, L. (2006) '"Law is life!" Flag wars, local government law, and the gentrification of Olde Towne East', *Fordham Intellectual Property, Media and Entertainment Law Journal* 16(3).

Bryant, K. and Vidal-Ortiz, S. (2008) 'Introduction to retheorizing homophobias', *Sexualities* 11(4).

Bullard, R. (1994) *Dumping in Dixie: Race, Class and Environmental Quality* (Boulder, CO: Westview Press).

Bumiller, K. (2008) *In an Abusive State: How Neoliberalism Appropriated the Feminist Movement against Sexual Violence* (Durham, NC: Duke University Press).

Bündnis 90/Die Grünen (2008) *Berliner Aktionsplan gegen die Homophobie*. Berlin Senate, Print matter 16/1966 (1 December), 16th election period.

Butler, J. (2007) 'Sexual politics: The limits of secularism, the time of coalition', *British Journal of Sociology* public lecture, London School of Economics, 30 October.

Çağlar, A. (2001) 'Stigmatisierende Metaphern und die Transnationalisierung sozialer Räume', in F. Gesemann (ed.) *Migration und Integration in Berlin* (Opladen: Leske+Budrich).

Castells, M. (1983) 'Cultural identity, sexual liberation and urban structure: The gay community in San Francisco', in *The City and the Grassroots: A Cross-cultural Theory of Urban Social Movements* (Berkeley: University of California Press).

Catungal, J.P. (2010) 'Commerce, community, citizenship: Changing political economies of Toronto's "Gay Village"', paper presented at Reinstating Transgression: Emerging Political Economies of Queer Space conference, American University, Washington, DC, 17–18 April.

Çetin, Z. (2011) 'Eine ökonomische Macht, die auf Normalisierung abzieht', in K. Yılmaz-Günay (ed.) *Karriere eines konstruierten Gegensatzes: Zehn Jahre 'Muslime versus Schwule'. Sexualpolitiken seit dem 11. September 2001* (Berlin: Self Publishing).

Chan, W., Chunn, D. and Menzies, R. (eds) (2005). *Women, Madness and the Law: A Feminist Reader* (London: Glass House).

Chávez, K. (2013) *Queer Migration Politics: Activist Rhetoric and Coalitional Possibilities* (Champaign: University of Illinois Press).

Cohen, C. (1997) 'Punks, bulldaggers and welfare queens: The radical potential of queer politics?', *GLQ: A Journal of Lesbian and Gay Studies* 3(4).

Cohen, C. (2010) 'Death and rebirth of a movement: Queering critical ethnic studies', *Social Justice* 37(4).

Collins, P.H. (1991) 'Mammies, matriarchs, and other controlling images', in *Black Feminist Thought: Knowledge, Consciousness, and the Politics of Empowerment* (New York: Routledge).

Combahee River Collective (1986 [1977]) *The Combahee River Collective Statement: Black Feminist Organizing in the Seventies and Eighties* (Boston, MA: Kitchen Table Press).

Conrad, R. (ed.) (2012) *Against Equality: Queer Critiques of Gay Marriage* (Lewiston, ME: Against Equality Publishing Collective).

Cortbus, C. (2014) 'Neo-Nazis celebrate shocking Holocaust Memorial desecration', *Israel National News*, 8 January. Available at: http://www.israelnationalnews.com/News/News. aspx/176074#.U5sQmY1dUSY (accessed 11 June 2014).

Coulthard, G. (2011) 'Keynote speech', at Critical Ethnic Studies and the Future of Genocide conference, University of Riverside, 10–12 March.

Coulthard, G. (2013) 'Polis nullius: Gentrification, settler-colonialism and indigenous sovereignty in the city', paper presented at Critical Ethnic Studies conference, University of Illinois, Chicago, 21 September.

Courant, S. (2006) 'Schwuler Krach um Muslim-Test', *Tageszeitung*, 21 January. Available at: www.taz.de/1/archiv/archiv-start/?dig=2006%2F01%2F21%2Fa0242&cHash=603c7934a6 (accessed 1 August 2014).

Crasshole, W. (2010) 'Getting your gay on', *The Exberliner*, 20 June. Available at: http://www.exberliner.com/culture/getting-your-gay-on/ (accessed 1 January 2014).

Critical Resistance Oakland Report (2011) *Betraying the Model City: How Gang Injunctions Fail Oakland*. Available at: http://crwp.live.radicaldesigns.org/wp-content/uploads/2012/04/CR_GangInjunctionsReport.pdf (accessed 1 August 2014).

Cruz, L.E. (2014) 'Two-spirit survival/resistance and rebellions to colonial corporate violences before & after "Stonewall Riots": A small and incomplete sample', 23 June. Available at: http://louisesmecruz.blogspot.ca/2014/06/two-spirit-survivalresistance-and.html (accessed 30 March 2015).

Cvetkovich, A. (2003) *An Archive of Feelings: Trauma, Sexuality, and Lesbian Public Cultures* (Durham, NC: Duke University Press).

da Silva, D.F. (2007) *Toward a Global Idea of Race* (Minneapolis: University of Minnesota Press).

Davis, A. (2003) *Are Prisons Obsolete?* (New York: Seven Stories Press).

Davis, A. and Rodriguez, D. (2000) 'The challenge of prison abolition: A conversation', *Social Justice* 27(3).

Decena, C. (2011) *Tacit Subjects: Belonging and Same-sex Desire among Dominican Immigrant Men* (Durham, NC: Duke University Press).

Decolonize Queer (2011) 'From Gay Pride to White Pride? Why it is racist to march on the East End', *Decolonize Queer*. Available at: www.decolonizingsexualities.org/decolonize-queer/ (accessed 17 May 2013).

d'Emilio, J. (1993 [1983]) 'Capitalism and gay identity', in H. Abelove, M. Barale and D. Halperin (eds) *The Lesbian and Gay Studies Reader* (New York: Routledge).

Dinshaw, C., Edelman, L., Ferguson, R.A., Freccero, C., Freeman, E., Halberstam, J. et al. (2007) 'Theorizing queer temporalities: A roundtable discussion', *GLQ: A Journal of Lesbian and Gay Studies* 13(2).

Dissidentenfunk (2005) *Massregelvollzug/Forensische Psychiatrie*, 13 January. Available at: http://www.dissidentenfunk.de/archiv/s0501/index.html (accessed 1 January 2014).

Doan, P.L. and Higgins, H. (2011) 'The demise of queer space? Resurgent gentrification and the assimilation of LGBT neighborhoods', *Journal of Planning Education and Research* 31(1).

Doinet, R., Götting, M. and Knobbe, M. (2008) 'Der Fall Serkan A.: Eine klassische Karriere', *Der Stern*, 13 January. Available at: http://www.stern.de/panorama/:Der-Fall-Serkan-A.-Eine-Karriere/607151.html (accessed 5 January 2010).

Douglas, S., Jivraj, S. and Lamble, S. (2011) *Liabilities of Queer Anti-racist Critique*, special issue of *Feminist Legal Studies* 19(2).

Drag Festival (2008a) Info. Available at: http://drag-festival.net/drag/?page_id=2 (accessed 1 June 2013).

Drag Festival (2008b) 'Homophober Überfall nach dem Drag Festival', press release 8 June.

Duggan, L. (2004). *The Twilight of Equality: Neoliberalism, Cultural Politics and the Attack on Democracy* (Boston, MA: Beacon Press).

Edelman, L. (2004) *No Future: Queer Theory and the Death Drive* (Durham, NC: Duke University Press).

Eick, V. (2003) '"Und das ist auch gut so ...": Polizieren im Berlin des 21. Jahrhundert', in S. Nissen (ed.) *Kriminalität und Sicherheitspolitik. Analysen aus London, Paris, Berlin und New York* (Opladen: Leske+Budrich).

Eicker, P. (2007) 'Küssen verboten?', *Hinnerk* 4.

Ekine, S. (2013) 'Contesting narratives of queer Africa', in S. Ekine and H. Abbas (eds) *Queer African Reader* (Dakar: Pambazuka Press).

El-Tayeb, F. (1999) *Schwarze Deutsche: Der Diskurs um 'Rasse' und nationale Identität 1890–1933* (Frankfurt a.M.: Campus).

El-Tayeb, F. (2011) *European Others: Queering Ethnicity in Postnational Europe* (Minneapolis: University of Minnesota Press).

El-Tayeb, F. (2012) '"Gays who cannot properly be gay": Queer Muslims in the neoliberal European city', *European Journal of Women's Studies* 19(1).

Eng, D. and Han, S. (2006) 'Desegregating love: Transnational adoption, racial reparation, and racial transitional objects', *Studies in Gender and Sexuality* 7(2).

Eng, D.L. and Kazanjian, D. (eds) (2003) *Loss: The Politics of Mourning* (Berkeley: University of California Press).

Freccero, C. (2007) 'Queer times', *South Atlantic Quarterly* 106(3).

Epstein, S. (1987) 'Gay politics, ethnic identity: The limits of social constructionism', *Socialist Review* 93/94.

Erdem, E. (2009) 'In der Falle einer Politik des Ressentiments. Feminismus und die Integrationsdebatte', in S. Hess, J, Binder and J. Moser (eds) *No Integration?! Kulturwissenschaftliche Beiträge zur Integrationsdebatte in Europa* (Bielefeld: Transcript).

Erevelles, N. (2010) 'Embattled pedagogies: Deconstructing terror from a transnational feminist disability studies perspective', in A. DeLeon and W. Ross (eds) *Critical Theories, Radical Pedagogies and Social Education* (Rotterdam: Sense Publishers).

Evans, J. (2014) 'Harmless kisses and infinite loops: Making space for queer place in twenty-first century Berlin', in M. Cook and J. Evans (eds) *Queer Cities, Queer Cultures: Europe since 1945* (London: Bloomsbury).

Farrow, K. (2010 [2004]) 'Is gay marriage antiblack???', in R. Conrad (ed.) *Against Equality: Queer Critiques of Gay Marriage* (Lewiston, ME: Against Equality Publishing Collective).

Feddersen, J. (2003) 'Was guckst du? Bist du schwul?', *Tageszeitung*, 8 November.

Fekete, L. (2006) 'Enlightened fundamentalism? Immigration, feminism and the right', *Race & Class* 48(2).

Fekete, L. (2014) 'Rechte Gewalt in Europa', *Rosa-Luxemburg-Stiftung*. Available at: www.nsu-watch.info/2014/11/rechte-gewalt-europa-das-konzept-des-anti-extremismus-schwaecht-den-antifaschistischen-widerstand/ (accessed 1 January 2015).

Feldman, A. (2004) 'Memory theatres, virtual witnessing, and the trauma-aesthetic', *Biography* 27(1).

Fenced Out, directed by FIERCE (USA, 2001).

Ferguson, R. (2004) *Aberrations in Black: Toward a Queer of Color Critique* (Minneapolis: University of Minnesota Press).

Ferreday, D. and Kuntsman, A. (2011) 'Introduction: Haunted futurities', *Borderlands E-Journal: New Spaces in the Humanities* 10(2).

Fertig, G. and Salka, S. (2009) 'Wehrt Euch!' (Defend yourselves), *Siegessäule*, November. Available at: www.siegessaeule.de/uploads/img/printausgaben/sis_11-09.pdf (accessed 1 April 2014).

Fest, N. (2014) 'Islam als Integrationshindernis', *Bild*, 27 July. Available at: www.bild. de/news/standards/religionen/islam-als-integrationshindernis-36990528.bild.html (accessed 1 August 2014).

FIERCE (2008) 'LGBTQ youth fight for a S.P.O.T. on Pier 40', 15 September. Available at: http://fiercenyc.org/media/docs/3202_PublicHearingPressRelease (accessed 1 April 2014).

Finley, C. (2014a) 'Decolonizing sexualized cultural images of Native peoples : "Bringing sexy back" to native studies', public lecture, University of Toronto, 26 March.

Finley, C. (2014b) 'Gay marriage and indigenous sovereignty: Making queer love legit and fun in the Colville Nation', paper presented at the American Studies Association, Los Angeles, 5–9 November.

Finley, C. et al. (2014) 'What's love got to do with it?', panel at the American Studies Association, Los Angeles, 5–9 November.

Fisher, M. (2015) 'Charlie Hebdo's most famous cover shows what makes the magazine so important', *Vox*, 17 January. Available at: www.vox.com/2015/1/7/7507729/the-satirical-cartoon-cover-that-defines-charlie-hebdo (accessed 18 January 2015).

Flag Wars (film, dir. Linda Goode Bryant, Laura Poitras, 2003).

Florida, R. (2002) *The Rise of the Creative Class* (New York: Basic Books).

Foucault, M. (1978) 'About the concept of the "dangerous individual" in 19th-century legal psychiatry', *International Journal of Law and Psychiatry* 1.

Foucault, M. (2004 [1978]) *The Birth of Biopolitics: Lectures at the Collège de France 1978–1979* (London: Palgrave).

Freeman, E. (2007) 'Still after', *South Atlantic Quarterly* 106(3).

Freeman, E. (2010) *Time Binds: Queer Temporalities, Queer Histories* (Durham, NC: Duke University Press).

Gayhane (n.d.). Available at: http://so36.de/events/gayhane/ (accessed 1 April 2014).

Geidner, C. (2013) 'Meet the trans scholar fighting against the campaign for out trans military service', *BuzzFeed*, 9 September. Available at: www.buzzfeed.com/chrisgeidner/meet-the-trans-scholar-fighting-against-the-campaign-for-out (accessed 6 January 2014).

Genderliste (2012) 'Morgen: Kameraspaziergang Neukölln', email announcement, 7 June.

GfK GeoMarketing (n.d.), *Europe-wide market data*. Available at: www.gfk- geomarketing. com/market_data.html (accessed 1 April 2010).

Ghaziani, A. (2010) 'There goes the gayborhood?', *Contexts* 9(4).

Ghorashi, H. (2003) 'Ayaan Hirsi Ali: Daring or dogmatic? Debates on multiculturalism and emancipation in the Netherlands', in T. van Meijl and H. Driessen (eds) *Multiple Identifications and the Self* (Utrecht: Stichting Focaal).

Gieseking, J. (2013) 'Queering the meaning of "neighborhood": Reinterpreting the lesbian-queer experience of Park Slope, Brooklyn, 1983–2008', in M. Addison and Y. Taylor (eds) *Queer Presences and Absences* (New York: Palgrave Macmillan).

Gilmore, R.W. (1999) 'Globalisation and US prison growth: From military Keynesianism to post-Keynesian militarism', *Race & Class* 40(2/3).

Gilmore, R.W. (2007) *Golden Gulag: Prisons, Surplus, Crisis, and Opposition in Globalizing California* (Berkeley: University of California Press).

Global LGBTQ Human Rights (2014) 'In conversation', University of Toronto, 20 June.

Göbel, M. (2009) 'Neue Küsse fürs Mahnmal', *Siegessäule* 12.

Göbel, M. (2013) 'Ärger im queeren Paradies: Transgenialer* CSD ohne Straßenfest auf der Oranienstraße', *Tageszeitung*, 11 July. Available at: www.siegessaeule.de/newscomments/article/aerger-im-queeren-paradies-transgenialer-csd-ohne-strassenfest-auf-der-oranienstrasse.html?PHPSESSID=c5ac01e3f8c1a8d839fab0146444ce6e (accessed 26 November 2013).

Goonewardena, K. and Kipfer, S. (2005) 'Spaces of difference: Reflections from Toronto on multiculturalism, bourgeois urbanism and the possibility of radical urban politics', *International Journal of Urban and Regional Research* 29(3).

Gordon, A. (1999) 'Globalism and the prison-industrial complex: An interview with Angela Davis', *Race & Class* 40.

Gordon, A. (2006) 'Abu Ghraib: Imprisonment and the War on Terror', *Race & Class* 48(1).

Gorman, R. (2013) 'Mad nation? Thinking through race, class, and mad identity politics', in B.A. LeFrançois, R. Menzies and G. Reaume (eds) *Mad Matters: A Critical Reader in Canadian Mad Studies* (Toronto: Canadian Scholars Press Inc.).

Gossett, R. (2012) 'Ten posts for Sylvia Rivera's ten-year anniversary', *The Spirit Was.* Available at: http://thespiritwas.tumblr.com/post/28415757544/ten-posts-for-sylvia-riveras-ten-year-memorial (accessed 1 August 2014).

Gossett, R. (2013) 'Happy birthday Marsha "pay it no mind" Johnson', Crunk Feminist Collective, 27 June. Available at: www.crunkfeministcollective.com/2013/06/27/happy-birthday-marsha-pay-it-no-mind-johnson/ (accessed 6 January 2014).

Gosine, A. (2009) 'Politics and passion: An interview with Gloria Wekker', *Caribbean Review of Gender Studies* 3. Available at: http://sta.uwi.edu/crgs/november2009/journals/CRGS%20Wekker.pdf (accessed 1 August 2014).

Gramsci, A. (1996) 'Aufzeichnungen und verstreute Notizen für eine Gruppe von Aufsätzen über die Geschichte der Intellektuellen, §§ 1–3', in *Gefängnisbriefe* 7(12–15) (Hamburg: Argument).

Grassmann, P. (2007) 'Migrantenkinder gegen Schwule: Homophobes Berlin', *Süddeutsche Zeitung*, 26 September. Available at: http://www.sueddeutsche.de/panorama/703/419467/text/ (accessed 1 June 2009).

Grewal, I. (2005) *Transnational America: Feminisms, Diasporas, Neoliberalisms* (Durham, NC: Duke University Press).

Grewal, I. and Kaplan, C. (1994) *Scattered Hegemonies: Postmodernity and Transnational Feminist Practices* (Minneapolis: University of Minnesota Press).

Grewal, I. and Kaplan, C. (2000) 'Postcolonial studies and transnational feminist practices', *Jouvert* 5(1).

Grewal, I. and Kaplan, C. (2001) 'Global identities: Theorizing transnational studies of sexuality', *GLQ: A Journal of Lesbian and Gay Studies* 7(4).

Grosfoguel, R., Oso, L. and Christou, A. (2014) '"Racism", intersectionality and migration studies: Framing some theoretical reflections', *Identities*.

GSW (2010) *WohnmarktReport 2010* (Housing Market Report 2010). Available at: www.businesslocationcenter.de/imperia/md/content/blc/leben/wmr_dt.pdf (accessed 1 April 2010).

Gumbs, A.P. (2010) *We Can Learn to Mother Ourselves: The Queer Survival of Black Feminism 1968–1996* (unpublished PhD dissertation, Duke University).

Gutiérrez Rodríguez, E. (2000) '"My traditional clothes are sweat-shirts and jeans": Über die Schwierigkeit, nicht different zu sein oder Gegen-Kultur als Zurichtung', European Institute for Progressive Cultural Politics. Available at: http://eipcp.net/transversal/0101/gutierrezrodriguez/de (accessed 17 July 2014).

Gutiérrez Rodríguez, E. (2010) 'Decolonizing postcolonial rhetoric', in E. Gutiérrez Rodríguez, M. Boatca and S. Costa (eds) *Decolonizing European Sociology* (Aldershot: Ashgate).

Ha, N. (2013) *Handel(n) und Wandel(n) – Urbane Informalität, städtische Repräsentation und migrantische Existenzsicherung in Berlin am Beispiel des mobilen Straßenhandel* (PhD dissertation, Technische Universität Berlin).

Haag, O. (2008) 'Inventing a tradition of oppression: On the commemoration of 'queer' Nazi victims in Austria', Paper presented at the Sex/ualities In and Out of Time conference, University of Edinburgh – St Andrews, 28–29 November.

Haakenson, T. (2009) 'Queers in space: The queer art of Michael Elmgreen and Ingar Dragset', paper presented at the Queer Futurities Symposium, Finland Institute, Berlin, 18–19 May.

Halberstam, J. (2005) *In a Queer Time and Place: Transgender Bodies, Subcultural Lives* (New York: New York University Press).

Hall, S. (1992) 'The West and the rest: Discourse and power', in S. Hall and B. Gieben (eds) *Formations of Modernity* (Cambridge: Polity Press).

Hall, S., Critcher, C., Jefferson, T., Clarke, J. and Roberts, B. (1978) *Policing the Crisis: Mugging, the State and Law and Order* (New York: Holmes and Meier).

Halmi, A. (2008) 'Kontinuitäten der Zwangspsychiatrie' (Master's dissertation, Freie Universität Berlin).

Hamburger Morgenpost (2007) 'Pulverfass St. Georg: Moslems gegen Schwule', 21 April.

Hanhardt, C.B. (2008) 'Butterflies, whistles, and fists: Gay safe streets patrols and the new gay ghetto, 1976–1981', *Radical History Review* 100.

Hanhardt, C.B. (2013) *Safe Space: Gay Neighborhood History and the Politics of Violence* (Durham, NC: Duke University Press).

Haritaworn, J. (2008a) 'Shifting positionalities: Empirical reflections on a queer/trans of colour methodology', *Sociological Research Online* 13(1). Available at: www.socresonline.org.uk/13/1/13.html (accessed 1 January 2015).

Haritaworn, J. (2008b) 'Loyal repetitions of the nation: Gay assimilation and the "war on terror"', *DarkMatter* 3.

Haritaworn, J. (2010a) 'Queer injuries: The racial politics of homophobic hate crime in Germany', in special issue on *Sexuality, Criminalization and Social Control, Social Justice* 37(1): 69–91.

Haritaworn, J. (2010b) 'Wounded subjects: Sexual exceptionalism and the moral panic on "migrant homophobia" in Germany', in M. Boatca, S. Costa and E. Gutiérrez Rodríguez (eds) *Decolonising European Sociology* (Aldershot: Ashgate).

Haritaworn, J. (2011) 'Colorful bodies in the *multikulti* metropolis: Vitality, victimology and transgressive citizenship in Berlin', in T. Cotton (ed.) *Trans-Migrations: Bodies, Borders, and the (Geo)politics of Gender Trans-ing* (New York: Routledge).

Haritaworn, J. (2012) *The Biopolitics of Mixing: Thai Multiracialities and Haunted Ascendancies.* (Aldershot: Ashgate).

Haritaworn, J. (2015) 'Decolonizing the non/human', *GLQ* 21(2/3).

Haritaworn, J. and Petzen, J. (2011) 'Invented traditions, new intimate publics: Tracing the German "Muslim homophobia" discourse', in S. Hutchings, C. Flood, G. Miazhevich and H. Nickels (eds) *Islam in Its International Context: Comparative Perspectives* (Cambridge: Cambridge Scholars Press).

Haritaworn, J. and Weheliye, A. (forthcoming) 'Ethnic studies in Deutschland? Über die Grenzen und Potenziale der universitären Institutionalisierung von minorisierten Wissensformen', in N. Ha and N. Ha (eds) *Geschlossene Gesellschaft* (Berlin: Heinrich-Böll-Stiftung).

Haritaworn, J., Kuntsman, A. and Posocco, S. (2013) 'Introduction: Murderous Inclusions', *International Feminist Journal of Politics* 15(4).

Haritaworn, J., Kuntsman, A. and Posocco, S. (2014) 'Introduction', in J. Haritaworn, A. Kuntsman and S. Posocco (eds) *Queer Necropolitics* (London: Routledge).

Haritaworn, J., Tauqir, T. and Erdem, E. (2008) "Gay imperialism: Gender and sexuality discourse in the 'war on terror'", in A. Kuntsman and E. Miyake (eds) *Out of Place: Interrogating Silences in Queerness/Raciality* (York: Raw Nerve Books).

Haug, S. (2010) *Jugendliche Migranten – Muslimische Jugendliche: Gewalttätigkeit und geschlechterspezifische Einstellungsmuster* (Berlin: Federal Ministry for Family, Seniors, Women and Youth).

Häußermann, H., Gornig, M., Hausmann, P., Kapphan, A. and Werwatz, A. (2007) *Monitoring Soziale Stadtentwicklung Berlin 2007. Fortschreibung für den Zeitraum 2005–2006* (Senate Administration for Urban Development Berlin, Department IA, Urban Development Planning and Terrain Management).

Heisig, K. (2010) *Das Ende der Geduld: Konsequent gegen jugendliche Gewalttäter* (Munich: Herder).

Herdt, G. (2009) 'Introduction: Moral panics, sexual rights, and cultural anger', in G. Herdt (ed.) *Moral Panics, Sex Panics: Fear and the Fight over Sexual Rights* (New York: New York University Press).

Heyl, M., Kaethner, G., Kiener, S., Öztürk, R., Riechers, K., Schlüter, D. et al. (2008) 'Mein Vater hat mich geprügelt: U-Bahn-Schläger spricht im Knast', *Bild*, 3 January. Available at: www.bild.de/news/vermischtes/vater/schlaeger-3399928.bild.html (accessed 1 August 2014).

Hieronymus, A. (2011 [2009]) 'Schwule und Muslim_innen zwischen Homophobie und Islamophobie', in K. Yılmaz-Günay (ed.) *Karriere eines konstruierten Gegensatzes: zehn Jahre 'Muslime versus Schwule'. Sexualpolitiken seit dem 11. September 2001* (Berlin: Self Publishing).

Himmelrath, A. (2012) '10 years of PISA testing: Taking stock', trans. C. Cave, Goethe Institute. Available at: www.goethe.de/wis/fut/sul/en8729860.htm (accessed 24 October 2012).

Hinnerk: Das schwule Magazin im Norden (2007) April–September.

Hirschfeld-Eddy-Stiftung (n.d.) 'A civil rights pioneer and a human rights advocate'. Available at: http://www.hirschfeld-eddy-stiftung.de/en/foundation/about-us/names/ (accessed 11 June 2014).

Hobsbawm, E. (1983) 'Introduction: Inventing traditions', in E. Hobsbawm and T. Ranger (eds) *The Invention of Tradition* (Cambridge: Cambridge University Press).

Holm, A. (2006) 'Urban renewal and the end of social housing in East Berlin', *Social Justice* 33(3).

Holm, A. (2008) 'Die Vergesellschaftung der Stadt: Neuordnungen des Städtischen in kapitalistischen Gesellschaften', *Marxistische Blätter* 5. Available at: http://www.linksnet. de/de/artikel/23801 (accessed on 1 April 2010).

Holm, A. (2009) 'Soziale Mischung: Zur Entstehung und Funktion eines Mythos', *Forum Wissenschaft* 1. Reposted at: http://gentrificationblog.wordpress.com/2009/07/29/ mythos-soziale-mischung/ (accessed on 13 July 2012).

Holm, A. (2010a) 'Hohe Mieten machen Kreuzberg pleite', *Gentrificationblog*. Available at: http://gentrificationblog.wordpress.com/2010/03/05/berlin-hohe-mieten-machen-kreuzberg-pleite/ (accessed 1 June 2013).

Holm, A. (2010b) 'Neukölln in den Kollwitzplatz verwandeln?' *Gentrificationblog*, Available at: http://gentrificationblog.wordpress.com/2010/03/10/berlin-neukoelln-in-den-kollwitzplatz- verwandeln-radiofeature / (accessed 1 June 2013).

Holm, A. (2011) 'Wohnungspolitik der rot-roten Regierungskoalition in Berlin', in A. Holm, K. Lederer and M. Naumann (eds) *Linke Metropolenpolitik: Erfahrungen und Perspektiven am Beispiel Berlin* (Münster: Westfälisches Dampfboot).

Holm, A. (2012) 'Vorwort', in A. Holm (ed.) *Manuell Castells: Kampf in den Städten. Gesellschaftliche Widersprüche und politische Macht* (Hamburg: VSA).

Holm, A. (n.d.) 'Mit "Pioniere" getaggte Artikel', *Gentrificationblog*. Available at: http://gentrificationblog.wordpress.com/tag/pioniere/ (accessed 1 June 2013).

Hong, G.K. (2008) '"The future of our worlds": Black feminism and the politics of knowledge in the university under globalization', *Meridians: Feminism, Race, Transnationalism* 8(2).

hooks, b. (1992) 'Eating the other: Desire and resistance', in *Black Looks: Race and Representation* (Boston, MA: South End Press).

hooks, b. (1996) *Killing Rage: Ending Racism* (London: Penguin).

Huck, W. (2011) 'Intensivtäter aus jugendpsychiatrischer Sicht', in A. Boeger (ed.) *Jugendliche Intensivtäter: Interdisziplinare Perspektiven* (Wiesbaden: VS).

Hutson, C. (2009) 'Unverschämt – Wir im Spannungsfeld von Rassismus, Hetero-/Sexismus und Ableism', paper given at Hamburg University, 13 May.

Incite! Women of Color Against Violence (eds) (2007) *The Revolution Will Not Be Funded: Beyond the Non-profit Industrial Complex* (Cambridge, MA: South End Press).

Incite! Women of Color Against Violence (2008) 'Critical lessons from the New Jersey 7', *New Left Turn*, September. Available at: www.incite-national.org/media/docs/9908_toolkitrev-nj7.pdf (accessed 1 August 2014).

Incite! Women of Color Against Violence (2011) (eds) *The Revolution Will Not Be Funded: Beyond the Non-profit Industrial Complex* (Cambridge, MA: South End Press)

Indymedia (2008) 'Homophober Angriff in Kreuzberg', 8 June. Available at: http://de.indymedia.org/2008/06/219458.shtml (accessed 20 August 2008).

Indymedia (2009) 'Task Force Okerstraße', 8 August. Available at: http://de.indymedia.org/2009/08/257756.shtml (accessed 30 March 2015).

Indymedia (2012) 'Bürgerwehr in Kreuzberg', 23 May. Available at: http://de.indymedia.org/2012/05/330358.shtml (accessed 1 November 2013).

Ingram, G.B. (2003) 'Returning to the scene of the crime: Uses of trial dossiers on consensual male homosexuality for urban research, with examples from twentieth-century British Columbia', *GLQ: A Journal of Lesbian and Gay Studies* 10(1).

Ingram, G.B., Boutillette, A.-M. and Retter, Y. (1997) 'Lost in space', in G. Ingram, A.-M. Boutillette and Y. Retter (eds) *Queers in Space: Communities, Public Places, Sites of Resistance* (Seattle, WA: Bay Press).

Jaffer, F. (2012) 'Homonationalist discourse, queer organizing and the media', in M. Smith and F. Jaffer (eds) *Beyond the Queer Alphabet: Conversations on Gender, Sexuality and Intersectionality*, Teaching Equity Matters Book Series. Available at: https://the-menace.s3.amazonaws.com/uploads/Beyond_the_Queer_Alphabet_20March2012-F.pdf (accessed 1 August 2014).

Jakob, C. (2014) 'Wissenschaftler über Islamophobie', *Tageszeitung*, 29 July. Available at: www.taz.de/Wissenschaftler-ueber-Islamophobie/!143233/ (accessed 1 August 2014).

Jameson, F. (1988) 'Cognitive mapping', in C. Nelson and L. Grossberg (eds) *Marxism and the Interpretation of Culture* (Chicago: University of Illinois Press).

Jivraj, S. and de Jong, A. (2011) 'The Dutch homo-emancipation policy and its silencing effects on queer Muslims', *Feminist Legal Studies* 19(2).

Jungle World (2008), issue 26, 26 June.

JVA Tegel (n.d.) *Statistische Angaben*. Available at: www.berlin.de/jva-tegel/02_UeberUns/03_Statistische_Angaben/Statistik.pdf (accessed 1 April 2010).

Kanani, N. (2011) 'Race and madness: Locating the experiences of racialized people with psychiatric histories in Canada and the United States', *Critical Disability Discourse/ Discours Critiques dans le Champ du Handicap* 3.

Kanani, N. (forthcoming) 'Thinking through disability and settler colonialism in Canada', in R. Gorman (ed.) *Disabling States* (Toronto: Canadian Scholars Press Inc.).

Kandaswamy, P. (2008) 'State austerity and the racial politics of same-sex marriage in the US', *Sexualities* 11(6).

Kapur, R. (2005) *Erotic Justice: Law and the New Politics of Postcolonialism* (London: Glasshouse Press).

Kedves, J. (2014) 'LOVE AIDS RIOT SEX I + II', *frieze*. Available at: http://frieze-magazin. de/archiv/kritik/love-aids-riot-sex-i-ii/?lang=en (accessed 1 December 2014).

Khalass!!! We're vex! (2013) *We Are Here – We Have Always Been Here! Wir sind da – wir waren schon immer da!* (unpublished manifesto, Berlin).

Kiliç, E. (2008) *Diskriminierung von Migranten bei der Wohnungssuche Eine Untersuchung in Berlin* (unpublished dissertation in Urban and Regional Sociology, Humboldt University, Berlin).

Kipfer, S. and Keil, R. (2002) 'Toronto Inc.? Planning the competitive city in the New Toronto', *Antipode* 34(2).

Klein, N. (2013) 'Dancing the world into being: A conversation with Idle No More's Leanne Simpson', posted at *Yes! Magazine*, 5 March. Available at: www.yesmagazine. org/peace-justice/dancing-the-world-into-being-a-conversation-with-idle-no-more-leanne-simpson (accessed 1 August 2014).

Knopp, L. (1990) 'Some theoretical implications of gay involvement in an urban land market', *Political Geography Quarterly* 9(4).

Kotti Camp (2012) 'Social Housing in a Post-Social Berlin', 22 September. Available at: http://kottiundco.net/2012/09/22/social-housing-in-a-post-social-berlin/ (accessed 1 June 2013).

Kotti Camp (n.d.) 'Unser Protest in Zeitungen/Radio/Fernsehen'. Available at: http:// kottiundco.net/kleine-presseschau/ (accessed 1 June 2013).

Kuntsman, A. (2009a) *Figurations of Violence and Belonging: Queerness, Migranthood and Nationalism in Cyberspace and Beyond* (Oxford: Peter Lang).

Kuntsman, A. (2009b) 'The currency of victimhood in uncanny homes: Russian-speaking queer immigrants in Israel confront homophobia', *Journal of Ethnic and Migration Studies* 35(1).

Kuumba, M.B. (2001) *Gender and Social Movements* (Lanham, MD: Rowman & Littlefield).

Lamble, S. (2008) 'Retelling racialized violence, remaking White innocence: The politics of interlocking oppressions in Transgender Day of Remembrance', *Sexuality Research & Social Policy* 5(1).

Lamble, S. (2014) 'Queer investments in punishment: Sexual citizenship, social movements and the expanding carceral state', in J. Haritaworn, A. Kuntsman and S. Posocco (eds) *Queer Necropolitics* (London: Routledge).

Lawrence, B. (2004) *'Real' Indians and Others: Mixed-blood Urban Native Peoples and Indigenous Nationhood* (Lincoln, NE: University of Nebraska Press).

Lees, L. (2008) 'Gentrification and social mixing: Towards an inclusive urban renaissance?', *Urban Studies* 45(12).

Lefebvre, H. (1991 [1974]) *The Production of Space*, trans. D. Nicholson-Smith (Oxford: Blackwell).

Lentin, A. and Titley, G. (2011) *The Crises of Multiculturalism: Racism in a Neoliberal Age* (London: Zed Books).

Levine, M. (1979) 'Gay ghetto', *Journal of Homosexuality* 4(4).

Long, S. (n.d.) Tag Archives: Sochi. Available at: http://paper-bird.net/tag/sochi/ (accessed 1 December 2014).

Love, H. (2007a) 'Compulsory happiness and queer existence', New Formations 63(1).

Love, H. (2007b) Feeling Backward: Loss and the Politics of Queer History (Cambridge, MA: Harvard University Press).

LSVD (2001) 'Denkmal für die homosexuellen NS-Opfer gefordert'. Available at: www.lsvd. de/gedenk-ort/pm101001.htm (accessed 15 August 2009).

LSVD (2003) 'Schluss mit Diskriminierung und Gewalt. Migranten müssen Verhältnis zu Homophobie klären', press release, 18 July.

LSVD (2009) 'Feier zum Tag des Gedenkens an die Opfer des Nationalsozialismus'. Available at: www.berlin.lsvd.de/cms/index.php?option=com_content&task=view&id =450&Itemid=82 (accessed 15 August 2009).

LSVD (2014) 'Veranstaltung 10. Todestag Hatun Sürücü', press release, 18 December.

LSVD (n.d.) 'Zeig Respekt!' Available at: http://zeig-respekt.lsvd.de/index.php?option=com_ content&view=frontpage&Itemid=133 (accessed 5 June 2011).

Luibhéid, E. (2008) 'Queer/migration: An unruly body of scholarship', GLQ: A Journal of Lesbian and Gay Studies 14(2).

Luig, J. (2008) 'Und dann werden wir behaart: Ein Tag als Drag King', Tageszeitung, 11 June. Available at: www.taz.de/!18557/ (accessed 1 August 2014).

Lury, C. (2000) 'The united colors of diversity', in S. Franklin, C. Lury and J. Stacey (eds) Global Nature, Global Culture (Thousand Oaks, CA: Sage).

MacDougall, C. (2011) Cold War Capital: Contested Urbanism in West Berlin, 1963–1989 (unpublished PhD dissertation, Rutgers University).

Manalansan IV, M.F. (2005) 'Race, violence, and neoliberal spatial politics in the global city', Social Text 23(3–4 84–5).

Maneo (2008a) 'Küssen für ein tolerantes Berlin – 1. MANEO Kuss-Marathon am Internationalen Tag gegen Homophobie 17. Mai'. Available at: www.maneo-toleranzkampagne.de/?cat=2&sub=3 (accessed 6 January 2014).

Maneo (2008b) '2. MANEO-Kussmarathon protect every kiss: Berlin küsste für mehr Toleranz', Maneo Toleranzkampagne, 17 May. Available at: www.maneo-toleranzkampagne.de/?cat=2&sub=3 (accessed 6 January 2014).

Maneo (2008c) '"Sei schwul, sei Opfer, sei Berlin? Die Stadt ist gefordert!"', press release, 31 October. Available at: www.m-ermisch.de/Downlod/Maneo-PM081031_ schwererUerbergriff_n.pdf (accessed 15 August 2009).

Maneo (2009) 'Protect every kiss: Berlins 3. MANEO Kuss-Marathon', Maneo Toleranzkampagne, 9 May. Available at: www.maneo.de/presse/archiv/year/2009/ article/protect-every-kiss.html (accessed 27 December 2013).

Maneo (2010a) 'Zum Tod von Kirsten Heisig'. Available at: http://www.maneo.de/presse/ archiv/select_category/1/article/zum-tod-von-kirsten-heisig.html (accessed 1 August 2014).

Maneo (2010b) 'Berlins 4. MANEO Kuss-Marathon – Protect Every Kiss – Berlin kisses for more tolerance', Maneo Toleranzkampagne, 5 May. Available at: www.maneo.de/ en/news/archiv/year/2010/article/berlins-4-maneo-kuss-marathon-protect-every-kiss-berlin-kisses-for-more-tolerance.html (accessed 27 December 2013).

Maneo (2011) 'The International Maneo Conference 2011'. Available at: www.maneo.de/ en/maneo-konferenz.html (accessed 1 November 2013).

Marcuse, P. and van Kempen, R. (2000) 'Conclusion: A changed spatial order', in P. Marcuse and R. van Kempen (eds) Globalizing Cities: A New Spatial Order? (Oxford: Blackwell).

Martin, R. (2007) An Empire of Indifference: American War and the Financial Logic of Risk Management (Durham, NC: Duke University Press).

Massad, J.A. (2007) *Desiring Arabs* (Chicago: University of Chicago Press).

Mbembe, A. (2003) 'Necropolitics', *Public Culture* 15(1).

McClintock, A. (1993) 'Family feuds: Gender, nationalism and the family', *Feminist Review* 44.

McKittrick, K. (2006) *Demonic Grounds: Black Women and the Cartographies of Struggle* (Minneapolis: University of Minnesota Press).

McNeill, J. (2014) Untitled presentation at the 'What the fuck is queer about settler colonialism, racism and homonationalism?' roundtable, Toronto, 23 July.

Mecheril, P. and Teo, T. (eds) (1994) *Andere Deutsche. Zur Lebenssituation von Menschen multiethnischer und multikultureller Herkunft* (Berlin: Dietz Verlag).

Melamed, J. (2011) 'Reading Tehran in Lolita: Making racialized and gendered difference work for neoliberal multiculturalism', in G. Hong and R. Ferguson (eds) *Strange Affinities: The Gender and Sexual Politics of Comparative Racialization* (Durham, NC: Duke University Press).

Melter, C. and Mecheril, P. (eds) (2009) *Rassismustheorie und -forschung in Deutschland. Kontur eines wissenschaftlichen Feldes* (Schwalbach: Wochenschau Verlag).

Migrationsrat (2014a) *Der NSU-Komplex. Drei Jahre nach der 'Selbstenttarnung' des NSU* (Newsletter No. 4). Available online: www.migrationsrat.de/dokumente/ pressemitteilungen/MRBB-NL-2014-04-Leben%20nach%20Migration.pdf (accessed 1 January 2015).

Migrationsrat (2014b) 'Migrant_innenselbstorganisationen übernehmen Verantwortung im Kampf gegen Homophobie und Transphobie', 17 May. Available at: www. migrationsrat.de/index.php?option=com_content&view=article&id=276:migrantinn enselbstorganisationen-verantwortung-im-kampf-gegen-homophobie-und-transphobie&catid=4:pressemitteilungen&Itemid=4 (accessed 1 January 2015).

Mock, J. (2013) 'Not all memoirs are created equal: The gate-keeping of trans women of color's stories'. Available at: http://janetmock.com/2013/06/05/memoir-trans-women-of-color/ (accessed 6 January 2014).

Moraga, C. and Anzaldúa, G. (eds) (1981) *This Bridge Called My Back: Writings by Radical Women of Color* (Watertown, NY: Persephone).

Morgensen, S. (2011) *Spaces Between Us: Queer Settler Colonialism and Indigenous Decolonization* (Minneapolis: University of Minnesota Press).

Mortimer-Sandilands, C. and Erickson, B. (2010) 'Introduction: A genealogy of queer ecologies', in C. Mortimer-Sandilands and B. Erickson (eds) *Queer Ecologies: Sex, Nature, Politics, Desire* (Bloomington: Indiana University Press).

Mosse, G. (1997) *Nationalism and Sexuality* (New York: Howard Fertig).

Moynihan, D.P. (1965) *The Negro Family: The Case for National Action* (Washington, DC: Office of Policy Planning and Research, U.S. Department of Labor).

Muñoz, J.E. (1999) *Disidentifications: Queers of Color and the Performance of Politics* (Minneapolis: University of Minnesota Press).

Muñoz, J.E. (2000) 'Feeling brown: Ethnicity and affect in Ricardo Bracho's *The Sweetest Hangover (and Other STDs)*', *Theatre Journal* 52(1).

Muñoz, J.E. (2007) 'Cruising the toilet: LeRoi Jones/Amiri Baraka, radical black traditions, and queer futurity', *GLQ: A Journal of Lesbian and Gay Studies* 13(2).

N., M. and Rage, R. (2013) 'Time-travelling brown bears: Intergenerational interviews with two transmasculine femmes of color on healing justice', *Heinrich Böll Stiftung*. Available at: http://heimatkunde.boell.de/2013/05/01/time-travelling-brown-bears-intergenerational-interviews-two-transmasculine-femmes-color (accessed 1 August 2014).

Naber, N. (2013) 'Transnational anti-imperialism and Middle East Women's Studies', *Jadaliyya*, 2 July. Available at: www.jadaliyya.com/pages/index/12584/transnational-anti-imperialism-and-middle-east-wom (accessed 1 August 2014).

Nair, Y. (2008) 'Why I won't come out on National Coming Out Day', 9 October. Available at: www.yasminnair.net/content/why-i-won%E2%80%99t-come-out-national-coming-out-day-9-october-2008 (accessed 1 June 2013).

Nair, Y. (2010) 'Against equality, against marriage: An introduction', in R. Conrad (ed.) *Against Equality: Queer Critiques of Gay Marriage* (Lewiston, ME: Against Equality Publishing Collective).

Namaste, K. (1996) 'Tragic misreadings: Queer theory's erasure of transgender subjectivity', in B. Beemyn and M. Eliason (eds) *Queer Studies: A Lesbian, Gay, Bisexual, and Transgender Anthology* (New York: New York University Press).

Nash, C. (2013) 'Queering neighbourhoods: Politics and practice in Toronto', *ACME* 12(2).

Nash, C. and Catungal, J.-P. (eds) (2013) 'Introduction', special issue *Sexual Landscapes, Lives and Livelihoods in Canada*, *ACME* 12(2).

Native Youth Sexual Health Network/Families of Sisters in Spirit/No More Silence (2014) 'Supporting the Resurgence of Community-based Responses to Violence'. Available at: www.nativeyouthsexualhealth.com/march142014.pdf (accessed 1 August 2014).

Negri, A. (2008) 'The labor of the multitude and the fabric of biopolitics', *Mediations* 23(2).

Offending the Clientele (2010) directed by Anonymous (Germany). Available at: http://vimeo.com/16116523 (accessed 1 June 2014).

Ohder, C. and Huck, L. (2006) *Intensivtäter in Berlin: Hintergründe und Folgen vielfacher strafrechtlicher Auffälligkeit. Teil 1: Eine Auswertung von Akten der Abteilung 47 der Berliner Staatsanwaltschaft* (Berliner Forum Gewaltprävention).

Opitz, M., Oguntoye, K. and Schultz, D. (eds) (1992 [1986]) *Showing Our Colors: Afro-German Women Speak Out* (Amherst: University of Massachusetts Press).

Özyürek, E. (2013) 'Creating parallel communities of perpetrators: Muslim-only Holocaust education and anti-Semitism prevention programs in Germany', presentation at the Kevorkian Center, New York University.

Panorama (2014) 'Kontaktversuch: "Lügenpresse" trifft Pegida', 18 December. Available at: www.youtube.com/watch?v=DDkB09hxG2w (accessed 1 February 2015).

Paris is Burning, dir. Jenny Livingston (1990, USA).

Partridge, D. (2010) 'Holocaust *mahnmal* (memorial): Monumental memory amidst contemporary race', *Comparative Studies in Society and History* 52(4).

Patai, R. (1973) *The Arab Mind* (New York: Charles Scribner's Sons).

Paterson, T. (2015) 'Pegida movement's marches attract thousands as hatred of Islam and immigrants sweeps across Germany in the wake of Paris attacks', *Independent*, 8 February. Available at: www.independent.co.uk/news/world/europe/pegida-movements-marches-attract-thousands-as-hatred-of-islam-and-immigrants-sweeps-across-germany-in-the-wake-of-paris-attacks-9978543.html (accessed 1 February 2015).

Petzen, J. (2005) 'Wer liegt oben? Türkische und deutsche Maskulinitäten in der schwulen Szene', in Ifade (ed.) *Insider – Outsider: Bilder, ethnisierte Räume und Partizipation im Migrationsprozess* (Bielefeld: Transcript).

Petzen, J. (2008) *Gender Politics in the New Europe: 'Civilizing' Muslim Sexualities* (PhD thesis, University of Washington).

Petzen, J. (2011) 'Silent echoes: The aftermath of Judith Butler's refusal of the Civil Courage Award', in K. Yılmaz-Günay (ed.) *Karriere eines konstruierten Gegensatzes: zehn Jahre "Muslime versus Schwule". Sexualpolitiken seit dem 11. September 2001* (Berlin: Self Publishing).

Phoenix, A. (1987) 'Theories of gender and black families', in G. Weiner and M. Arnot (eds) *Gender Under Scrutiny* (London: Hutchinson).

Pilling, M. (2011) '"Taking up space": Spatialized privilege in Toronto's "Queer West" scene', unpublished manuscript.

Polzer, P. (2004) 'Von Kebabgehege bis Türkenghetto: Wie man Denken verweigern und doch Chefredakteurin sein kann. Interview mit der Chefredaktion des Berliner Homo-Magazins Siegessäule, die im November 2003 ihr Heft mit dem Titel "Türken raus!" versahen', *Gigi*, 29.

Popoola, O. and Sezen, B. (1999) 'Vorwort', in *Talking Home: Heimat aus unserer eigenen Feder. Frauen of Color in Deutschland* (Amsterdam: Blue Moon Press).

Povinelli, E.A. (2008) 'The child in the broom closet: States of killing and letting die', *South Atlantic Quarterly* 107(3).

Prosser, J. (1998) *Second Skins: The Body Narratives of Transsexuality* (New York: Columbia University Press).

Puar, J. (2007) *Terrorist Assemblages: Homonationalism in Queer Times* (Durham, NC: Duke University Press).

Puar, J. (2011) 'The cost of getting better: Suicide, sensation, switchpoints', paper presented at Racialization, Neoliberalism and Queering Public Spheres symposium, University of California at San Diego, 22–3 April.

Puar, J. (2013) 'Homonationalism as assemblage: Viral travels, affective sexualities', *Jindal Global Law Review* 4(2).

Puar, J. and Rai, A. (2002) 'Monster, terrorist, fag: The war on terrorism and the production of docile patriots', *Social Text* 20(3).

Queer.de (2008) 'Umbenannt: Hirschfeld-Ufer in Berlin'. Available at: http://www.queer.de/detail.php?article_id=8704 (accessed 11 June 2014).

Razack, S. (2002a) 'When place becomes race', in S. Razack (ed.) *Space, Race and Law: Unmapping a White Settler Society* (Toronto: Between the Lines).

Razack, S. (2002b) 'Gendered racial violence and spatialized justice: The murder of Pamela George', in S. Razack (ed.) *Space, Race and Law: Unmapping a White Settler Society* (Toronto: Between the Lines).

Reddy, C. (2011) 'Neoliberalism and transnational publics: On queer of color critique', lecture at the Racialization, Neoliberalism and Queering Public Spheres symposium, University of California at San Diego, 22–3 April.

Reed, T.V. (2005) *The Art of Protest* (Minneapolis: University of Minnesota Press).

Rivera, S. (2002) 'Queens in exile: The forgotten ones', in J. Nestle, C. Howell and R. Wilchins (eds) *Genderqueer* (Los Angeles: Allyson Books).

Roberts, D. (1993) 'Crime, race, and reproduction', *Tulane Law Review* 67.

Roberts, D. (1997) *Killing the Black Body: Race, Reproduction, and the Meaning of Liberty* (New York: Pantheon Books).

Roberts, D. (2011) *Fatal Invention: How Science, Politics, and Big Business Re-create Race in the Twenty-first Century* (New York: The New Press).

Roberts, M. (2009) "Dan Savage, chill with your race baiting", *Bilerico Project*, 3 September. Available at: www.bilerico.com/2009/09/dan_savage_chill_with_your_race_baiting.php (accessed 6 January 2014).

Rose, N. (1989) *Governing the Soul: The Shaping of Private Life* (London: Routledge).

Rose, N. (2010) 'Screen and intervene: Governing risky brains', *History of the Human Sciences* 23(1).

Ross, L. (2003) 'Barbara Smith: Interviewed by Loretta J. Ross', Voices of Feminism Oral History Project, Smith College.

Roth, M. and Seiffge-Krenke, I. (2011) 'Frühe Delinquenz und familiäre Belastungen in der Kindheit', in A. Boeger (ed.) *Jugendliche Intensivtäter: Interdisziplinare Perspektiven* (Wiesbaden: VS).

Rothe, J. (forthcoming) 'The semiotics of gay imperialism' (working title), in S. Bakshi, S. Jivraj and S. Posocco (eds) *Decolonizing Sexualities: Postcolonial Perspectives* (London: Counterpress).

Rubin, G. (1984) 'Thinking sex: Notes for a radical theory of the politics of sexuality', in C. Vance (ed.) *Pleasure and Danger: Exploring Female Sexuality* (Boston, MA: Routledge and Kegan Paul).

Ruder, D. (2011) 'Opferlotto', in K. Yılmaz-Günay (ed.) *Karriere eines konstruierten Gegensatzes: Zehn Jahre 'Muslime gegen Schwule'. Sexualpolitiken seit dem 11. September 2001* (Berlin: Self Publishing).

Safra Project (2011) 'Safra Project Statement on East End Gay Pride', 13 March, posted at Nohomonationalism. Available at: http://nohomonationalism.blogspot.ca/2011/03/safra-project-statement-on-east-end-gay.html (accessed 1 August 2014).

Said, E. (1994 [1978]) *Orientalism* (New York: Vintage).

Sailiata, K. (2014) *The Samoan Cause: Colonialism, Culture and the Rule of Law* (PhD dissertation, University of Michigan).

Samour, N. (2012) 'Addressing Palestine as a race question', lecture at Critical Race Theory Europe symposium, Humboldt Universität, Berlin, 16 June.

Sarrazin, T. (2010) *Deutschland schafft sich ab: Wie wir unser Land aufs Spiel setzen* (Munich: DVA).

Saunders, P. and Kirby, J. (2010) 'Move along: Community-based research into the policing of sex work in Washington, DC', *Social Justice* 37(1).

Schneider, P. (2005) 'The new Berlin wall', *New York Times*, 4 December. Available at: www.nytimes.com/2005/12/04/magazine/04berlin.html (accessed 22 November 2009).

Schulman, S. (2012) *The Gentrification of the Mind: Witness to a Lost Imagination* (Berkeley: University of California Press).

Schütz, J. (2010) 'Kriminelle Ausländer: Diese mutige Richterin redet Klartext', *Bild*. Available at: www.bild.de/news/vermischtes/richterin/redet-klartext-ueber-kriminelle-auslaender-5879218.bild.html (accessed 1 August 2014).

Schwab, W. (2009) 'Homophobie-Expertin der Berliner Polizei: "Gewalt fängt nicht erst an, wenn es blutet"', *Tageszeitung*, 22 June. Available at: www.taz.de/!36454/ (accessed 1 August 2014).

SchwuZ (n.d.) Facebook page. Available at: www.facebook.com/schwuz?fref-ts (accessed 19 July 2013).

Seidman, S. (1996) 'Introduction', in S. Seidman (ed.) *Queer Theory/Sociology* (Oxford: Blackwell).

Shakhsari, S. (2014) 'Killing me softly with your rights: Queer death and the politics of rightful killing', in J. Haritaworn, A. Kuntsman and S. Posocco (eds) *Queer Necropolitics* (London: Routledge).

Shapira, A. (2014) 'The Holocaust Memorial that became a refuge for drunks and sunbathers', *Haaretz*, 28 April. Available at: www.haaretz.com/life/books/1.587863 (accessed 1 January 2015).

Shooman, Y. (2011) 'Der Topos "Deutschenfeindlichkeit" in rechtspopulistischen Diskursen', in Bündnis 'Rechtspopulismus stoppen' (ed.) *Rechtspopulismus in Berlin: Rassismus als Bindeglied zwischen der Mitte der Gesellschaft und Neonazismus?* (Berlin: Bündnis 'Rechtspopulismus stoppen').

Siegessäule (2008) October issue.

Siegessäule (2009) November issue.

Siegessäule (2011) 'Mehr Regenbogenkieze?', 28 November. Available at: www.siegessaeule.
de/artikel-archiv/berlin/mehr-regenbogenkieze.html (accessed 1 June 2013).

Siegessäule TV (2009) 'Transphobe Gewalt im Berliner Frobenkiez – Solidarität mit
den Sexarbeiterinnen'. Available at: www.t-videa.cz/youtube/336466-siegessauletv-
transphobe-gewalt-im-berliner-frobenkiez-solidaritat-mit-den-sexarbeiterinnen.html
(accessed 1 November 2013).

Simon, B. (2007) 'Einstellung zur Homosexualität'. Available at: http://arbeitsblaetter.
stangl-taller.at/news/104/einstellung-zur-homosexualitaet (accessed 1 August 2014).

Simon, B. (2008) 'Einstellungen zur Homosexualität', *Zeitschrift für Entwicklungspsychologie
und Pädagogische Psychologie* 40(2).

Simpson, L.B. (2014) 'Not Murdered, Not Missing'. Available at: http://leannesimpson.ca/
page/2/ (accessed 1 May 2014).

Singh, I. and Rose, N. (2009) 'Biomarkers in psychiatry'. *Nature* 460(7252).

Skeggs, B. (1997) *Formations of Class and Gender: Becoming Respectable* (London: Sage).

Skeggs, B. (2004) 'Uneasy alignments, resourcing respectable subjectivity', *Gay and Lesbian
Quarterly* 10(2).

Skeggs, B. (2010) 'The value of relationships: Affective scenes and emotional performances',
Feminist Legal Studies 18(1).

Smith, A. (2005) *Conquest: Sexual Violence and American Indian Genocide* (Cambridge,
MA: South End Press).

Smith, A. (2007a) 'Native studies and critical pedagogy: Beyond the academic-industrial
complex', in J. Sudbury and M. Okazawa-Rey (eds) *Activist Scholarship: Antiracism,
Feminism, and Social Change* (Boulder, CO: Paradigm).

Smith, A. (2007b) 'Unmasking the state: Racial/gender terror and hate crimes', *Australian
Feminist Law Review* 26.

Smith, A. (2011) 'Against the law: Indigenous feminism and the nation-state', *Affinities: A
Journal of Radical Theory, Culture, and Action* 5(1).

Smith, B. (ed.) (2000 [1983]) *Home Girls: A Black Feminist Anthology* (New Brunswick,
NJ: Rutgers University Press).

Smith, N. (1979) 'Toward a theory of gentrification: A back to the city movement by capital,
not people', *Journal of the American Planning Association* 45(4).

Smith, N. (1996) '"Class struggle on Avenue B": The lower East Side as wild wild West', in
The New Urban Frontier: Gentrification and the Revanchist City (New York: Routledge).

Smith, N. (2002) 'New globalism, new urbanism: Gentrification as global urban strategy',
Antipode 34(3).

Smith, N., Sambale, J. and Eick, V. (2007) 'Neil Smith: Gentrification in Berlin and the
Revanchist State'. Available at: http://www.policing-crowds.org/news/article/neil-smith-
gentrification-in-berlin-and-the-revanchist-state.html (accessed 1 April 2010).

Snorton, R. and Haritaworn, J. (2013) 'Trans necropolitics', in A. Aizura and S. Stryker (eds)
Transgender Studies Reader, vol. II (New York: Routledge).

Sow, N. (2014) 'The beast in the belly' (working title), *Heinrich-Böll-Stiftung*. Available
at: http://heimatkunde.boell.de/2014/12/08/beast-belly (accessed 1 December 2014).

Spade, D. (2004) 'Fighting to win', in M. Bernstein (ed.) *That's Revolting! Queer Strategies
for Resisting Assimilation* (Brooklyn, NY: Soft Skull Press).

Spade, D. (2011) *Normal Life: Administrative Violence, Critical Trans Politics and the Limits
of the Law* (Cambridge, MA: South End Press).

Spade, D. and Willse, C. (2000) 'Confronting the limits of gay hate crimes activism:
A radical critique', *UCLA Chicano-Latino Review* 21.

Spiegel (2011) 'Empörung im Vatikan: Benetton zieht Papst-Kussbild zurück'. Available at: www.spiegel.de/panorama/gesellschaft/empoerung-im-vatikan-benetton-zieht-papst-kussbild-zurueck-a-798293.html (accessed 6 January 2014).

Spiegel Online (2010) 'Kriminologische studies: Jung, muslimisch, brutal', 5 June. Available at: www.spiegel.de/panorama/justiz/kriminologische-studie-jung-muslimisch-brutal-a-698948.html (accessed 1 August 2014).

Spivak, G.C. (1999) *A Critique of Postcolonial Reason: Toward a History of the Vanishing Present* (Cambridge, MA: Harvard University Press).

Stanley, E. and Smith, N. (eds) (2011) *Captive Genders: Trans Embodiment and the Prison Industrial Complex* (Oakland, CA: AK Press).

Stehle, M. (2006) 'Narrating the ghetto, narrating Europe: From Berlin, Kreuzberg to the banlieues in Paris', *Westminster Papers in Communication and Culture* 3(3).

Stein, R. (2004), 'Introduction', in R. Stein (ed.) *New Perspectives on Environmental Justice: Gender, Sexuality, and Activism* (New Brunswick, NJ: Rutgers University Press).

Steyerl, H. and Gutiérrez Rodríguez, R. (eds) (2003) *Spricht die Subalterne deutsch? Migration und postcolonial Kritik* (Münster: Unrast).

Stone, J. (2015) 'Firebombs and pig heads thrown into mosques as anti-Muslim attacks increase after Paris shootings', *The Independent*, 14 January. Available at: www.independent.co.uk/news/world/europe/firebombs-and-pigs-heads-thrown-into-mosques-as-antimuslim-attacks-increase-after-paris-shootings-9977423.html (accessed 15 January 2015).

Sudbury, J. (2005) 'Celling black bodies: Black women in the global prison industrial complex', *Feminist Review* 80.

Sudbury, J. (2007) 'Challenging penal dependency: Activist scholars and the antiprison movement', in J. Sudbury and M. Okazawa-Rey (eds) *Activist Scholarship: Antiracism, Feminism, and Social Change* (Boulder, CO: Paradigm).

Sudbury, J. and Okazawa-Rey, M. (2007) 'Introduction: Activist scholarship and the neoliberal university after 9/11', in J. Sudbury and M. Okazawa-Rey (eds) *Activist Scholarship: Antiracism, Feminism, and Social Change* (Boulder, CO: Paradigm).

Support CeCe MacDonald (n.d.) 'Background'. Available at: http://supportcece.wordpress.com/about-2/background/ (accessed 1 August 2014).

SUSPECT (2010a) 'Where now? From Pride scandal to transnational movement', *Bully Bloggers*, 26 June. Available at: http://bullybloggers.wordpress.com/2010/06/26/where-now-from-pride-scandal-to-transnational-movement/ (accessed 1 August 2014).

SUSPECT (2010b) 'Active readings for organic intellectuals', *Nohomonationalism*. Available at: http://nohomonationalism.blogspot.com/2010/06/activist-writings-for-organic.html (accessed 1 August 2014).

SUSPECT (2011) 'SUSPECT dankt dem Safra Project', *Nohomonationalism*. Available at: http://nohomonationalism.blogspot.ca/2011/03/der-rassistische-east-end-gay-pride-in.html (accessed 1 August 2014).

Sylvia Rivera: Trans Movement Founder, directed by R. Wicker (USA: 2011). Available at: www.youtube.com/watch?v=ybnH0HB0lqc (accessed 1 June 2013).

Sylvia Rivera Law Project, FIERCE, Audre Lorde Project, The Peter Cicchino Youth Project, and Queers for Economic Justice (2009) 'SRLP announces non-support of the Gender Employment Non-Discrimination Act'. Available at: http://srlp.org/genda (accessed 5 January 2010).

Tadiar, N. (2012) 'Life-times in fate playing', *South Atlantic Quarterly* 111(4).

Tam, L. (2012) 'Governing through competency: Race, pathologization, and the limits of mental health outreach' (Master's Dissertation, University of Toronto).

TCSD (Transgenialer CSD Berlin) (2008) 'Despite the repetitive demand for its cancellation: The Transgenial Christopher Street Day will take place!' TCSD 2008. Available at: www. transgenialercsd.de/seite1.html (accessed 1 April 2010).

Teelucksingh, C. (2002) 'Spatiality and environmental justice in Parkdale (Toronto)', *Ethnologies* 24(1).

Thaemlitz, T. (2007) 'Transportation', in M.B. Sycamore (ed.) *Nobody Passes: Rejecting the Rules of Gender and Conformity* (San Francisco: Seal Press).

Thobani, S. (2007a) *Exalted Subjects: Studies in the Making of Race and Nation in Canada* (Toronto: University of Toronto).

Thobani, S. (2007b) 'White wars: Western feminisms and the War on Terror', *Feminist Theory* 8(2).

Thobani, S. (2014) 'Prologue', in J. Haritaworn, A. Kuntsman and S. Posocco (eds) *Queer Necropolitics* (London: Routledge).

Tongson, K. (2007) 'The light that never goes out: Butch intimacies and suburban sociabilities in "lesser Los Angeles"', in G. Haggerty and M. McGarry (eds) *A Companion to Lesbian, Gay, Bisexual, Transgender and Queer Studies* (Oxford: Blackwell).

TOPOS (2008) *Sozialstruktur und Mietentwicklung im Erhaltungsgebiet Luisenstadt (SO 36)* (Social Structure and Rent Development in the Protected Area Luisenstadt (SO 36)) (Berlin: Bezirksamt Friedrichshain-Kreuzberg). Available at: www.berlin.de/ imperia/md/content/bafriedrichshain- kreuzberg/abtstadtpg/amtstapl-verm_baa/stapl/ stadterneuerung/luise_endbericht.pdf?start&ts=1264082523&file=luise_endbericht. pdf (accessed 1 April 2010).

Toprak, A. (2011) 'Machtausübung', *Siegessäule*, November. Available at: www.siegessaeule. de/uploads-img-printausgaben-sis_11-09.pdf (accessed 25 October 2012).

Toprak, A. and Nowacki, K. (2010) *Gewaltphänomen bei männlichen, muslimischen Jugendlichen mit Migrationshintergrund und Präventionsstrategien* (Berlin: Federal Ministry for Family, Seniors, Women and Youth).

Trudelfisch (2010) 'Schuldfragen in Neukölln', *Steigende Mieten Stoppen*, 26 August. Available at: http://mietenstopp.blogsport.de/2010/08/26/schuldfragen-in-neukoelln/ (accessed 1 June 2013).

Tuck, E. and Yang, K.W. (2012) 'Decolonization is not a metaphor', *Decolonization: Indigeneity, Education & Society* 1(1). Available at: file:///Users/fesuser/Downloads/18630-43263-1-PB%20(1).pdf (accessed 1 April 2014).

UCL (2010) Backlash? The Resurgence of Homophobia in Contemporary Cities, Urban Laboratory workshop (11 February). Available at: www.ucl.ac.uk/intercultural-interaction/project-pages/backlash (accessed 1 April 2014).

Vergès, F. (1999) *Monsters and Revolutionaries: Colonial Family Romance and Métissage* (Durham, NC: Duke University Press).

Voronka, J. (2010) 'Rooting out the weeds: Resisting white settler and psychiatric supremacy through a critique of "The Review of the Roots of Youth Violence"', PsychOut Conference, University of Toronto, 7–8 May. Available at: http://individual.utoronto.ca/psychout/ papers/voronka.html (accessed 1 August 2014).

Wacquant, L. (2008) 'Ghettos and anti-ghettos: An anatomy of the new urban poverty', *Thesis Eleven* 94(1).

Weeks, J. (2014) *Sex, Politics and Society: The Regulation of Sexuality Since 1800* (London: Routledge).

Wekker, G. (2009) 'On homonostalgia and better times: Multiculturalism and postcolonialism/postcoloniality', George Mosse Lecture, University of Amsterdam, 16 September.

Werntz, K. (2012) 'Working the African bushes: Tales from Görli', *Exberliner*, 19 September. Available at: www.exberliner.com/features/people/working-the-african-bushes-tales-from-gorlitzer-park/ (accessed 1 June 2013).

Weston, K. (1995) 'Get thee to a big city: Sexual imaginary and the great gay migration', *GLQ: A Journal of Lesbian and Gay Studies* 2(3).

Wilchins, R. (2003) 'Airport insecurity?', *The Advocate*, 25 June.

Williams, R. (1978) *Marxism and Literature* (New York: Oxford University Press).

Willis, S. (1990) 'I want the black one: Is there a place for Afro-American culture in commodity culture?', *New Formations* 10.

Windy City Times (2011) 'International MANEO-Conference looked at LGBT neighborhoods worldwide: Chicago viewed as model for developing, sustaining LGBT neighborhoods', 9 December. Available at: http://windycitymediagroup.com/gay/lesbian/news/ARTICLE.php?AID=35180 (accessed 1 November 2013).

Winnicott, D.W. (1953) 'Transitional objects and transitional phenomena: A study of the first not-me possession', *International Journal of Psycho-Analysis* 34.

Wolter, S. (2011) 'Ist Krieg oder was? Queer nation building in Berlin-Schöneberg', in K. Yılmaz-Günay (ed.) *Karriere eines konstruierten Gegensatzes: Zehn Jahre 'Muslime versus Schwule'. Sexualpolitiken seit dem 11. September 2001* (Berlin: Self Publishing).

Yeğenoğlu, M. (1998) *Colonial Fantasies: Towards a Feminist Reading of Orientalism* (Cambridge: Cambridge University Press).

Yiğit, N., Vazquez, E. and Yazar, S. (2010) 'Versteckte Diskriminierung beweisen! TESTING als Instrument der Antidiskriminierungsarbeit am Beispiel Wohnungsmarkt', *Rassismus & Diskriminierung in Deutschland* 57.

Yıldız, Y. (2009) 'Turkish girls, Allah's daughters, and the contemporary German subject: Itinerary of a figure', *German Life and Letters* 62(4).

Yılmaz-Günay, K. and Wolter, S.A. (2013) 'Pink washing Germany? Der deutsche Homonationalismus und die "jüdische Karte"', in D. Gürsel, Z. Çetin and Allmende e.V. (eds) *Wer macht Demo_kratie. Kritische Migrationsforschung* (Münster: Edition Assemblage).

Yuval-Davis, N. (1997) *Gender and Nation* (London: Sage).

Zablotsky, V. (2012) 'Die Diasporisierung des "Anderen" in deutschen Erinnerungslandschaften: Zur Konstruktion Jüdischer Differenz in der Bundesrepublik Deutschland seit 1990' (unpublished Master's Diploma: Freie Universität Berlin).

Zimmermann, B. (2013) 'Politik, protest, party', *Tageszeitung*, 23 June. Available at: www.taz.de/Transgenialer-CSD-demonstriert/!118627/ (accessed 26 November 2013).

Zoé (2008) '"We break the gender binary every day at breakfast": Interview with Shuki (Jerusalem Kings) from Israel', Drag Festival Berlin.

Zuberi, T. and Bonilla-Silva, E. (eds) (2008) *White Logic, White Methods: Racism and Methodology* (Lanham, MD: Rowman and Littlefield).

INDEX